ERIES.

ERIES

· $1.00
· 1.00
· 1.00
· 1.00

ncil
not
ery

CH COURSE
GLISH.

BY

AVER WILKINSON.

NEW YORK:
HAUTAUQUA PRESS,
C. L. S. C. DEPARTMENT,
805 BROADWAY.
1886.

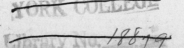

COPYRIGHT, 1886,

BY PHILLIPS & HUNT.

OTHER VOLUMES IN THE AFTER-SCHOOL S

BY THE SAME AUTHOR.

The required books of the C. L. S. C. are recommended by a Cou of six. It must, however, be understood that recommendation does involve an approval by the Council, or by any member of it, of ev principle or doctrine contained in the book recommended.

ELECTROTYPED AND PRINTED

BY RAND, AVERY, & COMPANY,

BOSTON.

PREFACE.

THE preparation of the present volume proposed to the author a task more difficult far than that undertaken in any one of the four preceding volumes of the group, THE AFTER-SCHOOL SERIES, to which it belongs. Those volumes dealt with literatures limited and finished: this volume deals with a literature indefinitely vast in extent, and still in vital process of growth. The selection of material to be used was, in the case of the earlier volumes, virtually made for the author beforehand, in a manner greatly to ease his sense of responsibility for the exercise of individual judgment and taste. Long prescription, joined to the winnowing effect of wear and waste through time and chance, had left little doubt what works of what writers, Greek and Roman, best deserved now to be shown to the general reader. Besides this, the prevalent custom of

iii

the schools of classical learning could then wisely be taken as a clew of guidance to be implicitly followed, whatever might be the path through which it should lead. There is here no similar avoidance of responsibility possible; for the schools have not established a custom, and French literature is a living body, from which no important members have ever yet been rent by the ravages of time.

The greater difficulty seen thus to inhere already in the nature itself of the task proposed for accomplishment, was gravely increased by the much more severe compression deemed to be in the present instance desirable. The room placed at the author's disposal for a display of French literature was less than half the room allowed him for the display of either the Greek or the Latin.

The plan, therefore, of this volume, imposed the necessity of establishing from the outset certain limits, to be very strictly observed. First, it was resolved to restrict the attention bestowed upon the national history, the national geography, and the national language, of the French, to such brief occasional notices as, in the course of the volume, it might seem necessary, for illustration of the particular author, from time to time to make. The only introductory general matter here to be found will accordingly consist of a rapid and summary review of that literature, as a whole, which is the subject of the book. It was next determined to limit the authors selected for representation to those of the finished centuries. A third decision was to make the number of authors small rather than large, choice rather than inclusive. The principle at this point adopted, was to choose those authors only whose merit, or whose fame, or whose influence, might be supposed unquestionably such that their names and their works would certainly be found surviving, though the language in which they wrote should, like its parent Latin, have perished from the tongues of men. The proportion of space severally allotted to the different authors was to be measured partly according to their relative importance, and partly according to their estimated relative capacity of interesting in translation the average intelligent reader of to-day.

In one word, the single inspiring aim of the author has here been to furnish enlightened readers, versed only in the English language, the means of acquiring, through the medium of their vernacular, some proportioned, trustworthy, and effective knowledge and appreciation, in its chief classics, of the great literature which has been written in French. This object has been sought, not through narrative and description, making books and authors the subject, but through the literature itself, in specimen extracts illuminated by the necessary explanation and criticism.

It is proposed to follow the present volume with a volume similar in general character, devoted to German literature.

CONTENTS.

Classic French Course in English.

I.

FRENCH LITERATURE.

Of French literature, taken as a whole, it may boldly be said that it is, not the wisest, not the weightiest, not certainly the purest and loftiest, but by odds the most brilliant and the most interesting, literature in the world. Strong at many points, at some points triumphantly strong, it is conspicuously weak at only one point, — the important point of poetry. In eloquence, in philosophy, even in theology; in history, in fiction, in criticism, in epistolary writing, in what may be called the pamphlet; in another species of composition, characteristically, peculiarly, almost uniquely, French, — the Thought and the Maxim; by eminence in comedy, and in all those related modes of written expression for which there is scarcely any name but a French name, — the *jeu d'esprit*, the *bon mot*, *persiflage*, the *phrase;* in social and political speculation; last, but not least, in scientific exposition elegant enough in form and in style to rise to the rank of literature proper, — the French language has abundant achievement to show, that puts it, upon the whole, hardly second in wealth of letters to any other language whatever, either ancient or modern.

What constitutes the charm — partly a perilous charm — of French literature is, before all else, its incomparable clearness, its precision, its neatness, its point; then, added to this, its lightness of touch, its sureness of aim; its vivacity, sparkle, life; its inexhaustible gayety; its impulsion toward wit, — impulsion so strong as often to land it in mockery; the sense of release that it breathes and inspires; its freedom from prick to the conscience; its exquisite study and choice of effect; its deference paid to decorum, — decorum, we mean, in taste, as distinguished from morals; its infinite patience and labor of art, achieving the perfection of grace and of ease, — in one word, its style.

We speak, of course, broadly and in the gross. There are plenty of French authors to whom some of the traits just named could by no means be attributed, and there is certainly not a single French author to whom one could truthfully attribute them all. Voltaire insisted that what was not clear was not French, — so much, to the conception of this typical Frenchman, was clearness the genius of the national speech. Still, Montaigne, for example, was sometimes obscure; and even the tragedist Corneille wrote here and there what his commentator, Voltaire, declared to be hardly intelligible.

So, too, Rabelais, coarsest of humorists, offending decorum in various ways, offended it most of all exactly in that article of taste, as distinguished from morals, which, with first-rate French authors in general, is so capital a point of regard. On the other hand, Pascal, — not to mention the moralists by profession, such as Nicole, and the preachers Bourdaloue and Massillon, — Pascal, quivering himself, like a soul unclad, with sense of responsibility to God, constantly probes you, reading him, to the inmost quick of your conscience. Rousseau, notably in the "Confessions," and in the Reveries supplementary to the "Confessions;" Chateaubriand, echoing Rousseau; and that wayward woman of genius, George Sand, disciple she to both, — were so far from being always light-heartedly gay, that not seldom they spread over their page a sombre atmosphere almost of gloom, — gloom flushed pensively, as with a clouded "setting sun's pathetic light." In short, when you speak of particular authors, and naturally still more when you speak of particular works, there are many discriminations to be made. Such exceptions, however, being duly allowed, the literary product of the French mind, considered in the aggregate, will not be misconceived if regarded as possessing the general characteristics in style that we have now sought briefly to indicate.

French literature, we have hinted, is comparatively poor in poetry. This is due in part, no doubt, to the genius of the people; but it is also due in part to the structure of the language. The language, which is derived chiefly from Latin, is thence in such a way derived as to have lost the regularity and stateliness of its ancient original, without having compensated itself with any richness and sweetness of sound peculiarly its own ; like, for instance, that canorous vowel quality of its sister derivative, the Italian. The French language, in short, is far from being an ideal language for the poet.

In spite, however, of this fact, disputed by nobody, it is true of French literature, as it is true of almost any national literature, that it took its rise in verse instead of in prose. Anciently, there were two languages subsisting together in France, which came to be distinguished from each other in name by the word of affirmation — *oc* or *oïl*, yes — severally peculiar to them, and thus to be known respectively as *langue d'oc*, and *langue d'oïl*. The future belonged to the latter of the two forms of speech, — the one spoken in the northern part of the country. This, the *langue d'oïl*, became at length the French language. But the *langue d'oc*, a soft and musical tongue, survived long enough to become the vehicle of lyric strains, mostly on subjects of love and gallantry, still familiar in mention, and famous as the songs of the troubadours. The flourishing time of the troubadours was in the eleventh and twelfth centuries. Provençal is an alternative name of the language.

Side by side with the southern *troubadours*, or a

little later than they, the *trouvères* of the north sang,
with more manly ambition, of national themes, and,
like Virgil, of arms and of heroes. Some productions of the *trouvères* may fairly be allowed an elevation of aim and of treatment entitling them to be
called epic in character. *Chansons de geste* (songs
of exploit), or *rómans*, is the native name by which
those primitive French poems are known. They
exist in three principal cycles, or groups, of productions, — one cycle composed of those pertaining to
Charlemagne ; one, of those pertaining to British
Arthur ; and a third, of those pertaining to ancient
Greece and Rome, notably to Alexander the Great.
The cycle revolving around the majestic legend of
Charlemagne for its centre was Teutonic, rather
than Celtic, in spirit as well as in theme. It tended
to the religious in tone. The Arthurian cycle was
properly Celtic. It dealt more with adventures of
love. The Alexandrian cycle, so named from one
principal theme celebrated, — namely, the deeds of
Alexander the Great, — mixed fantastically the traditions of ancient Greece and Rome with the then
prevailing ideas of chivalry, and with the figments
of fairy lore. (The metrical form employed in these
poems gave its name to the Alexandrine line later
so predominant in French poetry.) The volume of
this quasi-epical verse, existing in its three groups,
or cycles, is immense. So is that of the satire and
the allegory in metre that followed. From this
latter store of stock and example, Chaucer drew to

supply his muse with material. The *fabliaux*, so called, — fables, that is, or stories, — were still another form of early French literature in verse. It is only now, within the current decade of years, that a really ample collection of *fabliaux* — hitherto, with the exception of a few printed volumes of specimens, extant exclusively in manuscript — has been put into course of publication. Rutebeuf, a *trouvère* of the reign of St. Louis (Louis IX., thirteenth century), is perhaps as conspicuous a personal name as any that thus far emerges out of the sea of practically anonymous early French authorship. A frankly sordid and mercenary singer, Rutebeuf, always tending to mockery, was not seldom licentious, — in both these respects anticipating, as probably also to some extent by example conforming, the subsequent literary spirit of his nation. The *fabliaux* generally mingled with their narrative interest that spice of raillery and satire constantly so dear to the French literary appetite. Thibaud was, in a double sense, a royal singer of songs ; for he reigned over Navarre, as well as chanted sweetly in verse his love and longing, so the disputed legend asserts, for Queen Blanche of Castile. Thibaud bears the historic title of The Song-maker. He has been styled the Béranger of the thirteenth century. To Thibaud is said to be due the introduction of the feminine rhyme into French poetry, — a metrical variation of capital importance. The songs of Abélard, in the century preceding Thibaud, won a wide popularity.

Prose, meantime, had been making noteworthy approaches to form. Villehardouin must be named as first in time among French writers of history. His work is entitled, "Conquest of Constantinople." It gives an account of the Fourth Crusade. Joinville, a generation later, continues the succession of chronicles with his admiring story of the life of Saint Louis, whose personal friend he was. But Froissart of the fourteenth century, and Comines of the fifteenth, are greater names. Froissart, by his simplicity and his narrative art, was the Herodotus, as Philip de Comines, for his political sagacity, has been styled the Tacitus, of French historical literature. Up to the time of Froissart, the literature which we have been treating as French was different enough in form from the French of to-day to require what might be called translation in order to become generally intelligible to the living generation of Frenchmen. The text of Froissart is pretty archaic, but it definitely bears the aspect of French.

With the name of Comines, who wrote of Louis XI. (compare Walter Scott's "Quentin Durward"), we reach the fifteenth century, and are close upon the great revival of learning which accompanied the religious reformation under Luther and his peers. Now come Rabelais, boldly declared by Coleridge one of the great creative minds of literature; and Montaigne, with those Essays of his, still living, and, indeed, certain always to live. John Calvin, meantime, writes his "Institutes of the Christian Religion" in French as well as in Latin, showing once and for all, that in the right hands his vernacular tongue was as capable of gravity as many a writer before him had superfluously shown that it was capable of levity. Amyot, the translator of Plutarch, is a French writer of power, without whom the far greater Montaigne could hardly have been. The influence of Amyot on French literary history is wider in reach and longer in duration than we thus indicate; but Montaigne's indebtedness to him is alone enough to prove that a mere translator had in this man made a very important contribution to the forming prose literature of France.

"The Pleiades," so called, were a group of seven writers, who, about the middle of the sixteenth century, banded themselves together in France, with the express aim of supplying influential example to improve the French language for literary purposes. Their peculiar appellation, "The Pleiades," was copied from that of a somewhat similar group of Greek writers, that existed in the time of Ptolemy Philadelphus. Of course, the implied allusion in it is to the constellation of the Pleiades. The individual name by which the Pleiades of the sixteenth century may best be remembered is that of Ronsard the poet, associated with the romantic and pathetic memory of Mary, Queen of Scots. Never, perhaps, in the history of letters was the fame of a poet in the poet's own lifetime more universal and more splendid than was the fame of Ronsard. A high court of literary judicature formally decreed to Ronsard the title of The French Poet by eminence. This occurred in the youth of the poet. The wine of success so brilliant turned the young fellow's head. He soon began to play lord paramount of Parnassus, with every air of one born to the purple. The kings of the earth vied with each other to do him honor. Ronsard affected scholarship, and the foremost scholars of his time were proud to place him with Homer and with Virgil on the roll of the poets. Ronsard's peculiarity in style was the free use of words and constructions not properly French. Boileau indicated whence he enriched his vocabulary and his syntax, by satirically saying that Ronsard spoke Greek and Latin in French. At his death, Ronsard was almost literally buried under praises. Sainte-Beuve strikingly says that he seemed to go forward into posterity as into a temple.

Sharp posthumous reprisals awaited the extravagant fame of Ronsard. Malherbe, coming in the next generation, legislator of Parnassus, laughed the literary pretensions of Ronsard to scorn. This stern critic of form, such is the story, marked up his copy of Ronsard with notes of censure so many, that a friend of his, seeing the annotated volume, observed, " What here is not marked, will be understood to have been approved by you." Whereupon Malherbe, taking his pen, with one indiscriminate stroke drew it abruptly through the whole volume. " There I Ronsardized," the contemptuous critic would exclaim, when in reading his own verses to an acquaintance, — for Malherbe was poet himself, — he happened to encounter a word that struck him as harsh or improper. Malherbe, in short, sought to chasten and check the luxuriant overgrowth to which the example and method of the Pleiades were tending to push the language of poetry in French. The resultant effect of the two contrary tendencies — that of literary wantonness on the one hand, and that of literary prudery on the other — was at the same time to enrich and to purify French poetical diction. Balzac (the elder), close to Malherbe in time, performed a service for French prose similar to that which the latter performed for French verse. These two critical and literary powers brought in the reign of what is called classicism in France. French classicism had its long culmination under Louis XIV.

But it was under Louis XIII., or rather under that monarch's great minister, Cardinal Richelieu, that the rich and splendid Augustan age of French literature was truly prepared. Two organized forces, one of them private and social, the other official and public, worked together, though sometimes perhaps not in harmony, to produce the magnificent literary result that illustrated the time of Louis XIV. Of these two organized forces, the Hôtel de Rambouillet was one, and the French Academy was the other. The Hôtel de Rambouillet has become the adopted name of a literary society, presided over by the fine inspiring genius of the beautiful and accomplished

Italian wife of the Marquis de Rambouillet, a lady who generously conceived the idea of rallying the feminine wit and virtue of the kingdom to exert a potent influence for regenerating the manners and morals, and indeed the literature, of France. At the high court of blended rank and fashion and beauty and polish and virtue and wit, thus established in the exquisitely builded and decorated saloons of the Rambouillet mansion, the selectest literary genius and fame of France were proud and glad to assemble for the discussion and criticism of literature. Here came Balzac and Voiture; here Corneille read aloud his masterpieces before they were represented on the stage; here Descartes philosophized; here the large and splendid genius of Bossuet first unfolded itself to the world; here Madame de Sévigné brought her bright, incisive wit, trebly commended by stainless reputation, unwithering beauty, and charming address, in the woman who wielded it. The noblest blood of France added the decoration and inspiration of their presence. It is not easy to overrate the diffusive beneficent influence that hence went forth to change the fashion of literature, and to change the fashion of society, for the better. The Hôtel de Rambouillet proper lasted two generations only; but it had a virtual succession, which, though sometimes interrupted, was scarcely extinct until the brilliant and beautiful Madame Récamier ceased, about the middle of the present century, to hold her famous *salons* in Paris. The continuous fame and influence of the French Academy, founded by Richelieu, everybody knows. No other European language has been elaborately and sedulously formed and cultivated like the French.

But great authors are better improvers of a language than any societies, however influential. Corneille, Descartes, Pascal, did more for French style than either the Hôtel de Rambouillet or the Academy, — more than both these two great literary societies together. In verse, Racine, following Corneille, advanced in some important respects upon the example and lead of that great original master; but in prose, when Pascal published his "Provincial Letters," French style reached at once a point of perfection beyond which it never since has gone. Bossuet, Bourdaloue, Fénelon, Massillon, Molière, La Fontaine, Boileau, La Rochefoucauld, La Bruyère, — what a constellation of names are these, to glorify the age of Louis XIV.! And Louis XIV. himself, royal embodiment of a literary good sense carried to the pitch of something very like real genius in judgment and taste, — what a sun was he (with that talent of his for kingship, probably never surpassed), to balance and to sway, from his unshaken station, the august intellectual system of which he alone constituted the despotic centre to attract and repel! Seventy-two years long was this sole individual reign. Louis XIV. still sat on the throne of France when the seventeenth century became the eighteenth.

The eighteenth century was an age of universal reaction in France. Religion, or rather ecclesiasticism, — for, in the France of those times, religion was the Church, and the Church was the Roman Catholic hierarchy, — had been the dominant fashion under Louis XIV. Infidelity was a broad literary mark, written all over the face of the eighteenth century. It was the hour and power of the Encyclopædists and the Philosophers, — of Voltaire, of Diderot, of D'Alembert, of Rousseau. Montesquieu, though contemporary, belongs apart from these writers. More really original, more truly philosophical, he was far less revolutionary, far less destructive, than they. Still, his influence was, on the whole, exerted in the direction, if not of infidelity, at least of religious indifferentism. The French Revolution was laid in train by the great popular writers whom we have now named, and by their fellows. It needed only the spark, which the proper occasion would be sure soon to strike out, and the awful, earth-shaking explosion would follow. After the Revolution, during the First Empire, so called, — the usurpation, that is, of Napoleon Bonaparte, — literature was well-nigh extinguished in France. The names, however, then surpassingly brilliant, of Chateaubriand and Madame de Staël, belong to this period.

Three centuries have now elapsed since the date of "The Pleiades." Throughout this long period, French literature has been chiefly under the sway of that spirit of classicism in style which the reaction against Ronsardism, led first by Malherbe and afterwards by Boileau, had established as the national standard in literary taste and aspiration. But Rousseau's genius acted as a powerful solvent of the classic tradition. Chateaubriand's influence was felt on the same side, continuing Rousseau's. George Sand, too, and Lamartine, were forces that strengthened this component. Finally, the great personality of Victor Hugo proved potent enough definitively to break the spell that had been so long and so heavily laid on the literary development of France. The bloodless warfare was fierce between the revolutionary Romanticists and the conservative Classicists in literary style, but the victory seemed at last to remain with the advocates of the new romantic revival. It looked, on the face of the matter, like a signal triumph of originality over prescription, of genius over criticism, of power over rule. We still live in the midst of the dying echoes of this resonant strife. Perhaps it is too early, as yet, to determine on which side, by the merit of the cause, the advantage truly belongs. But, by the merit of the respective champions, the result was, for a time at least, triumphantly decided in favor of the Romanticists, against the Classicists. The weighty authority, however, of Sainte-Beuve, at first thrown into the scale that at length would sink, was thence withdrawn, and at last, if not resolutely cast upon the opposite side of the balance, was left wavering in a kind of equipoise between the one and the other. But our preliminary sketch has already passed the limit within which our choice of authors for representation is necessarily confined.

With first a few remarks, naturally suggested, that may be useful, on the general subject thus rather touched merely than handled, the present writer gives way to let now the representative authors themselves, selected for the purpose, supply to the reader a just and lively idea of French literature.

The first thing, perhaps, to strike the thoughtful mind in a comprehensive view of the subject, is not so much the length — though this is remarkable — as the long *continuity* of French literary history. From its beginning down to the actual moment, French literature has suffered no serious break in the course of its development. There have been periods of greater, and periods of less, prosperity and fruit; but wastes of marked suspension and barrenness, there have been none.

The second thing noticeable is, that French literature has, to a singular degree, lived an independent life of its own. It has found copious springs of health and growth within its own bosom.

But then, a third thing to be also observed, is that, on the other hand, the touch of foreign influence, felt and acknowledged by this most proudly and self-sufficiently national of literatures, has proved to it, at various epochs, a sovereign force of revival and elastic expansion. Thus, the great renascence in the sixteenth century of ancient Greek and Latin letters was new life to French literature. So, again, Spanish literature, brought into contact with French through Corneille and Molière with others, gave to the national mind of France a new literary launch. But the most recent and perhaps the most remarkable example of foreign influence quickening French literature to make it freshly fruitful, is supplied in the great romanticizing movement under the lead of Victor Hugo. English literature — especially Shakspeare — was largely the pregnant cause of this attempted emancipation of the French literary mind from the burden of classicism.

A fourth very salient trait in French literary history consists in the self-conscious, elaborate, persistent efforts put forth from time to time by individuals, and by organizations, both public and private, in France, to improve the language, and to elevate the literature, of the nation. We know of nothing altogether comparable to this anywhere else in the literature of the world.

A fifth striking thing about French literature is, that it has to a degree, as we believe beyond parallel, exercised a real and vital influence on the character and the fortune of the nation. The social, the political, the moral, the religious, history of France is from age to age a faithful reflex of the changing phases of its literature. Of course, a reciprocal influence has been constantly reflected back and forth from the nation upon its literature, as well as from its literature upon the nation. But where else in the world has it ever been so extraordinarily, we may say so appallingly, true as in France, that the nation was such because such was its literature ?

French literature, it will at once be seen, is a study possessing, beyond the literary, a social, a political, and even a religious, interest.

Readers desiring to push their conversance with the literary history of France farther than the present volume will enable them to do, will consult with profit either the Primer, or the Short History, of French Literature, by Mr. George Saintsbury. Mr. Saintsbury is a well-informed writer, who, if the truth must be told, diffuses himself too widely to do his best possible work. He has, however, made French literature a specialty, and he is in general a trustworthy authority on the subject.

Another writer on the subject is Mr. H. Van Laun. Him, although a predecessor of his own in the field, Mr. Saintsbury severely ignores, by claiming that he is himself the first to write in English a history of French literature based on original and independent reading of the authors. We are bound to say that Mr. Van Laun's work is of very poor quality. It offers, indeed, to the reader one advantage not afforded by either of Mr. Saintsbury's works, the advantage, namely, of illustrative extracts from the authors treated, — extracts, however, not unfrequently marred by wretched translation.

The cyclopædias are, some of them, both in articles on particular authors and in their sketches of French literary history as a whole, good sources of general information on the subject. Readers who command the means of comparing several different cyclopædias, or several successive editions of some one cyclopædia, as, for example, the " Encyclopædia Britannica," will find enlightening and stimulating the not always harmonious views presented on the same topics. Hallam's " History of Literature in Europe " is an additional authority by no means to be overlooked.

II.

FROISSART.

1337-1410.

FRENCH literature, for the purposes of the present volume, may be said to commence with Froissart. Froissart is a kind of mediæval Herodotus. His time is, indeed, almost this side the middle ages ; but he belongs by character and by sympathy rather to the mediæval than to the modern world. He is delightfully like Herodotus in the style and the spirit of his narrative. Like Herodotus, he became a traveller in order to become an historian. Like Herodotus, he was cosmopolite enough not to be narrowly patriotic. Frenchman though he was, he took as much pleasure in recounting English victories as he did in recounting French. His countrymen have even accused him of unpatriotic partiality for the English. His Chronicles have been, perhaps, more popular in their English form than in their original French. Two prominent English translations have been made, of which the later, that by Thomas Johnes, is now most read. Sir Walter Scott thought the earlier excelled in charm of style.

Jehan or Jean Froissart was a native of Valenciennes. His father meant to make a priest of him, but the boy had other tastes of his own. Before he was well out of his teens, he began writing history. This was under the patronage of a great noble. Froissart was all his life a natural courtier. He throve on the patronage of the great. It was probably not a fawning spirit in him that made him this kind of man ; it was rather an innate love of splendor and high exploit. He admired chivalry, then in its last days, and he painted it with the passion of an idealizer. His father had been an heraldic painter, so it was perhaps an hereditary strain in the son that naturally attached him to rank and royalty. The people — that is, the promiscuous mass of mankind — hardly exist to Froissart. His pages, spacious as they are, have scarcely room for more than kings and nobles, and knights and squires. He is a picturesque and romantic historian, in whose chronicles the glories of the world of chivalry — a world, as we have said, already dying, and so soon to disappear — are fixed forever on an ample canvas, in moving form and shifting color, to delight the backward-looking imagination of mankind.

Froissart, besides being chronicler, was something of a poet. It would still be possible to confront one who should call this in question, with thirty thousand surviving verses from the chronicler's pen. Quantity, indeed, rather than quality, is the strong point of Froissart as poet.

He had no sooner finished the first part of his Chronicles, a compilation from the work of an earlier hand, than he posted to England for the purpose of formally presenting his work to the Queen, a princess of Hainault. She rewarded him handsomely. Woman enough, too, she was, woman under the queen, duly to despatch him back again to his native land, where the young fellow's heart, she saw, was lost to a noble lady, whom, from his inferior station, he could woo only as a moth might woo the moon. He subsequently returned to Great Britain, and rode about on horseback gathering materials of history. He visited Italy under excellent auspices, and, together with Chaucer and with Petrarch, witnessed a magnificent marriage ceremonial in Milan. Froissart continued to travel far and wide, always a favorite with princes, but always intent on achieving his projected work. He finally died at Chimay, where he had spent his closing years in rounding out to their completeness his "Chronicles of England, France, and the Adjoining Countries."

Froissart is the most leisurely of historians, or, rather, he is a writer who presupposes the largest allowance of leisure at the command of his readers. He does not seek proportion and perspective. He simply tells us all he had been able to find out respecting each transaction in its turn as it successively comes up in the progress of his narrative. If he goes wrong to-day, he will perhaps correct himself to-morrow, or day after to-morrow, — this not by changing the first record where it stands, to make it right, but by inserting a note of his mistake at the point, whatever it may be, which he shall chance to have reached in the work of composition when the new and better light breaks in on his eyes. The student is thus never quite certain but that what he is at one moment reading in his author, may be an error of which at some subsequent moment he will be faithfully advised. A little discomposing, this, but such is Froissart; and it is the philosophical way to take your author as he is, and make the best of him.

Of such an historian, an historian so diffuse, and so little selective, it would obviously be difficult to give any suitably brief specimen that should seem to present a considerable historic action in full. We go to Froissart's account of the celebrated battle of Poitiers (France). This was fought in 1356, between Edward the Black Prince on the English side, and King John on the side of the French.

King John of the French was, of course, a great
prize to be secured by the victorious English.
There was eager individual rivalry as to what particular warrior should be adjudged his true captor.
Froissart thus describes the strife and the issue : —

There was much pressing at this time, through eagerness to take the king; and those who were nearest to him,
and knew him, cried out, "Surrender yourself, surrender
yourself, or you are a dead man!" In that part of the field
was a young knight from St. Omer, who was engaged by a
salary in the service of the King of England; his name was
Denys de Morbeque; who for five years had attached himself
to the English, on account of having been banished in his
younger days from France, for a murder committed in an
affray at St. Omer. It fortunately happened for this knight,
that he was at the time near to the King of France, when he
was so much pulled about. He, by dint of force, for he was
very strong and robust, pushed through the crowd, and said
to the king, in good French, "Sire, sire, surrender yourself!"
The king, who found himself very disagreeably situated,
turning to him, asked, "To whom shall I surrender myself?
to whom? Where is my cousin, the Prince of Wales? If
I could see him, I would speak to him." — "Sire," replied Sir
Denys, "he is not here; but surrender yourself to me, and I
will lead you to him." — "Who are you?" said the king.
"Sire, I am Denys de Morbeque, a knight from Artois; but I
serve the King of England because I cannot belong to France,
having forfeited all I possessed there." The king then
gave him his right-hand glove, and said, "I surrender myself to you." There was much crowding and pushing about;
for every one was eager to cry out, "I have taken him!"
Neither the king nor his youngest son Philip were able to
get forward, and free themselves from the throng. . . .

The Prince [of Wales] asked them [his marshals] if they
knew any thing of the King of France: they replied, "No,

sir, not for a certainty; but we believe he must be either killed or made prisoner, since he has never quitted his battalion." The prince then, addressing the Earl of Warwick and Lord Cobham, said, "I beg of you to mount your horses, and ride over the field, so that on your return you may bring me some certain intelligence of him." The two barons, immediately mounting their horses, left the prince, and made for a small hillock, that they might look about them. From their stand they perceived a crowd of men-at-arms on foot, who were advancing very slowly. The King of France was in the midst of them, and in great danger; for the English and Gascons had taken him from Sir Denys de Morbeque, and were disputing who should have him, the stoutest bawling out, "It is I that have got him." — "No, no," replied the others: "we have him." The king, to escape from this peril, said, "Gentlemen, gentlemen, I pray you conduct me and my son in a courteous manner to my cousin the prince; and do not make such a riot about my capture, for I am so great a lord that I can make all sufficiently rich." These words, and others which fell from the king, appeased them a little; but the disputes were always beginning again, and they did not move a step without rioting. When the two barons saw this troop of people, they descended from the hillock, and, sticking spurs into their horses, made up to them. On their arrival, they asked what was the matter. They were answered, that it was the King of France, who had been made prisoner, and that upward of ten knights and squires challenged him at the same time, as belonging to each of them. The two barons then pushed through the crowd by main force, and ordered all to draw aside. They commanded, in the name of the prince, and under pain of instant death, that every one should keep his distance, and not approach unless ordered or desired so to do. They all retreated behind the king; and the two barons, dismounting, advanced to the king with profound reverences, and conducted him in a peaceable manner to the Prince of Wales.

We continue our citation from Froissart with the brief chapter in which the admiring chronicler tells the gallant story of the Black Prince's behavior as host toward his royal captive, King John of France (it was the evening after the battle): —

When evening was come, the Prince of Wales gave a supper in his pavilion to the King of France, and to the greater part of the princes and barons who were prisoners. The prince seated the King of France, and his son the Lord Philip, at an elevated and well-covered table: with them were Sir James de Bourbon, the Lord John d'Artois, the earls of Tancarville, of Estampes, of Dammartin, of Graville, and the Lord of Partenay. The other knights and squires were placed at different tables. The prince himself served the king's table, as well as the others, with every mark of humility, and would not sit down at it, in spite of all his entreaties for him so to do, saying that "he was not worthy of such an honor, nor did it appertain to him to seat himself at the table of so great a king, or of so valiant a man as he had shown himself by his actions that day." He added, also, with a noble air, "Dear sir, do not make a poor meal, because the Almighty God has not gratified your wishes in the event of this day; for be assured that my lord and father will show you every honor and friendship in his power, and will arrange your ransom so reasonably, that you will henceforward always remain friends. In my opinion, you have cause to be glad that the success of this battle did not turn out as you desired; for you have this day acquired such high renown for prowess, that you have surpassed all the best knights on your side. I do not, dear sir, say this to flatter you; for all those of our side who have seen and observed the actions of each party, have unanimously allowed this to be your due, and decree you the prize and garland for it." At the end of this speech, there were murmurs of praise heard from every one; and the French said

the prince had spoken nobly and truly, and that he would
be one of the most gallant princes in Christendom if God
should grant him life to pursue his career of glory.

A splendid and a gracious figure the Black Prince
makes in the pages of Froissart. It was great good
fortune for the posthumous fame of chivalry, that the
institution should have come by an artist so gifted
and so loyal as this Frenchman, to deliver its fea-
tures in portrait to after-times, before the living
original vanished forever from the view of history.
How much the fiction of Sir Walter Scott owes to
Froissart, and to Philip de Comines after Froissart,
those only can understand who have read both the
old chronicles and the modern romances.

It was one of the congenial labors of Sidney
Lanier — pure flame of genius that late burned itself out so swiftly among us ! — to edit a reduction
or abridgment of Froissart's Chronicles dedicated
especially to the use of the young. " The Boy's
Froissart," he called it. This book is enriched with
a wise and genial appreciation of Froissart's quality
by his American editor.

Whoever reads Froissart needs to remember that
the old chronicler is too much enamoured of chivalry,
and is too easily dazzled by splendor of rank, to be
a rigidly just censor of faults committed by knights
and nobles and kings. Froissart, in truth, seems
to have been nearly destitute of the sentiment of
humanity. War to him was chiefly a game and a
spectacle.

Our presentation of Froissart must close with a single passage additional, a picturesque one, in which the chronicler describes the style of living witnessed by him at the court — we may not unfitly so apply a royal word — of the Count de Foix. The reader must understand, while he reads what we here show, that Froissart himself, in close connection, relates at full, in the language of an informant of his, how this magnificent Count de Foix had previously killed, with a knife at his throat, his own and his only son. "I was truly sorry," so, at the conclusion of the story, Froissart, with characteristic direction of his sympathy, says, "for the count his father, whom I found a magnificent, generous, and courteous lord, and also for the country that was discontented for want of an heir." Here is the promised passage; it occurs in the ninth chapter of the third volume : —

Count Gaston Phœbus de Foix, of whom I am now speaking, was at that time fifty-nine years old ; and I must say, that although I have seen very many knights, kings, princes, and others, I have never seen any so handsome, either in the form of his limbs and shape, or in countenance, which was fair and ruddy, with gray and amorous eyes, that gave delight whenever he chose to express affection. He was so perfectly formed, one could not praise him too much. He loved earnestly the things he ought to love, and hated those which it was becoming him so to hate. He was a prudent knight, full of enterprise and wisdom. He had never any men of abandoned character with him, reigned prudently, and was constant in his devotions. There were regular nocturnals from the Psalter, prayers from the rituals to the

Virgin, to the Holy Ghost, and from the burial service. He had every day distributed as alms, at his gate, five florins in small coin, to all comers. He was liberal and courteous in his gifts, and well knew how to take when it was proper, and to give back where he had confidence. He mightily loved dogs above all other animals, and during the summer and winter amused himself much with hunting. . . .

When he quitted his chamber at midnight for supper, twelve servants bore each a lighted torch before him, which were placed near his table, and gave a brilliant light to the apartment. The hall was full of knights and squires, and there were plenty of tables laid out for any person who chose to sup. No one spoke to him at his table, unless he first began a conversation. He commonly ate heartily of poultry, but only the wings and thighs; for in the daytime, he neither ate nor drank much. He had great pleasure in hearing minstrels; as he himself was a proficient in the science, and made his secretaries sing songs, ballads, and roundelays. He remained at table about two hours, and was pleased when fanciful dishes were served up to him, which having seen, he immediately sent them to the tables of his knights and squires.

In short, every thing considered, though I had before been in several courts of kings, dukes, princes, counts, and noble ladies, I was never at one that pleased me more, nor was I ever more delighted with feats of arms, than at this of the Count de Foix. There were knights and squires to be seen in every chamber, hall, and court, going backwards and forwards, and conversing on arms and amours. Every thing honorable was there to be found. All intelligence from distant countries was there to be learnt, for the gallantry of the count had brought visitors from all parts of the world. It was there I was informed of the greater part of those events which had happened in Spain, Portugal, Arragon, Navarre, England, Scotland, and on the borders of Languedoc ; for I saw, during my residence, knights and squires arrive from every nation. I therefore made inquiries from them, or from the count himself, who cheerfully conversed with me.

The foregoing is one of the most celebrated passages of description in Froissart. At the same time that it discloses the form and spirit of those vanished days, which will never come again to the world, it discloses likewise the character of the man, who must indeed have loved it all well, to have been able so well to describe it.

We take now a somewhat long forward step, in going, as we do, at once from Froissart to Rabelais. Comines, lying between, we must reluctantly pass, with thus barely mentioning his name.

III.

RABELAIS.

1495-1553.

RABELAIS is one of the most famous of writers. But he is at the same time incomparably the coarsest.

The real quality of such a writer, it is evidently out of the question to exhibit at all adequately here. But equally out of the question it is to omit Rabelais altogether from an account of French literature.

Of the life of François Rabelais the man, these

few facts will be sufficient to know. In early youth he joined the monastic order of the Franciscans. That order hated letters ; but Rabelais loved them. He, in fact, conceived a voracious ambition of knowledge. He became immensely learned. This fact, with what it implies of long labor patiently achieved, is enough to show that Rabelais was not without seriousness of character. But he was much more a merry-andrew than a pattern monk. He made interest enough with influential friends to get himself transferred from the Franciscans to the Benedictines, an order more favorable to studious pursuits. But neither among the Benedictines was this roistering spirit at ease. He left them irregularly, but managed to escape punishment for his irregularity. At last, after various vicissitudes of occupation, he settled down as curate of Meudon, where (the place, however, is doubtful, as also the date) in 1553 he died. He was past fifty years of age before he finished the work which has made him famous.

This work is "The Life of Gargantua and Pantagruel," a grotesque and nondescript production, founded, probably, on some prior romance or traditionary tale of giants. The narrative of Rabelais is a tissue of adventures shocking every idea of verisimilitude, and serving only as a vehicle for the strange humor of the writer. The work is replete with evidences of Rabelais's learning. It would be useless to attempt giving any abstract or analysis of a book which is simply a wild chaos of material jumbled together with little regard to logic, order, or method of whatever sort. We shall better represent its character by giving a few specimen extracts.

Rabelais begins his romance characteristically. According as you understand him here, you judge the spirit of the whole work. Either he now gives you a clew by which, amid the mazes of apparent sheer frivolity on his part, you may follow till you win your way to some veiled serious meaning that he had all the time, but never dared frankly to avow; or else he is playfully misleading you on a false scent, which, however long held to, will bring you out nowhere — in short, is quizzing you. Let the reader judge for himself. Here is the opening passage, — the "Author's Prologue," it is called in the English translation executed by Sir Thomas Urquhart and Motteux; a version, by the way, which, with whatever faults of too much freedom, is the work of minds and consciences singularly sympathetic with the genius of the original; the English student is perhaps hardly at all at disadvantage, in comparison with the French, for the full appreciation of Rabelais: —

Most noble and illustrious drinkers, and you thrice precious pockified blades (for to you, and none else, do I dedicate my writings), Alcibiades, in that dialogue of Plato's which is entitled, "The Banquet," whilst he was setting forth the praises of his schoolmaster Socrates (without all question the prince of philosophers), amongst other discourses to that purpose said that he resembled the Sileni. Sileni of old were little boxes, like those we now may see in the shops of apothecaries, painted on the outside with wanton toyish figures, as harpies, satyrs, bridled geese, horned hares, saddled ducks, flying goats, thiller harts, and other such counterfeited pictures, at pleasure, to excite people unto laughter, as Silenus himself, who was the foster-father of good Bacchus, was wont to do; but within those capricious caskets called Sileni, were carefully preserved and kept many rich and fine drugs, such as balm, ambergreese, amomon, musk, civet, with several kinds of precious stones, and other things of great price. Just such another thing was Socrates; for to have eyed his outside, and esteemed of him by his exterior appearance, you would not have given the peel of an onion for him, so deformed he was in body, and ridiculous in his gesture. . . . Opening this box, you would have found within it a heavenly and inestimable drug, a more than human understanding, an admirable virtue, matchless learning, invincible courage, inimitable sobriety, certain contentment of mind, perfect assurance, and an incredible disregard of all that for which men commonly do so much watch, run, sail, fight, travel, toil, and turmoil themselves.

Whereunto (in your opinion) doth this little flourish of a preamble tend? For so much as you, my good disciples, and some other jolly fools of ease and leisure, . . . are too ready to judge, that there is nothing in them but jests, mockeries, lascivious discourse, and recreative lies; . . . therefore is it, that you must open the book, and seriously consider of the matter treated in it. Then shall you find that it containeth things of far higher value than the box did promise; that is to say, that the subject thereof is not so foolish, as by the title at the first sight it would appear to be.

. . . Did you ever see a dog with a marrow-bone in his mouth? . . . Like him, you must, by a sedulous lecture [reading], and frequent meditation, break the bone, and suck out the marrow; that is, my allegorical sense, or the things I to myself propose to be signified by these Pythagorical symbols; . . . the most glorious doctrines and dreadful mysteries, as well in what concerneth our religion, as matters of the public state and life economical.

Up to this point, the candid reader has probably been conscious of a growing persuasion that this author must be at bottom a serious if also a humorous man, — a man, therefore, excusably intent not to be misunderstood as a mere buffoon. But now let the candid reader proceed with the following, and confess, upon his honor, if he is not scandalized and perplexed. What shall be said of a writer who thus plays with his reader?

Do you believe, upon your conscience, that Homer, whilst he was couching his Iliad and Odyssey, had any thought upon those allegories which Plutarch, Heraclides Ponticus, Eustathius, Phornutus, squeezed out of him, and which Politian filched again from them? If you trust it, with neither hand nor foot do you come near to my opinion, which judgeth them to have been as little dreamed of by Homer, as the gospel sacraments were by Ovid, in his Metamorphoses; though a certain gulligut friar, and true baconpicker, would have undertaken to prove it, if, perhaps, he had met with as very fools as himself, and, as the proverb says, "a lid worthy of such a kettle."

If you give any credit thereto, why do not you the same to these jovial new Chronicles of mine? Albeit, when I did dictate them, I thought thereof no more than you, who possibly were drinking the whilst, as I was. For, in the composing of this lordly book, I never lost nor bestowed any more, nor any other time, than what was appointed to serve me for taking of my bodily refection; that is, whilst I was eating and drinking. And, indeed, that is the fittest and most proper hour, wherein to write these high matters and deep sentences; as Homer knew very well, the paragon of all philologues, and Ennius, the father of the Latin poets, as Horace calls him, although a certain sneaking jobbernol alleged that his verses smelled more of the wine than oil.

Does this writer quiz his reader, or, in good faith, give him a needed hint? Who shall decide?

We have let our first extract thus run on to some length, both for the reason that the passage is as representative as any we could properly offer of the quality of Rabelais, and also for the reason that the key of interpretation is here placed in the hand of the reader, for unlocking the enigma of this remarkable book. The extraordinary horse-play of pleasantry, which makes Rabelais unreadable for the general public of to-day, begins so promptly, affecting the very prologue, that we could not present even that piece of writing entire in our extract. We are informed that the circulation in England of the works of Rabelais, in translation, has been interfered with by the English government, on the ground of their indecency. We are bound to admit, that, if any writings whatever were to be suppressed on that ground, the writings of Rabelais are certainly entitled to be of the number. It is safe to say that never, no, not even in the boundless license of the comedy of Aristophanes, was more flagrant indecency, and indecency proportionately more redun-

dant in volume, perpetrated in literature, than was
done by Rabelais.   Indecency, however, it is, rather
than strict lasciviousness.   Rabelais sinned against
manners, more than he sinned against morals.   But
his obscenity is an ocean, without bottom or shore.
Literally, he sticks at nothing that is coarse.   Nay,
this is absurdly short of expressing the fact.   The
genius of Rabelais teems with invention of coarseness, beyond what any one could conceive as possible, who had not taken his measure of possibility
from Rabelais himself.   And his diction was as
opulent as his invention.

Such is the character of Rabelais the author.
What, then, was it, if not fondness for paradox,
that could prompt Coleridge to say, " I could write
a treatise in praise of the moral elevation of Rabelais' works, which would make the church stare
and the conventicle groan, and yet would be truth,
and nothing but the truth "?   If any thing besides
fondness for paradox inspired Coleridge in saying
this, it must, one would guess, have been belief on
his part in the allegorical sense hidden deep under-
neath the monstrous mass of the Rabelaisian buffoonery.   A more judicial sentence is that of
Hallam, the historian of the literature of Europe :
" He [Rabelais] is never serious in a single page,
and seems to have had little other aim, in his first
two volumes, than to pour out the exuberance of
his animal gayety."

The supply of animal gayety in this man was

something portentous. One cannot, however, but feel that he forces it sometimes, as sometimes did Dickens those exhaustless animal spirits of his. A very common trick of the Rabelaisian humor is to multiply specifications, or alternative expressions, one after another, almost without end. From the second book of his romance, — an afterthought, probably, of continuation to his unexpectedly successful first book, — we take the last paragraph of the prologue, which shows this. The veracious historian makes obtestation of the strict truth of his narrative, and imprecates all sorts of evil upon such as do not believe it absolutely. We cleanse our extract a little : —

And, therefore, to make an end of this Prologue, even as I give myself to an hundred thousand panniers-full of fair devils, body and soul, . . . in case that I lie so much as one single word in this whole history; after the like manner, St. Anthony's fire burn you, Mahoom's disease whirl you, the squinance with a stitch in your side, and the wolf in your stomach truss you, the bloody flux seize upon you, the cursed sharp inflammations of wild fire, as slender and thin as cow's hair strengthened with quicksilver, enter into you, . . . and, like those of Sodom and Gomorrha, may you fall into sulphur, fire, and bottomless pits, in case you do not firmly believe all that I shall relate unto you in this present Chronicle.

So much for Rabelais's prologues. Our readers must now see something of what, under pains and penalties denounced so dire, they are bound to believe. We condense and defecate for this purpose the thirty-eighth chapter of the first book, which is staggeringly entitled, " How Gargantua did eat up Six Pilgrims in a Sallad " : —

The story requireth that we relate that which happened unto six pilgrims, who came from Sebastian near to Nantes; and who, for shelter that night, being afraid of the enemy, had hid themselves in the garden upon the chickling peas, among the cabbages and lettuces. Gargantua, finding himself somewhat dry, asked whether they could get any lettuce to make him a sallad; and, hearing that there were the greatest and fairest in the country, — for they were as great as plum trees, or as walnut trees, — he would go thither himself, and brought thence in his hand what he thought good, and withal carried away the six pilgrims, who were in so great fear that they did not dare to speak nor cough. Washing them, therefore, first at the fountain, the pilgrims said one to another, softly, "What shall we do? We are almost drowned here amongst these lettuce: shall we speak? But, if we speak, he will kill us for spies." And, as they were thus deliberating what to do, Gargantua put them, with the lettuce, into a platter of the house, as large as the huge tun of the White Friars of the Cistertian order; which done, with oil, vinegar, and salt, he ate them up, to refresh himself a little before supper, and had already swallowed up five of the pilgrims, the sixth being in the platter, totally hid under a lettuce, except his bourbon, or staff, that appeared, and nothing else. Which Grangousier [Gargantua's father] seeing, said to Gargantua, "I think that is the horn of a shell snail: do not eat it." — "Why not?" said Gargantua; "they are good all this month:" which he no sooner said, but, drawing up the staff, and therewith taking up the pilgrim, he ate him very well, then drank a terrible draught of excellent white wine. The pilgrims, thus devoured, made shift to save themselves, as well as they could, by drawing their bodies out of the reach of the grinders of his teeth, but could not escape from thinking they had been put in the lowest dungeon of a prison. And, when Gargantua whiffed the great draught, they thought to have drowned in his mouth, and the flood of wine had almost carried them away into the gulf of his stomach. Nevertheless, skipping with their bourbons, as St. Michael's palmers used to do, they sheltered themselves from the danger of that inundation under the banks of his teeth. But one of them, by chance, groping, or sounding the country with his staff, to try whether they were in safety or no, struck hard against the cleft of a hollow tooth, and hit the mandibulary sinew or nerve of the jaw, which put Gargantua to very great pain, so that he began to cry for the rage that he felt. To ease himself, therefore, of his smarting ache, he called for his tooth-picker, and, rubbing towards a young walnut-tree, where they lay skulking, unnestled you my gentlemen pilgrims. For he caught one by the legs, another by the scrip, another by the pocket, another by the scarf, another by the band of the breeches; and the poor fellow that had hurt him with the bourbon, him he hooked to him by [another part of his clothes]. . . . The pilgrims, thus dislodged, ran away.

Rabelais closes his story with jocose irreverent application of Scripture, — a manner of his which gives some color to the tradition of a biblical pun made by him on his death-bed.

The closest English analogue to Rabelais is undoubtedly Dean Swift. We probably never should have had " Gulliver's Travels " from Swift, if we had not first had Gargantua and Pantagruel from Rabelais. Swift, however, differs from Rabelais as well as resembles him. Whereas Rabelais is simply monstrous in invention, Swift in invention submits himself loyally to law. Give Swift his world of Liliput and Brobdingnag respectively, and all, after that, is quite natural and probable. The reduction or the exaggeration is made upon a mathematically calculated scale. For such verisimilitude Rabelais cares not a straw. His various inventions are recklessly independent one of another. A characteristic of Swift thus is scrupulous conformity to whimsical law. Rabelais is remarkable for whimsical disregard of even his own whimseys. Voltaire put the matter with his usual felicity, — Swift is Rabelais in his senses.

One of the most celebrated — justly celebrated — of Rabelais's imaginations is that of the Abbey of Thélème [Thelema]. This constitutes a kind of Rabelaisian Utopia. It was proper of the released monk to give his Utopian dream the form of an abbey, but an abbey in which the opposite should obtain of all that he had so heartily hated in his own monastic experience. A humorously impossible place and state was the Abbey of Thélème, — a kind of sportive Brook Farm set far away in a world unrealized. How those Thelemites enjoyed life, to be sure! It was like endless plum pudding — for everybody to eat, and nobody to prepare : —

All their life was spent not in laws, statutes, or rules, but according to their own free will and pleasure. They rose out of their beds when they thought good; they did eat, drink, labor, sleep, when they had a mind to it, and were disposed for it. None did awake them, none did offer to constrain them to eat, drink, nor to do any other thing;

for so had Gargantua established it. In all their rule, and
strictest tie of their order, there was but this one clause to
be observed, —

DO WHAT THOU WILT.

. . . By this liberty they entered into a very laudable emu-
lation, to do all of them what they saw did please one. If
any of the gallants or ladies should say, Let us drink, they
would all drink. If any one of them said, Let us play, they
all played. If one said, Let us go a walking into the fields,
they went all. . . . There was neither he nor she amongst
them, but could read, write, sing, play upon several musical
instruments, speak five or six several languages, and compose
in them all very quaintly, both in verse and prose. Never
were seen so valiant knights, so noble and worthy, so dex-
trous and skilful both on foot and a horseback, more brisk
and lively, more nimble and quick, or better handling all
manner of weapons than were there. Never were seen
ladies so proper and handsome, so miniard and dainty, less
forward, or more ready with their hand, and with their
needle, in every honest and free action belonging to that sex,
than were there. For this reason, when the time came, that
any man of the said abbey, either at the request of his
parents, or for some other cause, had a mind to go out of it,
he carried along with him one of the ladies, namely her who
had before that accepted him as her lover, and they were
married together.

The foregoing is one of the most purely sweet
imaginative passages in Rabelais's works. The representation, as a whole, sheathes, of course, a keen
satire on the religious houses. Real religion, Rabelais nowhere attacks.

The same colossal Gargantua who had that eating
adventure with the six pilgrims, is made, in Rabelais's
second book, to write his youthful son Pantagruel —

also a giant, but destined to be, when mature, a model of all princely virtues — a letter on education, in which the most pious paternal exhortation occurs. The whole letter reads like some learned Puritan divine's composition. Here are a few specimen sentences : —

Fail not most carefully to peruse the books of the Greek, Arabian, and Latin physicians, not despising the Talmudists and Cabalists; and by frequent anatomies get thee the perfect knowledge of that other world, called the microcosm, which is man. And at some of the hours of the day apply thy mind to the study of the Holy Scriptures: first, in Greek, the New Testament, with the Epistles of the Apostles; and then the Old Testament in Hebrew. In brief, let me see thee an abyss and bottomless pit of knowledge. . . .

. . . It behoveth thee to serve, to love, to fear God, and on him to cast all thy thoughts and all thy hope, and, by faith formed in charity, to cleave unto him, so that thou mayst never be separated from him by thy sins. Suspect the abuses of the world. Set not thy heart upon vanity, for this life is transitory; but the Word of the Lord endureth forever.

"Friar John" is a mighty man of valor, who figures equivocally in the story of Gargantua and Pantagruel. The Abbey of Thélème is given him in reward of his services. Some have identified this fighting monk with Martin Luther. The representation is, on the whole, so conducted as to leave the reader's sympathies at least half enlisted in favor of the fellow, rough and roistering as he is.

Panurge is the hero of the romance of Pantagruel, — almost more than Pantagruel himself. It would

be unpardonable to dismiss Rabelais without first
making our readers know Panurge by, at least, a few
traits of his character and conduct. Panurge was
a shifty but unscrupulous adventurer, whom Pantagruel, pious prince as he was, coming upon him by
chance, took and kept under his patronage. Panurge
was an arch-imp of mischief, — mischief indulged in
the form of obscene and malicious practical jokes.
Rabelais describes his accomplishments in a long
strain of discourse, from which we purge our selection to follow, — thereby transforming Panurge into
a comparatively proper and virtuous person : —

He had threescore and three tricks to come by it
[money] at his need, of which the most honorable and most
ordinary was in manner of thieving, secret purloining, and
filching, for he was a wicked, lewd rogue, a cozener, drinker,
roysterer, rover, and a very dissolute and debauched fellow,
if there were any in Paris; otherwise, and in all matters else,
the best and most virtuous man in the world; and he was
still contriving some plot, and devising mischief against the
serjeants and the watch.

At one time he assembled three or four especial good
hacksters and roaring boys; made them in the evening
drink like Templars, afterwards led them till they came
under St. Genevieve, or about the college of Navarre, and,
at the hour that the watch was coming up that way, — which
he knew by putting his sword upon the pavement, and his
ear by it, and, when he heard his sword shake, it was an
infallible sign that the watch was near at that instant, —
then he and his companions took a tumbrel or garbage-cart,
and gave it the brangle, hurling it with all their force down
the hill, and then ran away upon the other side; for in less
than two days he knew all the streets, lanes, and turnings
in Paris, as well as his *Deus det.*

At another time he laid, in some fair place where the said watch was to pass, a train of gunpowder, and, at the very instant that they went along, set fire to it, and then made himself sport to see what good grace they had in running away, thinking that St. Anthony's fire had caught them by the legs. . . . In one of his pockets he had a great many little horns full of fleas and lice, which he borrowed from the beggars of St. Innocent, and cast them, with small canes or quills to write with, into the necks of the daintiest gentlewomen that he could find, yea, even in the church; for he never seated himself above in the choir, but always in the body of the church amongst the women, both at mass, at vespers, and at sermon.

Coleridge, in his metaphysical way, keen at the moment on the scent of illustrations for the philosophy of Kant, said, " Pantagruel is the Reason ; Panurge the Understanding." Rabelais himself, in the fourth book of his romance, written in the last years of his life, defines the spirit of the work. This fourth book, the English translator says, is " justly thought his masterpiece." The same authority adds with enthusiasm, " Being wrote with more spirit, salt, and flame than the first part." Here, then, is Rabelais's own expression, sincere or jocular, as you choose to take it, for what constitutes the essence of his writing. We quote from the " Prologue " : —

By the means of a little Pantagruelism (which, you know, is *a certain jollity of mind, pickled in the scorn of fortune*), you see me now [" at near seventy years of age," his translator says], hale and cheery, as sound as a bell, and ready to drink, if you will.

It is impossible to exaggerate the mad, rollicking humor, sticking at nothing, either in thought or in expression, with which especially this last book of Rabelais's work is written. But we have no more space for quotation.

Coleridge's theory of interpretation for Rabelais's writings is hinted in his "Table Talk," as follows: "After any particularly deep thrust, . . . Rabelais, as if to break the blow, and to appear unconscious of what he has done, writes a chapter or two of pure buffoonery."

The truth seems to us to be, that Rabelais's supreme taste, like his supreme power, lay in the line of humorous satire. He hated monkery, and he satirized the system as openly as he dared, — this, however, not so much in the love of truth and freedom, as in pure fondness for exercising his wit. That he was more than willing to make his ribald drollery the fool's mask from behind which he might aim safely his shafts of ridicule at what he despised and hated, is indeed probable. But in this is supplied to him no sufficient excuse for his obscene and blasphemous pleasantry. Nor yet are the manners of the age an excuse sufficient. Erasmus belonged to the same age, and he disliked the monks not less. But what a contrast, in point of decency, between Rabelais and Erasmus!

IV.

MONTAIGNE.

1533-1592.

MONTAIGNE is signally the author of one book. His " Essays " are the whole of him. He wrote letters, to be sure, and he wrote journals of travel in quest of health and pleasure. But these are chiefly void of interest. Montaigne the Essayist alone is emphatically the Montaigne that survives. " Montaigne the Essayist," — that has become, as it were, a personal name in literary history.

The " Essays " are one hundred and seven in number, divided into three books. They are very unequal in length ; and they are on the most various topics, — topics often the most whimsical in character. We give a few of his titles, taking them as found in Cotton's translation : —

That men by various ways arrive at the same end ; Whether the governor of a place ought himself to go out to parley ; Of liars ; Of quick or slow speech ; A proceeding of some ambassadors ; Various events from the same counsel ; Of cannibals ; That we laugh and cry from the same thing ; Of smells ; That the mind hinders itself ; Of thumbs ; Of virtue ; Of coaches ; Of managing the will ; Of cripples ; Of experience.

Montaigne's titles cannot be trusted to indicate the nature of the essays to which they belong. The author's pen will not be bound. It runs on at its own pleasure. Things the most unexpected are incessantly turning up in Montaigne, — things, probably, that were as unexpected to the writer when he was writing, as they will be to the reader when he is reading. The writing, on whatever topic, in whatever vein, always revolves around the writer for its pivot. Montaigne, from no matter what apparent diversion, may constantly be depended upon to bring up in due time at himself. The tether is long and elastic, but it is tenacious, and it is securely tied to Montaigne. This, as we shall presently let the author himself make plain, is no accident, of which Montaigne was unconscious. It is the express idea on which the " Essays " were written. Montaigne, in his " Essays," is a pure and perfect egotist, naked, and not ashamed. Egotism is Montaigne's note, his *differentia*, in the world of literature. Other literary men have been egotists — since. But Montaigne may be called the first, and he is the greatest.

Montaigne was a Gascon, and Gasconisms adulterate the purity of his French. But his style — a little archaic now, and never finished to the nail — had virtues of its own which have exercised a wholesome influence on classic French prose. It is simple, direct, manly, genuine. It is fresh and racy of the writer. It is flexible to every turn, it is sensitive

to every rise or fall, of the thought. It is a stead-
fast rebuke to rant and fustian. It quietly laughs
to scorn the folly of that style which writhes in an
agony of expression, with neither thought nor feeling
present to be expressed. Montaigne's "Essays"
have been a great and a beneficent formative force
in the development of prose style in French.

For substance, Montaigne is rich in practical
wisdom, his own by original reflection, or by discreet purveyal. He had read much, he had observed much, he had experienced much. The result
of all, digested in brooding thought, he put into his
"Essays." These grew as he grew. He got himself transferred whole into them. Out of them, in
turn, the world has been busy ever since dissolving
Montaigne.

Montaigne's "Essays" are, as we have said,
himself. Such is his own way of putting the fact.
To one admiring his essays to him, he frankly replied, "You will like me, if you like my essays, for
they are myself." The originality, the creative
character and force, of the "Essays," lies in this
autobiographical quality in them. Their fascina-
tion, too, consists in the self-revelation they contain.
This was, first, self-revelation on the part of the
writer; but no less it becomes, in each case, self-
revelation in the experience of the reader. For, as
face answereth to face in the glass, so doth the
heart of man to man, — from race to race, and from
generation to generation. If Montaigne, in his

" Essays," held the mirror up to himself, he, in the same act, held up the mirror to you and to me. The image that we, reading, call Montaigne, is really ourselves. We never tire of gazing on it. We are all of us Narcissuses. This is why Montaigne is an immortal and a universal writer.

Here is Montaigne's Preface to his " Essays ; " " The Author to the Reader," it is entitled : —

Reader, thou hast here an honest book; it doth at the outset forewarn thee that, in contriving the same, I have proposed to myself no other than a domestic and private end: I have had no consideration at all either to thy service or to my glory. My powers are not capable of any such design. I have dedicated it to the particular commodity of my kinsfolk and friends, so that, having lost me (which they must do shortly), they may therein recover some traits of my conditions and humors, and by that means preserve more whole, and more life-like, the knowledge they had of me. Had my intention been to seek the world's favor, I should surely have adorned myself with borrowed beauties. I desire therein to be viewed as I appear in mine own genuine, simple, and ordinary manner, without study and artifice; for it is myself I paint. My defects are therein to be read to the life, and my imperfections and my natural form, so far as public reverence hath permitted me. If I had lived among those nations which (they say) yet dwell under the sweet liberty of nature's primitive laws, I assure thee I would most willingly have painted myself quite fully, and quite naked. Thus, reader, myself am the matter of my book. There's no reason thou shouldst employ thy leisure about so frivolous and vain a subject. Therefore, farewell.

From Montaigne, the 12th of June, 1580.

Michel Eyquem de Montaigne, our author, as the

foregoing date will have suggested, derived his most familiar name from the place at which he was born and at which he lived. Readers are not to take too literally Montaigne's notice of his dispensing with "borrowed beauties." He was, in fact, a famous borrower. He himself warns his readers to be careful how they criticise him; they may be flouting unawares Seneca, Plutarch, or some other, equally redoubtable, of the reverend ancients. Montaigne is perhaps as signal an example as any in literature, of the man of genius exercising his prescriptive right to help himself to his own wherever he may happen to find it. But Montaigne has in turn been freely borrowed from. Bacon borrowed from him, Shakspeare borrowed from him, Dryden, Pope, Hume, Burke, Byron, — these, with many more, in England; and, in France, Pascal, La Rochefoucauld, Voltaire, Rousseau, — directly or indirectly, almost every writer since his day. No modern writer, perhaps, has gone in solution into subsequent literature more widely than Montaigne. But no writer remains more solidly and insolubly entire.

We go at once to chapter twenty-five of the first book of the "Essays," entitled, in the English translation, "Of the education of children." The translation we use henceforth throughout is the classic one of Charles Cotton, in a text of it edited by Mr. William Carew Hazlitt. The "preface," already given, Cotton omitted to translate. We have allowed Mr. Hazlitt to supply the deficiency.

Montaigne addresses his educational views to a countess. Several others of his essays are similarly inscribed to women. Mr. Emerson's excuse of Montaigne for his coarseness, — that he wrote for a generation in which women were not expected to be readers, — is thus seen to be curiously impertinent to the actual case that existed. Of a far worse fault in Montaigne than his coarseness, — we mean his outright immorality, — Mr. Emerson makes no mention, and for it, therefore, provides no excuse. We shall ourselves, in due time, deal more openly with our readers on this point.

It was for a "boy of quality" that Montaigne aimed to adapt his suggestions on the subject of education. In this happy country of ours, all boys are boys of quality; and we shall go nowhere amiss in selecting from the present essay: —

For a boy of quality, then, I say, I would also have his friends solicitous to find him out a tutor who has rather a well-made than a well-filled head, seeking, indeed, both the one and the other, but rather of the two to prefer manners and judgment to mere learning, and that this man should exercise his charge after a new method.

'Tis the custom of pedagogues to be eternally thundering in their pupil's ears, as they were pouring into a funnel, whilst the business of the pupil is only to repeat what the others have said: now, I would have a tutor to correct this error, and that, at the very first, he should, according to the capacity he has to deal with, put it to the test, permitting his pupil himself to taste things, and of himself to discern and choose them, sometimes opening the way to him, and sometimes leaving him to open it for himself; that is, I would not have him alone to invent and speak, but that he should also hear his pupil speak in turn. . . . Let him make him put what he has learned into a hundred several forms, and accommodate it to so many several subjects, to see if he yet rightly comprehends it, and has made it his own. . . . 'Tis a sign of crudity and indigestion to disgorge what we eat in the same condition it was swallowed: the stomach has not performed its office, unless it have altered the form and condition of what was committed to it to concoct. . . .

Let him make him examine and thoroughly sift every thing he reads, and lodge nothing in his fancy upon simple authority and upon trust. Aristotle's principles will then be no more principles to him than those of Epicurus and the Stoics: let this diversity of opinions be propounded to, and laid before, him; he will himself choose, if he be able; if not, he will remain in doubt.

> "Che, non men che saper, dubbiar m'aggrata."
> > DANTE, *Inferno*, xl. 93.

> ["That doubting pleases me, not less than knowing."
> > LONGFELLOW'S *Translation*.]

For, if he embrace the opinions of Xenophon and Plato, by his own reason, they will no more be theirs, but become his own. Who follows another, follows nothing, finds nothing, nay, is inquisitive after nothing. "Non sumus sub rege; sibi quisque se vindicet." ["We are under no king; let each look to himself." — SENECA, *Ep.* 33.] Let him, at least, know that he knows. It will be necessary that he imbibe their knowledge, not that he be corrupted with their precepts; and no matter if he forget where he had his learning, provided he know how to apply it to his own use. Truth and reason are common to every one, and are no more his who spake them first, than his who speaks them after; 'tis no more according to Plato, than according to me, since both he and I equally see and understand them. Bees cull their several sweets from this flower and that blossom, here and there where they find them; but themselves afterward make the honey, which is all and purely their own, and no more thyme and marjoram: so the several fragments he borrows from others he will transform and shuffle together, to compile a work that shall be absolutely his own; that is to say, his judgment: his instruction, labor, and study tend to nothing else but to form that. . . . Conversation with men is of very great use, and travel into foreign countries; . . . to be able chiefly to give an account of the humors, manners, customs, and laws of those nations where he has been, and that we may whet and sharpen our wits by rubbing them against those of others. . . .

In this conversing with men, I mean also, and principally, those who live only in the records of history: he shall, by reading those books, converse with the great and heroic souls of the best ages.

It is difficult to find a stopping-place in discourse so wise and so sweet. We come upon sentences like Plato for height and for beauty. An example: "The most manifest sign of wisdom is a continual cheerfulness; her state is like that of things in the regions above the moon, always clear and serene." But the genius of Montaigne does not often soar, though even one little flight like that shows that it has wings. Montaigne's garnishes of quotation from foreign tongues are often a cold-blooded device of afterthought with him. His first edition was without them, in many places where subsequently they appear. Readers familiar with Emerson will be reminded of him in perusing Montaigne. Emerson himself said, " It seemed to me [in read-

ing the "Essays" of Montaigne] as if I had myself
written the book in some former life, so sincerely it
spoke to my thoughts and experience." The rich
old English of Cotton's translation had evidently a
strong influence on Emerson, to mould his own style
of expression. Emerson's trick of writing " 'tis,"
was apparently caught from Cotton. The following
sentence, from the present essay of Montaigne,
might very well have served Mr. Emerson for his
own rule of writing: " Let it go before, or come
after, a good sentence, or a thing well said, is
always in season; if it neither suit well with what
went before, nor has much coherence with what follows after, it is good in itself." Montaigne, at any
rate, wrote his " Essays " on that easy principle.
The logic of them is the logic of mere chance association in thought. But, with Montaigne, — whatever is true of Emerson, — the association at least
is not occult; and it is such as pleases the reader,
not less than it pleased the writer. So this Gascon
gentleman of the olden time never tires us, and
never loses us out of his hand. We go with him
cheerfully where he so blithely leads.

Montaigne tells us how he was himself trained
under his father. The elder Montaigne, too, had his
ideas on education, — the subject which his son, in
this essay, so instructively treats. The essayist leads
up to his autobiographical episode by an allusion to
the value of the classical languages, and to the question of method in studying them. He says : —

In my infancy, and before I began to speak, he [my father] committed me to the care of a German, . . . totally ignorant of our language, but very fluent, and a great critic, in Latin. This man, whom he had fetched out of his own country, and whom he entertained with a very great salary, for this only end, had me continually with him: to him there were also joined two others, of inferior learning, to attend me, and to relieve him, who all of them spoke to me in no other language but Latin. As to the rest of his family, it was an inviolable rule, that neither himself nor my mother, man nor maid, should speak any thing in my company, but such Latin words as every one had learned only to gabble with me. It is not to be imagined how great an advantage this proved to the whole family: my father and my mother by this means learned Latin enough to understand it perfectly well, and to speak it to such a degree as was sufficient for any necessary use, as also those of the servants did, who were most frequently with me. In short, we Latined it at such a rate, that it overflowed to all the neighboring villages, where there yet remain, that have established themselves by custom, several Latin appellations of artisans and their tools. As for what concerns myself, I was above six years of age before I understood either French or Perigordin ["Perigordin" is Montaigne's name for the dialect of his province, Perigord (Gascony)], any more than Arabic; and, without art, book, grammar, or precept, whipping, or the expense of a tear, I had, by that time, learned to speak as pure Latin as my master himself, for I had no means of mixing it up with any other.

We are now to see how, helped by his wealth, the father was able to gratify a pleasant whimsey of his own in the nurture of his boy. Highly æsthetic was the matin *reveillé* that broke the slumbers of this hopeful young heir of Montaigne : —

Some being of opinion that it troubles and disturbs the brains of children suddenly to wake them in the morning, and to snatch them violently and over-hastily from sleep, wherein they are much more profoundly involved than we, he [the father] caused me to be wakened by the sound of some musical instrument, and was never unprovided of a musician for that purpose. . . . The good man, being extremely timorous of any way failing in a thing he had so wholly set his heart upon, suffered himself at last to be overruled by the common opinions: . . . he sent me, at six years of age, to the College of Guienne, at that time the best and most flourishing in France.

In short, as in the case of Mr. Tulliver, the world was " too many " for Eyquem *père;* and, in the education of his son, the stout Gascon, having started out well as dissenter, fell into dull conformity at last.

We ought to give some idea of the odd instances, classic and other, with which Montaigne plentifully bestrews his pages. He is writing of the " Force of Imagination." He says : —

A woman, fancying she had swallowed a pin in a piece of bread, cried and lamented as though she had an intolerable pain in her throat, where she thought she felt it stick; but an ingenious fellow that was brought to her, seeing no outward tumor nor alteration, supposing it to be only a conceit taken at some crust of bread that had hurt her as it went down, caused her to vomit, and, unseen, threw a crooked pin into the basin, which the woman no sooner saw, but, believing she had cast it up, she presently found herself eased of her pain. . . .

Such as are addicted to the pleasures of the field, have,

I make no question, heard the story of the falconer, who, having earnestly fixed his eyes upon a kite in the air, laid a wager that he would bring her down with the sole power of his sight, and did so, as it was said; for *the tales I borrow, I charge upon the consciences of those from whom I have them.*

We italicize the last foregoing words, to make readers see that Montaigne is not to be read for the truth of his instances. He uses what comes to hand. He takes no trouble to verify. "The discourses are my own," he says; but even this, as we have hinted, must not be pressed too hard in interpretation. Whether a given reflection of Montaigne's is strictly his own, in the sense of not having been first another's, who gave it to him, is not to be determined except upon very wide reading, very well remembered, in all the books that Montaigne could have got under his eye. That was full fairly his own, he thought, which he had made his own by intelligent appropriation. And this, perhaps, expresses in general the sound law of property in the realm of mind. At any rate, Montaigne will wear no yoke of fast obligation. He will write as pleases him. Above all things else, he likes his freedom.

Here is one of those sagacious historical scepticisms, in which Montaigne was so fond of poising his mind between opposite views. It occurs in his essay entitled, "Of the Uncertainty of our Judgments."

Amongst other oversights Pompey is charged withal at the battle of Pharsalia, he is condemned for making his army stand still to receive the enemy's charge, "by reason that" (I shall here steal Plutarch's own words, which are better than mine) "he by so doing deprived himself of the violent impression the motion of running adds to the first shock of arms, and hindered that clashing of the combatants against one another, which is wont to give them greater impetuosity and fury, especially when they come to rush in with their utmost vigor, their courages increasing by the shouts and the career; 'tis to render the soldiers' ardor, as a man may say, more reserved and cold." This is what he says. But, if Cæsar had come by the worse, why might it not as well have been urged by another, that, on the contrary, the strongest and most steady posture of fighting is that wherein a man stands planted firm, without motion; and that they who are steady upon the march, closing up, and reserving their force within themselves for the push of the business, have a great advantage against those who are disordered, and who have already spent half their breath in running on precipitately to the charge? Besides that, an army is a body made up of so many individual members, it is impossible for it to move in this fury with so exact a motion as not to break the order of battle, and that the best of them are not engaged before their fellows can come on to help them.

The sententiousness of Montaigne may be illustrated by transferring here a page of brief excerpts from the "Essays," collected by Mr. Bayle St. John in his biography of the author. This apothegmatic or proverbial quality in Montaigne had a very important sequel of fruitful influence on subsequent French writers, as chapters to follow in this volume will abundantly show. In reading the sentences sub-

joined, you will have the sensation of coming suddenly upon a treasure-trove of coined proverbial
wisdom : —

Our minds are never at home, but ever beyond home.

I will take care, if possible, that my death shall say nothing that my life has not said.

Life in itself is neither good nor bad: it is the place of
what is good or bad.

Knowledge should not be stuck on to the mind, but incorporated in it.

Irresolution seems to me the most common and apparent
vice of our nature.

Age wrinkles the mind more than the face.

Habit is a second nature.

Hunger cures love.

It is easier to get money than to keep it.

Anger has often been the vehicle of courage.

It is more difficult to command than to obey.

A liar should have a good memory.

Ambition is the daughter of presumption.

To serve a prince, you must be discreet and a liar.

We learn to live when life has passed.

The mind is ill at ease when its companion has the colic.

We are all richer than we think, but we are brought up
to go a-begging.

The greatest masterpiece of man is . . . to be born at
the right time.

We append a saying of Montaigne's not found in Mr. St. John's collection : —

There is no so good man who so squares all his thoughts and actions to the laws, that he is not faulty enough to deserve hanging ten times in his life.

Montaigne was too intensely an egotist, in his character as man no less than in his character as writer, to have many personal relations that exhibit him in aspects engaging to our love. But one friendship of his is memorable, — is even historic. The name of La Boëtie is forever associated with the name of Montaigne. La Boëtie is remarkable for being, as we suppose, absolutely the first voice raised in France against the idea of monarchy. His little treatise " Contr' Un " (literally, " Against One"), or " Voluntary Servitude," is by many esteemed among the most important literary productions of modern times. Others, again, Mr. George Saintsbury for example, consider it an absurdly overrated book. For our own part, we are inclined to give it conspicuous place in the history of free thought in France. La Boëtie died young ; and his " Contr' Un " was published posthumously, — first by the Protestants, after the terrible day of St. Bartholomew. Our readers may judge for themselves whether a pamphlet in which such passages as the following could occur, must not have had an historic effect upon the inflammable sentiment of the French people. We take

Mr. Bayle St. John's translation, bracketing a hint or two of correction suggested by comparison of the original French. The treatise of La Boëtie is sometimes now printed with Montaigne's "Essays," in French editions of our author's works: La Boëtie says: —

You sow your fruits [crops] that he [the king] may ravage them; you furnish and fill your houses that he may have something to steal; you bring up your daughters that he may slake his luxury; you bring up your sons that he may take them to be butchered in his wars, to be the ministers of his avarice, the executors of his vengeance; you disfigure your forms by labor [your own selves you inure to toil] that he may cocker himself in delight, and wallow in nasty and disgusting pleasure.

Montaigne seems really to have loved this friend of his, whom he reckoned the greatest man in France. His account of La Boëtie's death is boldly, and not presumptuously, paralleled by Mr. St. John with the "Phædon" of Plato. Noble writing, it certainly is, though its stateliness is a shade too self-conscious, perhaps.

We have thus far presented Montaigne in words of his own such as may fairly be supposed likely to prepossess the reader in his favor. We could multiply our extracts indefinitely in a like unexceptionable vein of writing. But to do so, and to stop with these, would misrepresent Montaigne. Montaigne is very far from being an innocent writer. His moral tone generally is low, and often it is execrable. He is coarse, but coarseness is not the worst of him. Indeed, he is cleanliness itself compared with Rabelais. But Rabelais is morality itself compared with Montaigne. Montaigne is corrupt and corrupting. This feature of his writings, we are necessarily forbidden to illustrate. In an essay written in his old age, — which we will not even name, its general tenor is so evil, — Montaigne holds the following language : —

I gently turn aside, and avert my eyes from the stormy and cloudy sky I have before me, which, thanks be to God, I regard without fear, but not without meditation and study, and amuse myself in the remembrance of my better years : —

" Animus quod perdidit, optat,
Atque in præterita se totus imagine versat."
PETRONIUS, c. 128.

["The mind desires what it has lost, and in fancy flings itself wholly into the past."]

Let childhood look forward, and age backward: is not this the signification of Janus' double face ? Let years haul me along if they will, but it shall be backward; as long as my eyes can discern the pleasant season expired, I shall now and then turn them that way; though it escape from my blood and veins, I shall not, however, root the image of it out of my memory : —

" Hoc est
Vivere bis, vita posse priore frui."
MARTIAL, x. 23, 7.

[" 'Tis to live twice to be able to enjoy former life again."]

Harmlessly, even engagingly, pensive seems the

foregoing strain of sentiment. Who could suppose it a prelude to detailed reminiscence on the author's part of sensual pleasures — the basest — enjoyed in the past? The venerable voluptuary keeps himself in countenance for his lascivious vein, by writing as follows : —

I have enjoined myself to dare to say all that I dare to do; even thoughts that are not to be published, displease me; the worst of my actions and qualities do not appear to me so evil, as I find it evil and base not to dare to own them. . . .
. . . I am greedy of making myself known, and I care not to how many, provided it be truly. . . . Many things that I would not say to a particular individual, I say to the people; and, as to my most secret thoughts, send my most intimate friends to my book. . . . For my part, if any one should recommend me as a good pilot, as being very modest, or very chaste, I should owe him no thanks [because the recommendation would be false].

We must leave it — as, however, Montaigne himself is far enough from leaving it — to the imagination of readers to conjecture what " pleasures " they are, of which this worn-out debauchee (nearing death, and thanking God that he nears it " without fear ") speaks in the following sentimental strain : —

In farewells, we oftener than not heat our affections towards the things we take leave of: I take my last leave of the pleasures of this world; these are our last embraces.

Mr. Emerson, in his " Representative Men,"

makes Montaigne stand for The Sceptic. Sceptic
Montaigne was. He questioned, he considered, he
doubted. He stood poised in equilibrium, in indifference, between contrary opinions. He saw reasons on this side, but he saw reasons also on that,
and he did not clear his mind. "*Que sçai-je?*"
was his motto ("What know I?"), a question as
of hopeless ignorance, — nay, as of ignorance also
void of desire to know. His life was one long in-
terrogation, a balancing of opposites, to the end.

Such, speculatively, was Montaigne. Such, too,
speculatively, was Pascal. The difference, however,
was greater than the likeness, between these two
minds. Pascal, doubting, gave the world of spiritual things the benefit of his doubt. Montaigne,
on the other hand, gave the benefit of his doubt to
the world of sense. He was a sensualist, he was a
glutton, he was a lecher. He, for his portion, chose
the good things of this life. His body he used to
get him pleasures of the body. In pleasures of the
body he sunk and drowned his conscience, — if he
ever had a conscience. But his intelligence survived. He became, at last, — if he was not such
from the first, — almost pure sense, without soul.

Yet we have no doubt Montaigne was an agreeable gentleman. We think we should have got on
well with him as a neighbor of ours. He was a
tolerably decent father, provided the child were
grown old enough to be company for him. His
own lawful children, while infants, had to go out

of the house for their nursing ; so it not unnaturally happened that all but one died in their infancy. Five of such is the number that you can count in his own journalistic entries of family births and deaths. But, speaking as "moral philosopher," in his "Essays," he says, carelessly, that he had lost "two or three" "without repining." This, perhaps, is affectation. But what affectation !

Montaigne was well-to-do ; and he ranked as a gentleman, if not as a great nobleman. He lived in a castle, bequeathed to him, and by him bequeathed, — a castle still standing, and full of personal association with its most famous owner. He occupied a room in the tower, fitted up as a library. Over the door of this room may still, we believe, be read Montaigne's motto, " *Que sçai-je?* " Votaries of Montaigne perform their pious pilgrimages to this shrine of their idolatry, year after year, century after century.

For, remember, it is now three centuries since Montaigne wrote. He was before Bacon and Shakspeare. He was contemporary with Charles IX., and with Henry of Navarre. But date has little to do with such a writer as Montaigne. His quality is sempiternal. He overlies the ages, as the long hulk of "The Great Eastern" overlay the waves of the sea, stretching from summit to summit. Not that, in the form of his literary work, he was altogether independent of time and of circumstance. Not that he was uninfluenced by his historic place, in the essential spirit of his work. But, more than often happens, Montaigne may fairly be judged out of himself alone. His message he might, indeed, have delivered differently; but it would have been substantially the same message if he had been differently placed in the world, and in history. We need hardly, therefore, add any thing about Montaigne's outward life. His true life is in his book.

Montaigne the Essayist is the consummate, the ideal, expression, practically incapable of improvement, of the spirit and wisdom of the world. This characterization, we think, fairly and sufficiently sums up the good and the bad of Montaigne. We might seem to describe no very mischievous thing. But to have the spirit and wisdom of this world expressed, to have it expressed as in a last authoritative form, a form to commend it, to flatter it, to justify it, to make it seem sufficient, to erect it into a kind of gospel, — that means much. It means hardly less than to provide the world with a new Bible, — a Bible of the world's own, a Bible that shall approve itself as better than the Bible of the Old and New Testaments. Montaigne's " Essays " constitute, in effect, such a book. The man of the world may, — and, to say truth, does, — in this volume, find all his needed texts. Here is *viaticum* — daily manna — for him, to last the year round, and to last year after year; an inexhaustible breviary for the church of this world ! It is of the gravest historical significance that Rabelais and Montaigne, but especially Montaigne, should, to such an extent, for now three full centuries, have been furnishing the daily intellectual food of Frenchmen.

Pascal, in an interview with M. de Saci (carefully reported by the latter), in which the conversation was on the subject of Montaigne and Epictetus contrasted, — these two authors Pascal acknowledged to be the ones most constantly in his hand, — said gently of Montaigne, "Montaigne is absolutely pernicious to those who have any inclination toward irreligion, or toward vicious indulgences." We, for our part, are prepared, speaking more broadly than Pascal, to say that, to a somewhat numerous class of naturally dominant minds, Montaigne's "Essays," in spite of all that there is good in them, — nay, greatly because of so much good in them, — are, by their subtly insidious persuasion to evil, upon the whole quite the most powerfully pernicious book known to us in literature, either ancient or modern.

V.

LA ROCHEFOUCAULD: 1613-1680 (La Bruyère: 1646 (?)-1696; Vauvenargues: 1715-1747).

In La Rochefoucauld we meet another eminent example of the author of one book. "Letters," "Memoirs," and "Maxims" indeed name productions in three kinds, productions all of them notable, and all still extant, from La Rochefoucauld's pen. But the "Maxims" are so much more famous than either the "Letters" or the "Memoirs," that their author may be said to be known only by those. If it were not for the "Maxims," the "Letters" and the "Memoirs" would probably now be forgotten. We here may dismiss these from our minds, and concentrate our attention exclusively upon the "Maxims." Voltaire said, "The 'Memoirs' of the Duc de La Rochefoucauld are read, but we know his 'Maxims' by heart."

La Rochefoucauld's "Maxims" are detached sentences of reflection and wisdom on human character and conduct. They are about seven hundred in number, but they are all comprised in a very small volume; for they generally are each only two or three lines in length, and almost never does a single maxim occupy more than the half of a moderate-sized page. The "Maxims," detached, as we have described them, have no very marked logical sequence in the order in which they stand. They all, however, have a profound mutual relation. An unvarying monotone of sentiment, in fact, runs through them. They are so many different expressions, answering to so many different observations taken at different angles, of one and the same persisting estimate of human nature. 'Self-love is the mainspring and motive of every thing we do, or say, or feel, or think : ' that is the total result of the " Maxims " of La Rochefoucauld.

The writer's qualifications for treating his theme were unsurpassed. He had himself the right character, moral and intellectual ; his scheme of conduct in life corresponded ; he wrote in the right language, French ; and he was rightly situated in time, in place, and in circumstance. He needed but to look closely within him and without him, — which he was gifted with eyes to do, — and then report what he saw, in the language to which he was born. This he did, and his " Maxims " are the fruit. His method was largely the sceptical method of Montaigne. His result, too, was much the same result as his master's. But the pupil surpassed the master in the quality of his work. There is a fineness, an exquisiteness, in the literary form of La Rochefoucauld, which Montaigne might indeed have disdained to seek, but which he could never, even with seeking, have attained. Each maxim of La Rochefoucauld is a " gem of purest ray serene," wrought to the last degree of perfection in form with infinite artistic pains. Purity, precision, clearness, density, point, are perfectly reconciled in La Rochefoucauld's style with ease, grace, and brilliancy of expression. The influence of such literary finish, well bestowed on thought worthy to receive it, has been incalculably potent in raising the standard of French production in prose. It was Voltaire's testimony, "One of the works which has most contributed to form the national taste, and give it a spirit of accuracy and precision, was the little collection of 'Maxims' by François Duc de La Rochefoucauld."

There is a high-bred air about La Rochefoucauld the writer, which well accords with the rank and character of the man La Rochefoucauld. He was of one of the noblest families in France. His instincts were all aristocratic. His manners and his morals were those of his class. Brave, spirited, a touch of chivalry in him, honorable and amiable as the world reckons of its own, La Rochefoucauld ran a career consistent throughout with his own master-principle, self-love. He had a wife whose conjugal fidelity her husband seems to have thought a sufficient supply in that virtue for both himself and her. He behaved himself accordingly. His illicit relations with other women were notorious. But they unhappily did not make La Rochefoucauld in that respect at all peculiar among the distinguished men of his time. His brilliant female friends collaborated with him in working out his "Maxims."

These were the labor of years. They were published in successive editions, during the lifetime of the author; and some final maxims were added from his manuscripts after his death.

Using, for the purpose, a very recent translation, that of A. S. Bolton (which, in one or two places, we venture to conform more exactly to the sense of the original), we give almost at hazard a few specimens of these celebrated apothegms. We adopt the numbering given in the best Paris edition of the " Maxims : " —

No. 11. The passions often beget their contraries. Avarice sometimes produces prodigality, and prodigality avarice: we are often firm from weakness, and daring from timidity.

No. 13. Our self-love bears more impatiently the condemnation of our tastes than of our opinions.

How much just detraction from all mere natural human greatness is contained in the following penetrative maxim ! —

No. 18. Moderation is a fear of falling into the envy and contempt which those deserve who are intoxicated with their good fortune; it is a vain parade of the strength of our mind; and, in short, the moderation of men in their highest elevation is a desire to appear greater than their fortune.

What effectively quiet satire in these few words !—

No. 19. We have strength enough to bear the ills of others.

This man had seen the end of all perfection in the apparently great of this world. He could not bear

that such should flaunt a false plume before their
fellows : —

No. 20. The steadfastness of sages is only the art of
locking up their uneasiness in their hearts.

Of course, had it lain in the author's chosen line
to do so, he might, with as much apparent truth,
have pointed out, that to lock up uneasiness in the
heart requires steadfastness no less — nay, more —
than not to feel uneasiness.

The inflation of " philosophy " vaunting itself is
thus softly eased of its painful distention : —

No. 22. Philosophy triumphs easily over troubles passed
and troubles to come, but present troubles triumph over
it.

When Jesus once rebuked the fellow-disciples of
James and John for blaming those brethren as self-
seekers, he acted on the same profound principle
with that disclosed in the following maxim : —

No. 34. If we had no pride, we should not complain of
that of others.

How impossible it is for that Proteus, self-love, to
elude the presence of mind, the inexorable eye, the
fast hand, of this incredulous Frenchman : —

No. 39. Interest [self-love] speaks all sorts of languages,
and plays all sorts of parts, even that of disinterestedness.

No. 49. We are never so happy, or so unhappy, as we
imagine.

No. 78. The love of justice is, in most men, only the fear
of suffering injustice.

What a subtly unsoldering distrust the following maxim introduces into the sentiment of mutual friendship! —

No. 83. What men have called friendship, is only a partnership, a mutual accommodation of interests, and an exchange of good offices: it is, in short, only a traffic, in which self-love always proposes to gain something.

No. 89. Every one complains of his memory, and no one complains of his judgment.

How striking, from its artful suppression of strikingness, is the first following, and what a wide, easy sweep of well-bred satire it contains! —

No. 93. Old men like to give good advice, to console themselves for being no longer able to give bad examples.

No. 119. We are so much accustomed to disguise ourselves to others, that, at last, we disguise ourselves to ourselves.

No. 127. The true way to be deceived, is to think one's self sharper than others.

The plain-spoken proverb, "A man that is his own lawyer, has a fool for his client," finds a more polished expression in the following: —

No. 132. It is easier to be wise for others, than to be so for one's self.

How pitilessly this inquisitor pursues his prey, the human soul, into all its useless hiding-places! —

No. 138. We would rather speak ill of ourselves, than not talk of ourselves.

The following maxim, longer and less felicitously phrased than is usual with La Rochefoucauld, recalls that bitter definition of the bore, — "One who insists on talking about himself all the time that you are wishing to talk about yourself : " —

No. 139. One of the causes why we find so few people who appear reasonable and agreeable in conversation, is, that there is scarcely any one who does not think more of what he wishes to say, than of replying exactly to what is said to him. The cleverest and the most compliant think it enough to show an attentive air; while we see in their eyes and in their mind a wandering from what is said to them, and a hurry to return to what they wish to say, instead of considering that it is a bad way to please or to persuade others, to try so hard to please one's self, and that to listen well is one of the greatest accomplishments we can have in conversation.

If we are indignant at the maxims following, it is probably rather because they are partly true than because they are wholly false : —

No. 144. We are not fond of praising, and, without interest, we never praise any one. Praise is a cunning flattery, hidden and delicate, which, in different ways, pleases him who gives and him who receives it. The one takes it as a reward for his merit: the other gives it to show his equity and his discernment.

No. 146. We praise generally only to be praised.

No. 147. Few are wise enough to prefer wholesome blame to treacherous praise.

No. 149. Disclaiming praise is a wish to be praised a second time.

No. 152. If we did not flatter ourselves, the flattery of others could not hurt us.

No. 184. We acknowledge our faults in order to atone, by our sincerity, for the harm they do us in the minds of others.

No. 199. The desire to appear able often prevents our becoming so.

No. 201. Whoever thinks he can do without the world, deceives himself much; but whoever thinks the world cannot do without him, deceives himself much more.

With the following, contrast Ruskin's noble paradox, that the soldier's business, rightly conceived, is self-sacrifice ; his ideal purpose being, not to kill, but to be killed : —

No. 214. Valor, in private soldiers, is a perilous calling, which they have taken to in order to gain their living.

Here is, perhaps, the most current of all La Rochefoucauld's maxims : —

No. 218. Hypocrisy is a homage which vice renders to virtue.

Of the foregoing maxim, it may justly be said, that its truth and point depend upon the assumption, implicit, that there is such a thing as virtue, — an assumption which the whole tenor of the "Maxims," in general, contradicts.

How incisive the following ! —

No. 226. Too great eagerness to requite an obligation is a kind of ingratitude.

No. 298. The gratitude of most men is only a secret desire to receive greater favors.

No. 304. We often forgive those who bore us, but we cannot forgive those whom we bore.

No. 313. Why should we have memory enough to retain even the smallest particulars of what has happened to us, and yet not have enough to remember how often we have told them to the same individual?

The first following maxim satirizes both princes and courtiers. It might be entitled, "How to insult a prince, and not suffer for your temerity": —

No. 320. To praise princes for virtues they have not, is to insult them with impunity.

No. 347. We find few sensible people, except those who are of our way of thinking.

No. 409. We should often be ashamed of our best actions, if the world saw the motives which cause them.

No. 424. We boast of faults the reverse of those we have: when we are weak, we boast of being stubborn.

Here, at length, is a maxim that does not depress, — that animates you: —

No. 432. To praise noble actions heartily, is in some sort to take part in them.

The following is much less exhilarating: —

No. 454. There are few instances in which we should make a bad bargain, by giving up the good that is said of us, on condition that nothing bad be said.

This, also: —

No. 458. Our enemies come nearer to the truth, in the opinions they form of us, than we do ourselves.

Here is a celebrated maxim, vainly "suppressed" by the author, after first publication: —

No. 583. In the adversity of our best friends, we always find something which does not displease us."

Before La Rochefoucauld, Montaigne had said, "Even in the midst of compassion, we feel within us an unaccountable bitter-sweet titillation of ill-natured pleasure in seeing another suffer;" and Burke, after both, wrote (in his " Sublime and Beautiful ") with a heavier hand, " I am convinced that we have a degree of delight, and that no small one, in the real misfortunes and pains of others."

La Rochefoucauld is not fairly cynical, more than is Montaigne. But, as a man, he wins upon you less. His maxims are like hard and sharp crystals, precipitated from the worldly wisdom blandly solute and dilute in Montaigne.

The wise of this world reject the dogma of human depravity, as taught in the Bible. They willingly accept it, — nay, accept it complacently, hugging themselves for their own penetration, — as taught in the " Maxims " of La Rochefoucauld.

Jean de La Bruyère is personally almost as little known as if he were an ancient of the Greek or Roman world, surviving, like Juvenal, only in his literary production. Bossuet got him employed to teach history to a great duke, who became his patron, and settled a life-long annuity upon him. He published his one book, the " Characters," in 1687, was made member of the French Academy in

1693, and died in 1696. That, in short, is La Bruyère's biography.

His book is universally considered one of the most finished products of the human mind. It is not a great work, — it lacks the unity and the majesty of design necessary for that. It consists simply of detached thoughts and observations on a variety of subjects. It shows the author to have been a man of deep and wise reflection, but especially a consummate master of style. The book is one to read in, rather than to read. It is full of food to thought. The very beginning exhibits a self-consciousness on the writer's part very different from that spontaneous simplicity in which truly great books originate. La Bruyère begins : —

Every thing has been said; and one comes too late, after more than seven thousand years that there have been men, and men who have thought.

La Bruyère has something to say, and that at length unusual for him, of pulpit eloquence. We select a few specimen sentences : —

Christian eloquence has become a spectacle. That gospel sadness, which is its soul, is no longer to be observed in it; its place is supplied by advantages of facial expression, by inflexions of the voice, by regularity of gesticulation, by choice of words, and by long categories. The sacred word is no longer listened to seriously; it is a kind of amusement, one among many; it is a game in which there is rivalry, and in which there are those who lay wagers.

Profane eloquence has been transferred, so to speak, from

the bar, . . . where it is no longer employed, to the pulpit, where it ought not to be found.

Matches of eloquence are made at the very foot of the altar, and in the presence of the mysteries. He who listens sits in judgment on him who preaches, to condemn or to applaud, and is no more converted by the discourse which he praises than by that which he pronounces against. The orator pleases some, displeases others, and has an understanding with all in one thing, — that as he does not seek to render them better, so they do not think of becoming better.

The almost cynical acerbity of the preceding is ostensibly relieved of an obvious application to certain illustrious contemporary examples among preachers by the following open allusion to Bossuet and Bourdaloue : —

The Bishop of Meaux [Bossuet] and Father Bourdaloue make me think of Demosthenes and Cicero. Both of them, masters of pulpit eloquence, have had the fortune of great models; the one has made bad critics, the other, bad imitators.

Here is a happy instance of La Bruyère's successful pains in redeeming a commonplace sentiment by means of a striking form of expression ; the writer is disapproving the use of oaths in support of one's testimony : —

An honest man who says, Yes, or No, deserves to be believed; his character swears for him.

Highly satiric in his quiet way, La Bruyère knew how to be. Witness the following thrust at a contemporary author, not named by the satirist, but, no doubt, recognized by the public of the time : —

He maintains that the ancients, however unequal and negligent they may be, have fine traits; he points these out; and they are so fine that they make his criticism readable.

How painstakingly, how self-consciously, La Bruyère did his literary work, is evidenced by the following : —

A good author, and one who writes with care, often has the experience of finding that the expression which he was a long time in search of without reaching it, and which at length he has found, is that which was the most simple, the most natural, and that which, as it would seem, should have presented itself at first, and without effort.

We feel that the quality of La Bruyère is such as to fit him for the admiration and enjoyment of but a comparatively small class of readers. He was somewhat over-exquisite. His art at times became artifice — infinite labor of style to make commonplace thought seem valuable by dint of perfect expression. We dismiss La Bruyère with a single additional extract, — his celebrated parallel between Corneille and Racine : —

Corneille subjects us to his characters and to his ideas; Racine accommodates himself to ours. The one paints men as they ought to be; the other paints them as they are. There is more in the former of what one admires, and of what one ought even to imitate; there is more in the latter of what one observes in others, or of what one experiences in one's self. The one inspires, astonishes, masters, instructs; the other pleases, moves, touches, penetrates. Whatever there is most beautiful, most noble, most imperial, in the reason is made use of by the former; by the latter, whatever is most seductive and most delicate in passion. You find in the former, maxims, rules, and precepts; in the latter, taste and sentiment. You are more absorbed in the plays of Corneille; you are more shaken and more softened in those of Racine. Corneille is more moral; Racine, more natural. The one appears to make Sophocles his model; the other owes more to Euripides.

Less than half a century after La Rochefoucauld and La Bruyère had shown the way, Vauvenargues followed in a similar style of authorship, promising almost to rival the fame of his two predecessors. This writer, during his brief life (he died at thirty-two), produced one not inconsiderable literary work more integral and regular in form, entitled, " Introduction to the Knowledge of the Human Mind "; but it is his disconnected thoughts and observations chiefly that continue to preserve his name.

Luc de Clapiers, Marquis de Vauvenargues, though nobly born, was poor. His health was frail. He did not receive a good education in his youth. Indeed, he was still in his youth when he went to the wars. His culture always remained narrow. He did not know Greek and Latin, when to know Greek and Latin was, as it were, the whole of scholarship. To crown his accidental disqualifications for literary work, he fell a victim to the small-pox, which left him wrecked in body. This occurred almost immediately after he abandoned a military career which had been fruitful to him of hardship, but not of promotion. In spite of all that was thus against him, Vauvenargues, in those years, few and evil, that were his, thought finely and justly enough to earn for himself a lasting place in the literary history of his nation. He was in the eighteenth century of France, without being of it. You have to separate him in thought from the infidels and the "philoso- phers" of his time. He belongs in spirit to an earlier age. His moral and intellectual kindred was with such as Pascal, far more than with such as Voltaire. Vauvenargues is, however, a writer for the few, instead of for the many. His fame is high, but it is not wide. Historically, he forms a step- ping-stone of transition to a somewhat similar nine- teenth-century name, that of Joubert. A very few sentences of his will suffice to indicate to our readers the quality of Vauvenargues. Self-evidently, the following antithesis drawn by him between Corneille and Racine is subtly and ingeniously thought, as well as very happily expressed — this, whatever may be considered to be its aptness in point of literary appreciation : —

Corneille's heroes often say great things without inspiring them; Racine's inspire them without saying them.

Here is a good saying : —

It is a great sign of mediocrity always to be moderate in praising.

There is worldly wisdom also here : —

He who knows how to turn his prodigalities to good account, practises a large and noble economy.

Virgil's "They are able, because they seem to themselves to be able," is recalled by this : —

The consciousness of our strength makes our strength greater.

So much for Vauvenargues.

VI.

LA FONTAINE.

1621–1695.

LA FONTAINE enjoys a unique fame. He has absolutely "no fellow in the firmament" of literature. He is the only fabulist, of any age or any nation, that, on the score simply of his fables, is admitted to be poet as well as fabulist. There is perhaps no other literary name whatever among the French, by long proof more secure, than is La Fontaine's, of universal and of immortal renown. Such a fame is, of course, not the most resplendent in the world ; but to have been the first, and to remain thus far the only, writer of fables enjoying recognition as true poetry, — this surely is an achievement entitling La

Fontaine to monumental mention in any sketch, however summary, of French literature.

Jean de La Fontaine was humbly born, at Château-Thierry in Champagne. His early education was sadly neglected. At twenty years of age he was still phenomenally ignorant. About this time, being now better situated, he developed a taste for the classics and for poetry. With La Fontaine the man, it is the sadly familiar French story of debauched manners in life and in literary production. We cannot acquit him, but we are to condemn him only in common with the most of his age and of his nation. As the world goes, La Fontaine was a "good fellow," never lacking friends. These were held fast in loyalty to the poet, not so much by any sterling worth of character felt in him, as by an exhaustless, easy-going good-nature, that, despite his social insipidity, made La Fontaine the most acceptable of every-day companions. It would be easy to repeat many stories illustrative of this personal quality in La Fontaine, while to tell a single story illustrative of any lofty trait in his character would be perhaps impossible. Still, La Fontaine seemed not ungrateful for the benefits he received from others ; and gratitude, no commonplace virtue, let us accordingly reckon to the credit of a man in general so slenderly equipped with positive claims to admiring personal regard. The mirror of *bonhomie* (easy-hearted good-fellowship), he always was. Indeed, that significant, almost untranslatable, French word might have been coined to fit La Fontaine's case. On his amiable side — a full hemisphere or more of the man — it sums him up completely. Twenty years long, this mirror of *bonhomie* was domiciliated, like a pet animal, under the hospitable roof of the celebrated Madame de la Sablière. There was truth as well as humor implied in what she said one day : " I have sent away all my domestics ; I have kept only my dog, my cat, and La Fontaine."

But La Fontaine had that in him which kept the friendship of serious men. Molière, a grave, even melancholy spirit, however gay in his comedies ; Boileau and Racine, decorous both of them, at least in manners, — constituted, together with La Fontaine, a kind of private " Academy," existing on a diminutive scale, which was not without its important influence on French letters. La Fontaine seems to have been a sort of Goldsmith in this club of wits, the butt of many pleasantries from his colleagues, called out by his habit of absent-mindedness. St. Augustine was one night the subject of an elaborate eulogy, which La Fontaine lost the benefit of, through a reverie of his own indulged meantime on a quite different character. Catching, however, at the name, La Fontaine, as he came to himself for a moment, betrayed the secret of his absent thoughts by asking, "Do you think St. Augustine had as much wit as Rabelais?"— "Take care, Monsieur La Fontaine : you have put one of your stockings on wrong side out," — he had actually done so, — was the only

answer vouchsafed to his question. The speaker in
this case was a doctor of the Sorbonne (brother to
Boileau), present as guest. The story is told of
La Fontaine, that egged on to groundless jealousy
of his wife, — a wife whom he never really loved, and
whom he soon would finally abandon, — he challenged
a military friend of his to combat with swords. The
friend was amazed, and, amazed, reluctantly fought
with La Fontaine, whom he easily put at his mercy.
"Now, what is this for?" he demanded. "The public says you visit my house for my wife's sake, not
for mine," said La Fontaine. "Then I never will
come again." "Far from it," responds La Fontaine, seizing his friend's hand. "I have satisfied
the public. Now you must come to my house every
day, or I will fight you again." The two went back
in company, and breakfasted together in mutual good
humor.

A trait or two more, and there will have been
enough of the man La Fontaine. It is said that
when, on the death of Madame de la Sablière, La
Fontaine was homeless, he was met on the street by
a friend, who exclaimed, "I was looking for you;
come to my house, and live with me!" "I was
on the way there," La Fontaine characteristically
replied. At seventy, La Fontaine went through a
process of "conversion," so called, in which he pro-
fessed repentance of his sins. On the genuineness
of this inward experience of La Fontaine, it is not
for a fellow-creature of his, especially at this dis-

tance of time, to pronounce. When he died, at seventy-three, Fénelon could say of him (in Latin), "La Fontaine is no more! He is no more; and with him have gone the playful jokes, the merry laugh, the artless graces, and the sweet Muses!"

La Fontaine's earliest works were *Contes*, so styled; that is, stories, tales, or romances. These are in character such that the subsequent happy change in manners, if not in morals, has made them unreadable, — for their indecency. We need concern ourselves only with the Fables, for it is on these that La Fontaine's fame securely rests. The basis of story in them was not generally original with La Fontaine. He took whatever fittest came to his hand. With much modesty, he attributed all to Æsop and Phædrus. But invention of his own is not altogether wanting to his books of fables. Still, it is chiefly the consummate artful artlessness of the form that constitutes the individual merit of La Fontaine's productions. With something, too, of the air of real poetry, he has undoubtedly invested his verse.

We give, first, the brief fable which is said to have been the prime favorite of the author himself. It is the fable of "The Oak and the Reed." Of this fable, French critics have not scrupled to speak in terms of almost the very highest praise. Chamfort says, "Let one consider, that, within the limit of thirty lines, La Fontaine, doing nothing but yield himself to the current of his story, has taken on

every tone, that of poetry the most graceful, that of
poetry the most lofty, and one will not hesitate to
affirm, that, at the epoch at which this fable appeared, there was nothing comparable to it in the
French language." There are, to speak precisely,
thirty-two lines in the fable. In this one case, let
us try representing La Fontaine's compression by
our English form. For the rest of our specimens,
we shall use Elizur Wright's translation, — a meri-
torious one, still master of the field which, near fifty
years ago, it entered as pioneer. Mr. Wright here
expands La Fontaine's thirty-two verses to forty-
four. The additions are not ungraceful, but they
encumber somewhat the Attic neatness and simplicity of the original. We ought to say, that La
Fontaine boldly broke with the tradition which had
been making Alexandrines — lines of six feet —
obligatory in French verse. He rhymes irregularly,
at choice, and makes his verses long or short, as
pleases him. The closing verse of the present piece
is, in accordance with the intended majesty of the
representation, an Alexandrine.

> The Oak one day said to the Reed,
> "Justly might you dame Nature blame:
> A wren's weight would bow down your frame;
> The lightest wind that chance may make
> Dimple the surface of the lake
> Your head bends low indeed,
> The while, like Caucasus, my front
> To meet the branding sun is wont,
> Nay, more, to take the tempest's brunt.

A blast you feel, I feel a breeze.
Had you been born beneath my roof,
Wide-spread, of leafage weather-proof,
    Less had you known your life to tease;
    I should have sheltered you from storm.
    But oftenest you rear your form
On the moist limits of the realm of wind.
Nature, methinks, against you sore has sinned."
    "Your pity," answers him the Reed,
"Bespeaks you kind; but spare your pain;
I more than you may winds disdain.
    I bend, and break not. You, indeed,
Against their dreadful strokes till now
Have stood, nor tamed your back to bow:
    But wait we for the end."
                    Scarce had he spoke,
When fiercely from the far horizon broke
The wildest of the children, fullest fraught
With terror, that till then the North had brought.
    The tree holds good; the reed it bends.
    The wind redoubled might expends,
And so well works that from his bed
Him it uproots who nigh to heaven his head
Held, and whose feet reached to the kingdom of the
        dead.

In the fable of the "Rat retired from the
World," La Fontaine rallies the monks. With French
finesse, he hits his mark by expressly avoiding it.
"What think you I mean by my disobliging rat? A
monk? No, but a Mahometan devotee; I take it
for granted that a monk is always ready with his
help to the needy!"

The sage Levantines have a tale
    About a rat that weary grew
Of all the cares which life assail,
    And to a Holland cheese withdrew.
His solitude was there profound,
Extending through his world so round.
Our hermit lived on that within;
And soon his industry had been
With claws and teeth so good,
    That in his novel heritage,
    He had in store for wants of age,
Both house and livelihood.
What more could any rat desire?
    He grew fat, fair, and round.
    God's blessings thus redound
To those who in his vows retire.
One day this personage devout,
Whose kindness none might doubt,
Was asked, by certain delegates
That came from Rat United States,
For some small aid, for they
To foreign parts were on their way,
For succor in the great cat-war:
Ratopolis beleaguered sore,
    Their whole republic drained and poor,
No morsel in their scrips they bore.
    Slight boon they craved, of succor sure
In days at utmost three or four.
"My friends," the hermit said,
"To worldly things I'm dead.
How can a poor recluse
To such a mission be of use?
What can he do but pray
That God will aid it on its way?
And so, my friends, it is my prayer
That God will have you in his care."

His well-fed saintship said no more,
But in their faces shut the door.
     What think you, reader, is the service,
For which I use this niggard rat ?
     To paint a monk ?   No, but a dervise.
A monk, I think, however fat,
Must be more bountiful than that.

The fable entitled " Death and the Dying " is much admired for its union of pathos with wit. " The Two Doves " is another of La Fontaine's more tender inspirations. " The Mogul's Dream " is a somewhat ambitious flight of the fabulist's muse. On the whole, however, the masterpiece among the fables of La Fontaine is that of " The Animals Sick of the Plague." Such at least is the opinion of critics in general. The idea of this fable is not original with La Fontaine. The homilists of the middle ages used a similar fiction to enforce on priests the duty of impartiality in administering the sacrament, so, called, of confession. We give this famous fable as our closing specimen of La Fontaine : —

     The sorest ill that Heaven hath
Sent on this lower world in wrath, —
The plague (to call it by its name),
     One single day of which
     Would Pluto's ferryman enrich,
Waged war on beasts, both wild and tame.
They died not all, but all were sick:
No hunting now, by force or trick,

To save what might so soon expire.
No food excited their desire:
Nor wolf nor fox now watched to slay
The innocent and tender prey.
> The turtles fled,
So love and therefore joy were dead.
The lion council held, and said,
" My friends, I do believe
This awful scourge for which we grieve,
Is for our sins a punishment
Most righteously by Heaven sent.
Let us our guiltiest beast resign,
A sacrifice to wrath divine.
Perhaps this offering, truly small,
May gain the life and health of all.
By history we find it noted
That lives have been just so devoted.
Then let us all turn eyes within,
And ferret out the hidden sin.
Himself, let no one spare nor flatter,
But make clean conscience in the matter.
For me, my appetite has played the glutton
Too much and often upon mutton.
What harm had e'er my victims done?
> I answer, truly, None.
Perhaps, sometimes, by hunger pressed,
> I've eat the shepherd with the rest.
> I yield myself if need there be;
> And yet I think, in equity,
Each should confess his sins with me;
For laws of right and justice cry,
The guiltiest alone should die."
" Sire," said the fox, " your majesty
Is humbler than a king should be,
And over-squeamish in the case.
> What! eating stupid sheep a crime?
> No, never, sire, at any time.

It rather was an act of grace,
A mark of honor to their race.
And as to shepherds, one may swear,
    The fate your majesty describes,
Is recompense less full than fair
    For such usurpers o'er our tribes."

    Thus Renard glibly spoke,
And loud applause from listeners broke.
Of neither tiger, boar, nor bear,
Did any keen inquirer dare
To ask for crimes of high degree ;
    The fighters, biters, scratchers, all
From every mortal sin were free;
    The very dogs, both great and small,
    Were saints, as far as dogs could be.

    The ass, confessing in his turn,
Thus spoke in tones of deep concern:
"I happened through a mead to pass;
The monks, its owners, were at mass:
Keen hunger, leisure, tender grass,
    And, add to these the devil, too,
    All tempted me the deed to do.
I browsed the bigness of my tongue:
Since truth must out, I own it wrong."
On this, a hue and cry arose,
As if the beasts were all his foes.
A wolf, haranguing lawyer-wise,
Denounced the ass for sacrifice, —
The bald-pate, scabby, ragged lout,
By whom the plague had come, no doubt.
His fault was judged a hanging crime.
    What! eat another's grass ? Oh, shame!
The noose of rope, and death sublime,
    For that offence were all too tame!
    And soon poor Grizzle felt the same.

> Thus human courts acquit the strong,
> And doom the weak, as therefore wrong.

It is suitable to add, in conclusion, that La Fontaine is a crucial author for disclosing the irreconcilable difference that exists, at bottom, between the Englishman's and the Frenchman's idea of poetry. No English-speaker, heir of Shakspeare and Milton, will ever be able to satisfy a Frenchman with admiration such as he can conscientiously profess for the poetry of La Fontaine.

VII.

MOLIÈRE.

1623-1673.

MOLIÈRE is confessedly the greatest writer of comedy in the world. Greek Menander might have disputed the palm; but Menander's works have perished, and his greatness must be guessed. Who knows but we guess him too great? Molière's works survive, and his greatness may be measured.

We have stinted our praise. Molière is not only the foremost name in a certain department of literature; he is one of the foremost names in literature. The names are few on which critics are willing to bestow this distinction. But critics generally agree in bestowing this distinction on Molière.

Molière's comedy is by no means mere farce. Farces he wrote, undoubtedly; and some element of farce, perhaps, entered to qualify nearly every comedy that flowed from his pen. But it is not for his farce that Molière is rated one of the few greatest producers of literature. Molière's comedy constitutes to Molière the patent that it does of high degree in genius, not because it provokes laughter, but because, amid laughter provoked, it not seldom reveals, as if with flashes of lightning, — lightning playful, indeed, but lightning that might have been deadly, — the "secrets of the nethermost abyss" of human nature. Not human manners merely, those of a time, or of a race, but human attributes, those of all times, and of all races, are the things with which, in his higher comedies, Molière deals. Some transient whim of fashion may in these supply to him the mould of form that he uses, but it is human nature itself that supplies to Molière the substance of his dramatic creations. Now and again, if you read Molière wisely and deeply, you find your laughter at comedy fairly frozen in your throat, by a gelid horror seizing you, to feel that these follies or these crimes displayed belong to that human nature, one and the same everywhere and always, of which also you yourself partake. Comedy, Dante, too, called his poem, which included the "Inferno." And a Dantesque quality, not of method, but of power, is to be felt in Molière.

This character in Molière the writer, accords

with the character of the man Molière. It might not have seemed natural to say of Molière, as was said of Dante, "There goes the man that has been in hell." But Molière was melancholy enough in temper and in mien to have well inspired an exclamation such as, 'There goes the man that has seen the human heart.'

A poet as well as a dramatist, his own fellow-countrymen, at least, feel Molière to be. In Victor Hugo's list of the eight greatest poets of all time, two are Hebrews (Job and Isaiah), two Greeks (Homer and Æschylus), one is a Roman (Lucretius), one an Italian (Dante), one an Englishman (Shakspeare), — seven. The eighth could hardly fail to be a Frenchman, and that Frenchman is Molière. Mr. Swinburne might perhaps make the list nine, but he would certainly include Victor Hugo himself.

Curiously enough, Molière is not this great writer's real name. It is a stage name. It was assumed by the bearer when he was about twenty-four years of age, on occasion of his becoming one in a strolling band of players, — in 1646 or thereabout. This band, originally composed of amateurs, developed into a professional dramatic company, which passed through various transformations, until, from being at first grandiloquently self-styled, L'Illustre Théâtre, it was, twenty years after, recognized by the national title of Théâtre Français. Molière's real name was Jean Baptiste Poquelin.

Young Poquelin's bent, early encouraged by seeing plays and ballets, was strongly toward the stage. The drama, under the quickening patronage of Louis XIII.'s lordly minister, Cardinal Richelieu, was a great public interest of those times in Paris. Molière's evil star, too, it was perhaps in part that brought him back to Paris, from Orleans. He admired a certain actress in the capital. She became the companion — probably not innocent companion — of his wandering life as actor. A sister of this actress — a sister young enough to be daughter, instead of sister — Molière finally married. She led her jealous husband a wretched conjugal life. A peculiarly dark tradition of shame, connected with Molière's marriage, has lately been to a good degree dispelled. But it is not possible to redeem this great man's fame to chastity and honor. He paid heavily, in like misery of his own, for whatever pangs of jealousy he inflicted. There was sometimes true tragedy for himself hidden within the comedy that he acted for others. (Molière, to the very end of his life, acted in the comedies that he wrote.) When some play of his represented the torments of jealousy in the heart of a husband, it was probably not so much acting, as it was real life, that the spectators saw proceeding on the stage between Molière and his wife, confronted with each other in performing the piece.

Despite his faults, Molière was cast in a noble, generous mould, of character as well as of genius.

Expostulated with for persisting to appear on the stage when his health was such that he put his life at stake in so doing, he replied that the men and women of his company depended for their bread on the play's going through, and appear he would. He actually died an hour or so after playing the part of the Imaginary Invalid in his comedy of that name. That piece was the last work of his pen.

Molière produced in all some thirty dramatic pieces, from among which we select a few of the most celebrated for brief description and illustration.

The "Bourgeois Gentilhomme" ("Shopkeeper turned Gentleman") partakes of the nature of the farce quite as much as it does of the comedy. But it is farce such as only a man of genius could produce. In it Molière ridicules the airs and affectations of a rich man vulgarly ambitious to figure in a social rank too exalted for his birth, his breeding, or his merit. Jourdain is the name under which Molière satirizes such a character. We give a fragment from one of the scenes. M. Jourdain is in process of fitting himself for that higher position in society to which he aspires. He will equip himself with the necessary knowledge. To this end he employs a professor of philosophy to come and give him lessons at his house : —

M. JOURDAIN. I have the greatest desire in the world to be learned; and it vexes me more than I can tell, that my father and mother did not make me learn thoroughly all the sciences when I was young.

PROFESSOR OF PHILOSOPHY. This is a praiseworthy feeling. *Nam sine doctrina vita est quasi mortis imago.* You understand this, and you have, no doubt, a knowledge of Latin ?

M. JOUR. Yes; but act as if I had none. Explain to me the meaning of it.

PROF. PHIL. The meaning of it is, that, without science, life is an image of death.

M. JOUR. That Latin is quite right.

PROF. PHIL. Have you any principles, any rudiments, of science ?

M. JOUR. Oh, yes! I can read and write.

PROF. PHIL. With what would you like to begin ? Shall I teach you logic ?

M. JOUR. And what may this logic be ?

PROF. PHIL. It is that which teaches us the three operations of the mind.

M. JOUR. What are they — these three operations of the mind?

PROF. PHIL. The first, the second, and the third. The first is to conceive well by means of universals; the second, to judge well by means of categories; and the third, to draw a conclusion aright by means of the figures Barbara, Celarent, Darii, Ferio, Baralipton, etc.

M. JOUR. Pooh! what repulsive words! This logic does not by any means suit me. Teach me something more enlivening.

PROF. PHIL. Will you learn moral philosophy ?

M. JOUR. Moral philosophy ?

PROF. PHIL. Yes.

M. JOUR. What does it say, this moral philosophy ?

PROF. PHIL. It treats of happiness, teaches men to moderate their passions, and —

M. JOUR. No, none of that. I am devilishly hot-tempered, and morality, or no morality, I like to give full vent to my anger whenever I have a mind to it.

Prof. Phil.   Would you like to learn physics?

M. Jour.   And what have physics to say for themselves?

Prof. Phil.   Physics are that science which explains the principles of natural things and the properties of bodies; which discourses of the nature of the elements, of metals, minerals, stones, plants, and animals; which teaches us the cause of all the meteors, the rainbow, the *ignis fatuus*, comets, lightning, thunder, thunderbolts, rain, snow, hail, and whirlwinds.

M. Jour.   There is too much hullaballoo in all that, too much riot and rumpus.

Prof. Phil.   Very good.

M. Jour.   And now I want to intrust you with a great secret.   I am in love with a lady of quality, and I should be glad if you would help me to write something to her in a short letter which I mean to drop at her feet.

Prof. Phil.   Very well.

M. Jour.   That will be gallant, will it not?

Prof. Phil.   Undoubtedly.   Is it verse you wish to write to her?

M. Jour.   Oh, no! not verse.

Prof. Phil.   You only wish prose?

M. Jour.   No.   I wish for neither verse nor prose.

Prof. Phil.   It must be one or the other.

M. Jour.   Why?

Prof. Phil.   Because, sir, there is nothing by which we can express ourselves except prose or verse.

M. Jour.   There is nothing but prose or verse?

Prof. Phil.   No, sir.   Whatever is not prose, is verse; and whatever is not verse, is prose.

M. Jour.   And when we speak, what is that, then?

Prof. Phil.   Prose.

M. Jour.   What! when I say, " Nicole, bring me my slippers, and give me my nightcap," is that prose?

PROF. PHIL. Yes, sir.

M. JOUR. Upon my word, I have been speaking prose these forty years without being aware of it; and I am under the greatest obligation to you for informing me of it. Well, then, I wish to write to her in a letter, "Fair Marchioness, your beautiful eyes make me die of love;" but I would have this worded in a genteel manner, and turned prettily.

PROF. PHIL. Say that the fire of her eyes has reduced your heart to ashes; that you suffer day and night for her, tortures —

M. JOUR. No, no, no, I don't any of that. I simply wish for what I tell you, — "Fair Marchioness, your beautiful eyes make me die of love."

PROF. PHIL. Still, you might amplify the thing a little.

M. JOUR. No, I tell you, I will have nothing but these very words in the letter; but they must be put in a fashionable way, and arranged as they should be. Pray show me a little, so that I may see the different ways in which they can be put.

PROF. PHIL. They may be put first of all, as you have said, "Fair Marchioness, your beautiful eyes make me die of love;" or else, "Of love die make me, fair Marchioness, your beautiful eyes;" or, "Your beautiful eyes of love make me, fair Marchioness, die;" or, "Die of love your beautiful eyes, fair Marchioness, make me;" or else, "Me make your beautiful eyes die, fair Marchioness, of love."

M. JOUR. But of all these ways, which is the best ?

PROF. PHIL. The one you said, — "Fair Marchioness, your beautiful eyes make me die of love."

M. JOUR. Yet I have never studied, and I did all right off at the first shot.

The "Bourgeois Gentilhomme" is a very amusing comedy throughout.

From "Les Femmes Savantes" ("The Learned

Women ") — " The Blue-Stockings," we might perhaps freely render the title — we present one scene to indicate the nature of the comedy. There had grown to be a fashion in Paris, among certain women high in social rank, of pretending to the distinction of skill in literary criticism, and of proficiency in science. It was the Hôtel de Rambouillet reduced to absurdity. That fashionable affectation Molière made the subject of his comedy, "The Learned Women."

In the following extracts, Molière satirizes, under the name of Trissotin, a contemporary writer, one Cotin. The poem which Trissotin reads for the learned women to criticise and admire, is an actual production of this gentleman. Imagine the domestic *coterie* assembled, and Trissotin, the poet, their guest. He is present, prepared to regale them with what he calls his sonnet. We need to explain that the original poem is thus inscribed: " To Mademoiselle de Longueville, now Duchess of Namur, on her Quartan Fever." The conceit of the sonneteer is that the fever is an enemy luxuriously lodged in the lovely person of its victim, and there insidiously plotting against her life : —

TRISSOTIN. Sonnet to the Princess Urania on her Fever.
          Your prudence sure is fast asleep,
          That thus luxuriously you keep
          And lodge magnificently so
          Your very hardest-hearted foe.
BÉLISE. Ah! what a pretty beginning!
ARMANDE. What a charming turn it has!

PHILAMINTE. He alone possesses the talent of making easy verses.

ARM. We must yield to *prudence fast asleep.*

BÉL. *Lodge one's very hardest-hearted foe* is full of charms for me.

PHIL. I like *luxuriously* and *magnificently :* these two adverbs joined together sound admirably.

BÉL. Let us hear the rest.

TRISS.   Your prudence sure is fast asleep,
          That thus luxuriously you keep
          And lodge magnificently so
          Your very hardest-hearted foe.

ARM. *Prudence fast asleep.*

BÉL. *To lodge one's foe.*

PHIL. *Luxuriously* and *magnificently.*

TRISS.   Drive forth that foe, whate'er men say,
          From out your chamber, decked so gay,
          Where, ingrate vile, with murderous knife,
          Bold she assails your lovely life.

BÉL. Ah! gently. Allow me to breathe, I beseech you.

ARM. Give us time to admire, I beg.

PHIL. One feels, at hearing these verses, an indescribable something which goes through one's inmost soul, and makes one feel quite faint.

ARM.   Drive forth that foe, whate'er men say,
        From out your chamber, decked so gay —
How prettily *chamber, decked so gay,* is said here! And with what wit the metaphor is introduced!

PHIL. Drive forth that foe, whate'er men say.
Ah! in what an admirable taste that *whate'er men say* is! To my mind, the passage is invaluable.

ARM. My heart is also in love with *whate'er men say.*

BÉL. I am of your opinion: *whate'er men say* is a happy expression.

ARM. I wish I had written it.

BÉL. It is worth a whole poem.

PHIL.   But do you, like me, thoroughly understand the wit of it ?

ARM. *and* BÉL.   Oh! Oh!

PHIL.   Drive forth that foe, whate'er men say.
Although another should take the fever's part, pay no attention; laugh at the gossips.

> Drive forth that foe, whate'er men say,
> Whate'er men say, whate'er men say.

This *whate'er men say*, says a great deal more than it seems. I do not know if every one is like me, but I discover in it a hundred meanings.

BÉL.   It is true that it says more than its size seems to imply.

PHIL. (*to* TRISSOTIN).   But when you wrote this charming *whate'er men say*, did you yourself understand all its energy ? Did you realize all that it tells us ? And did you then think that you were writing something so witty ?

TRISS.   Ah! ah!

ARM.   I have likewise the *ingrate* in my head, — this ungrateful, unjust, uncivil fever that ill-treats people who entertain her.

PHIL.   In short, both the stanzas are admirable. Let us come quickly to the triplets, I pray.

ARM.   Ah! once more, *whate'er men say*, I beg.

TRISS.   Drive forth that foe, whate'er men say, —

PHIL., ARM., *and* BÉL.   *Whate'er men say !*

TRISS.   From out your chamber, decked so gay, —

PHIL., ARM., *and* BÉL.   *Chamber decked so gay !*

TRISS.   Where, ingrate vile, with murderous knife, —

PHIL., ARM., *and* BÉL.   That *ingrate* fever!

TRISS.   Bold she assails your lovely life.

PHIL.   *Your lovely life !*

ARM. *and* BÉL.   Ah!

TRISS.   What! reckless of your ladyhood,
Still fiercely seeks to shed your blood, —

PHIL., ARM., *and* BÉL.   Ah!

TRISS. And day and night to work you harm.
> When to the baths sometime you've brought her,
> No more ado, with your own arm
> Whelm her and drown her in the water.

PHIL. Ah! It is quite overpowering.

BÉL. I faint.

ARM. I die from pleasure.

PHIL. A thousand sweet thrills seize one.

ARM. *When to the baths sometime you've brought her,*

BÉL. *No more ado, with your own arm*

PHIL. *Whelm her and drown her in the water.*

With your own arm, drown her there in the baths.

ARM. In your verses we meet at each step with charming beauty.

BÉL. One promenades through them with rapture.

PHIL. One treads on fine things only.

ARM. They are little lanes all strewn with roses.

TRISS. Then, the sonnet seems to you —

PHIL. Admirable, new; and never did any one make any thing more beautiful.

BÉL. (*to* HENRIETTE). What! my niece, you listen to what has been read without emotion! You play there but a sorry part!

HEN. We each of us play the best part we can, my aunt; and to be a wit does not depend on our will.

TRISS. My verses, perhaps, are tedious to you.

HEN. No. I do not listen.

PHIL. Ah! Let us hear the epigram.

But our readers, we think, will consent to spare the epigram. They will relish, however, a fragment taken from a subsequent part of the same protracted scene. The conversation has made the transition from literary criticism to philosophy, in Molière's time a fashionable study rendered such by the contemporary genius and fame of Descartes. Armande resents the limitations imposed upon her sex : —

ARM.   It is insulting our sex too grossly to limit our intelligence to the power of judging of a skirt, of the make of a garment, of the beauties of lace, or of a new brocade.

BÉL.   We must rise above this shameful condition, and bravely proclaim our emancipation.

TRISS.   Every one knows my respect for the fairer sex, and that, if I render homage to the brightness of their eyes, I also honor the splendor of their intellect.

PHIL.   And our sex does you justice in this respect: but we will show to certain minds who treat us with proud contempt, that women also have knowledge; that, like men, they can hold learned meetings — regulated, too, by better rules; that they wish to unite what elsewhere is kept apart, join noble language to deep learning, reveal nature's laws by a thousand experiments; and, on all questions proposed, admit every party, and ally themselves to none.

TRISS.   For order, I prefer peripateticism.

PHIL.   For abstractions, I love platonism.

ARM.   Epicurus pleases me, for his tenets are solid.

BÉL.   I agree with the doctrine of atoms; but I find it difficult to understand a vacuum, and I much prefer subtile matter.

TRISS.   I quite agree with Descartes about magnetism.

ARM.   I like his vortices.

PHIL.   And I, his falling worlds.

ARM.   I long to see our assembly opened, and to distinguish ourselves by some great discovery.

TRISS.   Much is expected from your enlightened knowledge, for nature has hidden few things from you.

PHIL.   For my part, I have, without boasting, already made one discovery; I have plainly seen men in the moon.

BÉL.   I have not, I believe, as yet quite distinguished men, but I have seen steeples as plainly as I see you.

ARM. In addition to natural philosophy, we will dive into grammar, history, verse, ethics, and politics.

PHIL. I find in ethics charms which delight my heart; it was formerly the admiration of great geniuses: but I give the preference to the Stoics, and I think nothing so grand as their founder.

"Les Précieuses Ridicules" is an earlier and lighter treatment of the same theme. The object of ridicule in both these pieces was a lapsed and degenerate form of what originally was a thing worthy of respect, and even of praise. At the Hôtel de Rambouillet, conversation was cultivated as a fine art. There was, no doubt, something overstrained in the standards which the ladies of that circle enforced. Their mutual communication was all conducted in a peculiar style of language, the natural deterioration of which was into a kind of euphuism, such as English readers will remember to have seen exemplified in Walter Scott's Sir Piercie Shafton. These ladies called each other, with demonstrative fondness, "Ma précieuse." Hence at last the term *précieuse* as a designation of ridicule. Madame de Sévigné was a *précieuse*. But she, with many of her peers, was too rich in sarcastic common sense to be a *précieuse ridicule*. Molière himself, thrifty master of policy that he was, took pains to explain that he did not satirize the real thing, but only the affectation.

"Tartuffe, or the Impostor," is perhaps the most celebrated of all Molière's plays. Scarcely comedy, scarcely tragedy, it partakes of both characters.

Like tragedy, serious in purpose, it has a happy ending like comedy. Pity and terror are absent; or, if not quite absent, these sentiments are present raised only to a pitch distinctly below the tragic. Indignation is the chief passion excited, or detestation, perhaps, rather than indignation. This feeling is provided at last with its full satisfaction in the condign punishment visited on the impostor.

The original "Tartuffe," like the most of Molière's comedies, is written in rhymed verse. We could not, with any effort, make the English-reading student of Molière sufficiently feel how much is lost when the form is lost which the creations of this great genius took, in their native French, under his own master hand. A satisfactory metrical rendering is out of the question. The sense, at least, if not the incommunicable spirit, of the original is very well given in Mr. C. H. Wall's version, which we use.

The story of "Tartuffe" is briefly this: Tartuffe, the hero, is a pure villain. He mixes no adulteration of good in his composition. He is hypocrisy itself, the strictly genuine article. Tartuffe has completely imposed upon one Orgon, a man of wealth and standing. Orgon, with his wife, and with his mother, in fact, believes in him absolutely. These people have received the canting rascal into their house, and are about to bestow upon him their daughter in marriage. The following scene from act first shows the skill with which Molière could exhibit, in a few strokes of bold exaggeration, the infatuation of Orgon's regard for Tartuffe. Orgon has been absent from home. He returns, and meets Cléante, his brother, whom, in his eagerness, he begs to excuse his not answering a question just addressed to him : —

ORGON (*to* CLÉANTE). Brother, pray excuse me: you will kindly allow me to allay my anxiety by asking news of the family. (*To* DORINE, *a maid-servant.*) Has every thing gone on well these last two days ? What has happened ? How is everybody ?

DOR. The day before yesterday our mistress was very feverish from morning to night, and suffered from a most extraordinary headache.

ORG. And Tartuffe ?

DOR. Tartuffe! He is wonderfully well, stout and fat, with blooming cheeks and ruddy lips.

ORG. Poor man!

DOR. In the evening she felt very faint, and the pain in her head was so great that she could not touch any thing at supper.

ORG. And Tartuffe ?

DOR. He ate his supper by himself before her, and very devoutly devoured a brace of partridges, and half a leg of mutton hashed.

ORG. Poor man!

DOR. She spent the whole of the night without getting one wink of sleep: she was very feverish, and we had to sit up with her until the morning.

ORG. And Tartuffe ?

DOR. Overcome by a pleasant sleepiness, he passed from the table to his room, and got at once into his warmed bed, where he slept comfortably till the next morning.

ORG. Poor man!

DOR. At last yielding to our persuasions, she consented to be bled, and immediately felt relieved.

ORG. And Tartuffe?

DOR. He took heart right valiantly, and fortifying his soul against all evils, to make up for the blood which our lady had lost, drank at breakfast four large bumpers of wine.

ORG. Poor man!

DOR. Now, at last, they are both well; and I will go and tell our lady how glad you are to hear of her recovery.

Tartuffe repays the trust and love of his benefactor by making improper advances to that benefactor's wife. Orgon's son, who does not share his father's confidence in Tartuffe, happens to be an unseen witness of the man's infamous conduct. He exposes the hypocrite to Orgon, with the result of being himself expelled from the house for his pains; while Tartuffe, in recompense for the injury done to his feelings, is presented with a gift-deed of Orgon's estate. But now Orgon's wife contrives to let her husband see and hear for himself the vileness of Tartuffe. This done, Orgon confronts the villain, and, with just indignation, orders him out of his house. Tartuffe reminds Orgon that the shoe is on the other foot; that he is himself now owner there, and that it is Orgon, instead of Tartuffe, who must go. Orgon has an interview with his mother, who is exasperatingly sure still that Tartuffe is a maligned good man : —

MADAME PERNELLE. I can never believe, my son, that he would commit so base an action.

ORG. What ?

PER. Good people are always subject to envy.

ORG. What do you mean, mother?

PER. That you live after a strange sort here, and that I am but too well aware of the ill will they all bear him.

ORG. What has this ill will to do with what I have just told you?

PER. I have told it you a hundred times when you were young, that in this world virtue is ever liable to persecution, and that, although the envious die, envy never dies.

ORG. But what has this to do with what has happened to-day?

PER. They have concocted a hundred foolish stories against him.

ORG. I have already told you that I saw it all myself.

PER. The malice of evil-disposed persons is very great.

ORG. You would make me swear, mother! I tell you that I saw his audacious attempt with my own eyes.

PER. Evil tongues have always some venom to pour forth; and here below, there is nothing proof against them.

ORG. You are maintaining a very senseless argument. I saw it, I tell you,—saw it with my own eyes! what you can call s-a-w, saw! Must I din it over and over into your ears, and shout as loud as half a dozen people?

PER. Gracious goodness! appearances often deceive us! We must not always judge by what we see.

ORG. I shall go mad!

PER. We are by nature prone to judge wrongly, and good is often mistaken for evil.

ORG. I ought to look upon his desire of seducing my wife as charitable?

PER. You ought to have good reasons before you accuse another, and you should have waited till you were quite sure of the fact.

ORG. Heaven save the mark! how could I be more sure? I suppose, mother, I ought to have waited till—you will make me say something foolish.

PER. In short, his soul is possessed with too pure a zeal; and I cannot possibly conceive that he would think of attempting what you accuse him of.

ORG. If you were not my mother, I really don't know what I might now say to you, you make me so savage.

The short remainder of the scene has for its important idea, the suggestion that under the existing circumstances some sort of peace ought to be patched up between Orgon and Tartuffe. Meantime one LOYAL is observed coming, whereupon the fourth scene of act fifth opens : —

LOY. (*to* DORINE *at the farther part of the stage*). Goodday, my dear sister; pray let me speak to your master.

DOR. He is with friends, and I do not think he can see any one just now.

LOY. I would not be intrusive. I feel sure that he will find nothing unpleasant in my visit: in fact, I come for something which will be very gratifying to him.

DOR. What is your name?

LOY. Only tell him that I come from Mr. Tartuffe, for his benefit.

DOR. (*to* ORGON). It is a man who comes in a civil way from Mr. Tartuffe, on some business which will make you glad, he says.

CLÉ. (*to* ORGON). You must see who it is, and what the man wants.

ORG. (*to* CLÉANTE). He is coming, perhaps, to settle matters between us in a friendly way. How, in this case, ought I to behave to him?

CLÉ. Don't show any resentment, and, if he speaks of an agreement, listen to him.

LOY. (*to* ORGON). Your servant, sir! May heaven punish whoever wrongs you! and may it be as favorable to you, sir, as I wish!

ORG. (*aside to* CLÉANTE). This pleasant beginning agrees with my conjectures, and argues some sort of reconciliation.

LOY. All your family was always dear to me, and I served your father.

ORG. Sir, I am sorry and ashamed to say that I do not know who you are, neither do I remember your name.

LOY. My name is Loyal; I was born in Normandy, and am a royal bailiff in spite of envy. For the last forty years I have had the good fortune to fill the office, thanks to Heaven, with great credit; and I come, sir, with your leave, to serve you the writ of a certain order.

ORG. What! you are here —

LOY. Gently, sir, I beg. It is merely a summons, — a notice for you to leave this place, you and yours; to take away all your goods and chattels, and make room for others, without delay or adjournment, as hereby decreed.

ORG. I! leave this place?

LOY. Yes, sir; if you please. The house incontestably belongs, as you are well aware, to the good Mr. Tartuffe. He is now lord and master of your estates, according to a deed I have in my keeping. It is in due form, and cannot be challenged.

DAMIS (*to* MR. LOYAL). This great impudence is, indeed, worthy of all admiration.

LOY. (*to* DAMIS). Sir, I have nothing at all to do with you. (*Pointing to* ORGON.) My business is with this gentleman. He is tractable and gentle, and knows too well the duty of a gentleman to try to oppose authority.

ORG. But —

LOY. Yes, sir: I know that you would not, for any thing, show contumacy; and that you will allow me, like a reasonable man, to execute the orders I have received. . . .

The scene gives in conclusion some spirited by-play of asides and interruptions from indignant mem-

bers of the family. Then follows scene fifth, one
exchange of conversation from which will sufficiently
indicate the progress of the plot : —

ORG. Well, mother, you see whether I am right; and you
can judge of the rest by the writ. Do you at last acknowledge his rascality ?

PER. I am thunderstruck, and can scarcely believe my
eyes and ears.

The next scene introduces Valère, the noble lover
of that daughter whom the infatuated father was
bent on sacrificing to Tartuffe. Valère comes to
announce that Tartuffe, the villain, has accused Orgon to the king. Orgon must fly. Valère offers
him his own carriage and money, — will, in fact,
himself keep him company till he reaches a place of
safety. As Orgon, taking hasty leave of his family,
turns to go, he is encountered by — the following
scene will show whom : —

TAR. (*stopping* ORGON). Gently, sir, gently; not so fast,
I beg. You have not far to go to find a lodging, and you are
a prisoner in the king's name.

ORG. Wretch ! you had reserved this shaft for the last;
by it you finish me, and crown all your perfidies.

TAR. Your abuse has no power to disturb me, and I
know how to suffer every thing for the sake of Heaven.

CLÉ. Your moderation is really great, we must acknowledge.

DA. How impudently the infamous wretch sports with
Heaven!

TAR. Your anger cannot move me. I have no other
wish but to fulfil my duty.

MARIANNE. You may claim great glory from the performance of this duty: it is a very honorable employment for you.

TAR. The employment cannot be otherwise than glorious, when it comes from the power that sends me here.

ORG. But do you remember that my charitable hand, ungrateful scoundrel, raised you from a state of misery?

TAR. Yes, I know what help I have received from you; but the interest of my king is my first duty. The just obligation of this sacred duty stifles in my heart all other claims; and I would sacrifice to it friend, wife, relations, and myself with them.

ELMIRE. The impostor!

DOR. With what treacherous cunning he makes a cloak of all that men revere! . . .

TAR. (*to the* OFFICER). I beg of you, sir, to deliver me from all this noise, and to act according to the orders you have received.

OFFICER. I have certainly put off too long the discharge of my duty, and you very rightly remind me of it. To execute my order, follow me immediately to the prison in which a place is assigned to you.

TAR. Who? I, sir?

OFFICER. Yes, you.

TAR. Why to prison?

OFFICER. To you I have no account to render. (*To* ORGON.) Pray, sir, recover from your great alarm. We live under a king [Louis XIV.] who is an enemy to fraud, — a king who can read the heart, and whom all the arts of impostors cannot deceive. His great mind, endowed with delicate discernment, at all times sees things in their true light. . . . He annuls, by his sovereign will, the terms of the contract by which you gave him [Tartuffe] your property. He moreover forgives you this secret offence in which you were involved by the flight of your friend. This to reward the zeal which you once showed for him in maintaining his rights, and to prove that his heart, when it is least expected, knows how to recompense a good action. Merit with him is never lost, and he remembers good better than evil.

DOR. Heaven be thanked!

PER. Ah! I breathe again.

EL. What a favorable end to our troubles!

MAR. Who would have foretold it?

ORG. (*to* TARTUFFE, *as the* OFFICER *leads him off*). Ah, wretch! now you are —

Tartuffe thus disposed of, the play promptly ends, with a vanishing glimpse afforded us of a happy marriage in prospect for Valère with the daughter.

Molière is said to have had a personal aim in drawing the character of Tartuffe. This, at least, was like Dante. There is not much sweet laughter in such a comedy. But there is a power that is dreadful.

Each succeeding generation of Frenchmen supplies its bright and ingenious wits who produce comedy. But as there is no second Shakspeare, so there is but one Molière.

VIII.

PASCAL.

1623–1662.

Pascal's fame is distinctly the fame of a man of genius. He achieved notable things. But it is what he might have done, still more than what he did, that fixes his estimation in the world of mind. Blaise Pascal is one of the chief intellectual glories of France.

Pascal, the boy, had a strong natural bent toward mathematics. The story is that his father, in order to turn his son's whole force on the study of languages, put out of the lad's reach all books treating his favorite subject. Thus shut up to his own resources, the masterful little fellow, about his eighth year, drawing charcoal diagrams on the floor, made perceptible progress in working out geometry for himself. At sixteen he produced a treatise on conic sections that excited the wonder and incredulity of Descartes. Later, he experimented in barometry, and pursued investigations in mechanics. Later still, he made what seemed to be approaches toward Newton's binomial theorem.

Vivid religious convictions meantime deeply affected Pascal's mind. His health, never robust, began to give way. His physicians prescribed mental diversion, and forced him into society. That medicine, taken at first with reluctance, proved dangerously delightful to Pascal's vivacious and susceptible spirit. His pious sister Jacqueline warned her brother that he was going too far. But he was still more effectively warned by an accident, in which he almost miraculously escaped from death. Withdrawing from the world, he adopted a course of ascetic practices, in which he continued till he died — in his thirty-ninth year. He wore about his waist an iron girdle armed with sharp points; and this he would press smartly with his elbow when he detected himself at fault in his spirit.

Notwithstanding what Pascal did or attempted, worthy of fame, in science, it was his fortune to become chiefly renowned by literary achievement. His, in fact, would now be a half-forgotten name if he had not written the "Provincial Letters" and the "Thoughts."

The "Provincial Letters" is an abbreviated title. The title in full originally was, "Letters written by Louis de Montalte to a Provincial, one of his friends, and to the Reverend Fathers, the Jesuits, on the subject of the morality and the policy of those Fathers."

Of the "Provincial Letters," several English translations have been made. No one of these that we have been able to find, seems entirely satisfactory. There is an elusive quality to Pascal's style, and in losing this you seem to lose something of

Pascal's thought. For with Pascal the thought and the style penetrate each other inextricably and almost indistinguishably. You cannot print a smile, an inflection of the voice, a glance of the eye, a French shrug of the shoulders. And such modulations of the thought seem everywhere to lurk in the turns and phrases of Pascal's inimitable French. To translate them is impossible.

Pascal is beyond question the greatest modern master of that indescribably delicate art in expression, which, from its illustrious ancient exemplar, has received the name of the Socratic irony. With this fine weapon, in great part, it was, wielded like a magician's invisible wand, that Pascal did his memorable execution on the Jesuitical system of morals and casuistry, in the "Provincial Letters." In great part, we say; for the flaming moral earnestness of the man could not abide only to play with his adversaries, to the end of the famous dispute. His lighter cimeter blade he flung aside before he had done, and, toward the last, brandished a sword that had weight as well as edge and temper. The skill that could halve a feather in the air with the sword of Saladin was proved to be also strength that could cleave a suit of mail with the brand of Richard the Lion-hearted.

It is universally acknowledged, that the French language has never in any hands been a more obedient instrument of intellectual power than it was in the hands of Pascal. He is rated the earliest writer to produce what may be called the final French prose. "The creator of French style," Villemain boldly calls him. Pascal's style remains to this day almost perfectly free from adhesions of archaism in diction and in construction. Pascal showed, as it were at once, what the French language was capable of doing in response to the demands of a master. It was the joint achievement of genius, of taste, and of skill, working together in an exquisite balance and harmony.

But let us be entirely frank. The "Provincial Letters" of Pascal are now, to the general reader, not so interesting as from their fame one would seem entitled to expect. You cannot read them intelligently without considerable previous study. You need to have learned, imperfectly, with labor, a thousand things that every contemporary reader of Pascal perfectly knew, as if by simply breathing, — the necessary knowledge being then, so to speak, abroad in the air. Even thus, you cannot possibly derive that vivid delight from perusing in bulk the "Provincial Letters" now, which the successive numbers of the series, appearing at brief irregular intervals, communicated to the eagerly expecting French public, at a time when the topics discussed were topics of a present and pressing practical interest. Still, with whatever disadvantage unavoidably attending, we must give our readers a taste of the quality of Pascal's "Provincial Letters."

We select a passage at the commencement of the

Seventh Letter. We use the translation of Mr. Thomas M'Crie. This succeeds very well in conveying the sense, though it necessarily fails to convey either the vivacity or the eloquence, of the incomparable original. The first occasion of the "Provincial Letters" was a championship proposed to Pascal to be taken up by him on behalf of his beleaguered and endangered friend Arnauld, the Port-Royalist. (Port Royal was a Roman-Catholic abbey, situated some eight miles to the south-west of Versailles, and therefore not very remote from Paris.) Arnauld was "for substance of doctrine" really a Calvinist, though he quite sincerely disclaimed being such; and it was for his defence of Calvinism (under its ancient form of Augustinianism) that he was threatened, through Jesuit enmity, with condemnation for heretical opinion. The problem was to enlist the sentiment of general society in his favor. The friends in council at Port Royal said to Pascal, "You must do this." Pascal said, "I will try." In a few days, the first letter of a series destined to such fame, was submitted for judgment to Port Royal and approved. It was printed — anonymously. The success was instantaneous and brilliant. A second letter followed, and a third. Soon, from strict personal defence of Arnauld, the writer went on to take up a line of offence and aggression. He carried the war into Africa. He attacked the Jesuits as teachers of immoral doctrine.

The plan of these later letters was, to have a Paris

gentleman write to a friend of his in the country (the "provincial"), detailing interviews held by him with a Jesuit priest of the city. The supposed Parisian gentleman, in his interviews with the supposed Jesuit father, affects the air of a very simple-hearted seeker after truth. He represents himself as, by his innocent-seeming docility, leading his Jesuit teacher on to make the most astonishingly frank exposures of the secrets of the casuistical system held and taught by his order.

The Seventh Letter tells the story of how Jesuit confessors were instructed to manage their penitents in a matter made immortally famous by the wit and genius of Pascal, the matter of "directing the intention." There is nothing in the "Provincial Letters" better suited than this at the same time to interest the general reader, and to display the quality of these renowned productions. (We do not scruple to change our chosen translation a little, at points where it seems to us susceptible of some easy improvement.) Remember it is an imaginary Parisian gentleman who now writes to a friend of his in the country : —

"You know," he said, "that the ruling passion of persons in that rank of life [the rank of gentleman] is 'the point of honor,' which is perpetually driving them into acts of violence apparently quite at variance with Christian piety; so that, in fact, they would be almost all of them excluded from our confessionals, had not our fathers relaxed a little from the strictness of religion, to accommodate themselves to the weakness of humanity. Anxious to keep on good terms, both with the gospel, by doing their duty to God, and with the men of the world, by showing charity to their neighbor, they needed all the wisdom they possessed to devise expedients for so nicely adjusting matters as to permit these gentlemen to adopt the methods usually resorted to for vindicating their honor without wounding their consciences, and thus reconcile things apparently so opposite to each other as piety and the point of honor.". . .

"I should certainly [so replies M. Montalte, with the most exquisite irony couched under a cover of admiring simplicity], — I should certainly have considered the thing perfectly impracticable, if I had not known, from what I have seen of your fathers, that they are capable of doing with ease what is impossible to other men. This led me to anticipate that they must have discovered some method for meeting the difficulty, — a method which I admire, even before knowing it, and which I pray you to explain to me."

"Since that is your view of the matter," replied the monk, "I cannot refuse you. Know, then, that this marvellous principle is our grand method of *directing the intention* — the importance of which, in our moral system, is such, that I might almost venture to compare it with the doctrine of probability. You have had some glimpses of it in passing, from certain maxims which I mentioned to you. For example, when I was showing you how servants might execute certain troublesome jobs with a safe conscience, did you not remark that it was simply by diverting their intention from the evil to which they were accessory, to the profit which they might reap from the transaction ? Now, that is what we call *directing the intention*. You saw, too, that, were it not for a similar divergence of *the mind*, those who give money for benefices might be downright simoniacs. But I will now show you this grand method in all its glory, as it applies to the subject of homicide, — a crime which it justifies in a thousand instances, — in order that, from this startling result, you may form an idea of all that it is calculated to effect."

"I foresee already," said I, "that, according to this mode, every thing will be permitted: it will stick at nothing."

"You always fly from the one extreme to the other," replied the monk; "prithee avoid that habit. For just to show you that we are far from permitting every thing, let me tell you that we never suffer such a thing as a formal intention to sin, with the sole design of sinning; and, if any person whatever should persist in having no other end but evil in the evil that he does, we break with him at once; such conduct is diabolical. This holds true, without exception of age, sex, or rank. But when the person is not of such a wretched disposition as this, we try to put in practice our method of *directing the intention*, which consists in his proposing to himself, as the end of his actions, some allowable object. Not that we do not endeavor, as far as we can, to dissuade men from doing things forbidden; but, when we cannot prevent the action, we at least purify the motive, and thus correct the viciousness of the mean by the goodness of the end. Such is the way in which our fathers have contrived to permit those acts of violence to which men usually resort in vindication of their honor. They have no more to do than to turn off their intention from the desire of vengeance, which is criminal, and direct it to a desire to defend their honor, which, according to us, is quite warrantable. And in this way our doctors discharge all their duty towards God and towards man. By permitting the action, they gratify the world; and by purifying the intention, they give satisfaction to the gospel. This is a secret, sir, which was entirely unknown to the ancients; the world is indebted for the discovery entirely to our doctors. You understand it now, I hope?"

"Perfectly," was my reply. "To men you grant the outward material effect of the action, and to God you give the inward and spiritual movement of the intention; and, by this equitable partition, you form an alliance between the laws of God and the laws of men. But, my dear sir, to be frank with you, I can hardly trust your premises, and I suspect that your authors will tell another tale."

"You do me injustice," rejoined the monk ; "I advance nothing but what I am ready to prove, and that by such a rich array of passages, that altogether their number, their authority, and their reasonings, will fill you with admiration. To show you, for example, the alliance which our fathers have formed between the maxims of the gospel and those of the world, by thus regulating the intention, let me refer you to Reginald. (*In praxi.*, liv. xxi., num. 62, p. 260.) [These, and all that follow, are verifiable citations from real and undisputed Jesuit authorities, not to this day repudiated by that order.] 'Private persons are forbidden to avenge themselves ; for St. Paul says to the Romans (ch. 12th), "Recompense to no man evil for evil;" and Ecclesiasticus says (ch. 28th), "He that taketh vengeance shall draw on himself the vengeance of God, and his sins will not be forgotten." Besides all that is said in the gospel about forgiving offences, as in the 6th and 18th chapters of St. Matthew.'"

"Well, father, if after that, he [Reginald] says any thing contrary to the Scripture, it will, at least, not be from lack of scriptural knowledge. Pray, how does he conclude ? "

"You shall hear," he said. "From all this it appears that a military man may demand satisfaction on the spot from the person who has injured him — not, indeed, with the intention of rendering evil for evil, but with that of preserving his honor — *non ut malum pro malo reddat, sed ut conservat honorem.* See you how carefully, because the Scripture condemns it, they guard against the intention of rendering evil for evil ? This is what they will tolerate on no account. Thus Lessius observes (De Just., liv. ii., c. 9, d. 12, n. 79), that, 'If a man has received a blow on the face, he must on no account have an intention to avenge himself ; but he may lawfully have an intention to avert infamy, and may, with that view, repel the insult immediately, even at the point of the sword — *etiam cum gladio.*' So far are we from permitting any one to cherish the design of taking vengeance on his enemies, that our fathers will not allow any even to *wish their death* — by a movement of hatred. 'If your enemy is disposed to injure you,' says Escobar, 'you have no right to wish his death, by a movement of hatred; though you may, with a view to save yourself from harm.' So legitimate, indeed, is this wish, with such an intention, that our great Hurtado de Mendoza says that 'we may *pray God* to visit with speedy death those who are bent on persecuting us, if there is no other way of escaping from it.'" (In his book, De Spe, vol. ii., d. 15, sec. 4, 48.)

"May it please your reverence," said I, "the Church has forgotten to insert a petition to that effect among her prayers."

"They have not put every thing into the prayers that one may lawfully ask of God," answered the monk. "Besides, in the present case, the thing was impossible, for this same opinion is of more recent standing than the Breviary. You are not a good chronologist, friend. But, not to wander from the point, let me request your attention to the following passage, cited by Diana from Gaspar Hurtado (De Sub. Pecc., diff. 9; Diana, p. 5; tr. 14, r. 99), one of Escobar's four-and-twenty fathers : 'An incumbent may, without any mortal sin, desire the decease of a life-renter on his benefice, and a son that of his father, and rejoice when it happens ; provided always it is for the sake of the profit that is to accrue from the event, and not from personal aversion.'"

"Good," cried I. "That is certainly a very happy hit, and I can easily see that the doctrine admits of a wide application. But yet there are certain cases, the solution of which, though of great importance for gentlemen, might present still greater difficulties."

"Propose such, if you please, that we may see," said the monk.

"Show me, with all your directing of the intention," returned I, "that it is allowable to fight a duel."

"Our great Hurtado de Mendoza," said the father, "will satisfy you on that point in a twinkling. 'If a gentleman,' says he, in a passage cited by Diana, 'who is challenged to fight a duel, is well known to have no religion, and if the vices to which he is openly and unscrupulously addicted, are such as would lead people to conclude, in the event of his refusing to fight, that he is actuated, not by the fear of God, but by cowardice, and induce them to say of him that he was a *hen*, and not a man — *gallina, et non vir ;* in that case he may, to save his honor, appear at the appointed spot — not, indeed, with the express intention of fighting a duel, but merely with that of defending himself, should the person who challenged him come there unjustly to attack him. His action in this case, viewed by itself, will be perfectly indifferent ; for what moral evil is there in one's stepping into a field, taking a stroll in expectation of meeting a person, and defending one's self in the event of being attacked ? And thus the gentleman is guilty of no sin whatever ; for in fact, it cannot be called accepting a challenge at all, his intention being directed to other circumstances, and the acceptance of a challenge consisting in an express intention to fight, which we are supposing the gentleman never had.' "

The humorous irony of Pascal, in the " Provincial Letters," plays like the diffusive sheen of an aurora borealis over the whole surface of the composition. It does not often deliver itself startlingly in sudden discharges as of lightning. You need to school your sense somewhat, not to miss a fine effect now and then. Consider the broadness and coarseness in pleasantry, that, before Pascal, had been common, almost universal, in controversy, and you will better understand what a creative touch it was of genius, of feeling, and of taste, that brought into literature the far more than Attic, the ineffable Christian, purity of that wit and humor in the "Provincial Letters" which will make these writings live as long as men anywhere continue to read the productions of past ages. Erasmus, perhaps, came the nearest of all modern predecessors to anticipating the purified pleasantry of Pascal.

It will be interesting and instructive to see Pascal's own statement of his reasons for adopting the bantering style which he did in the "Provincial Letters," as well as of the sense of responsibility to be faithful and fair, under which he wrote. Pascal says : —

I have been asked why I employed a pleasant, jocose, and diverting style. I reply . . . I thought it a duty to write so as to be comprehended by women and men of the world, that they might know the danger of their maxims and propositions which were then universally propagated. . . . I have been asked, lastly, if I myself read all the books which I quoted. I answer, No. If I had done so, I must have passed a great part of my life in reading very bad books; but I read Escobar twice through, and I employed some of my friends in reading the others. But I did not make use of a single passage without having myself read it in the book from which it is cited, without having examined the subject of which it treats, and without having read what went before and followed, so that I might run no risk of quoting an objection as an answer, which would have been blameworthy and unfair.

Of the wit of the "Provincial Letters," their wit and their controversial effectiveness, the specimens given will have afforded readers some approximate idea. We must deny ourselves the gratification of presenting a brief passage, which we had selected and translated for the purpose, to exemplify from the same source Pascal's serious eloquence. It was Voltaire who said of these productions : " Molière's best comedies do not excel them in wit, nor the compositions of Bossuet in sublimity." Something of Bossuet's sublimity, or of a sublimity perhaps finer than Bossuet's, our readers will discover in citations to follow from the " Thoughts."

Pascal's " Thoughts," the printed book, has a remarkable history. It was a posthumous publication. The author died, leaving behind him a considerable number of detached fragments of composition, first jottings of thought on a subject that had long occupied his mind. These precious manuscripts were almost undecipherable. The writer had used for his purpose any chance scrap of paper, — old wrapping, for example, or margin of letter, — that, at the critical moment of happy conception, was nearest his hand. Sentences, words even, were often left unfinished. There was no coherence, no sequence, no arrangement. It was, however, among his friends perfectly well understood that Pascal for years had meditated a work on religion designed to demonstrate the truth of Christianity. For this he had been thinking arduously. Fortunately he had even, in a memorable conversation, sketched his project at some length to his Port Royal friends. With so much, scarcely more, in the way of clew, to guide their editorial work, these friends prepared and issued a volume of Pascal's "Thoughts." With the most loyal intentions, the Port-Royalists unwisely edited too much. They pieced out incompletenesses, they provided clauses or sentences of connection, they toned down expressions deemed too bold, they improved Pascal's style! After having suffered such things from his friends, the posthumous Pascal, later, fell into the hands of an enemy. The infidel Condorcet published an edition of the "Thoughts." Whereas the Port-Royalists had suppressed to placate the Jesuits, Condorcet suppressed to please the "philosophers." Between those on the one side, and these on the other, Pascal's "Thoughts" had experienced what might well have killed any production of the human mind that could die. It was not till near the middle of the present century that Cousin called the attention of the world to the fact that we had not yet, but that we still might have, a true edition of Pascal's "Thoughts." M. Faugère took the hint, and consulting the original manuscripts, preserved in the national library at Paris, produced, with infinite editorial labor, almost two hundred years after the thinker's death, the first satisfactory edition of Pascal's "Thoughts." Since Faugère, M. Havet has also published an edition of Pascal's works entire, by him now first adequately annotated and explained. The arrangement of the "Thoughts" varies in order, according to the varying judgment of editors.

We use, for our extracts, a current translation, which we modify at our discretion, by comparison of the original text as given in M. Havet's elaborate work.

Our first extract is a passage in which the writer supposes a sceptic of the more shallow, trifling sort, to speak. This sceptic represents his own state of mind in the following strain as of soliloquy :—

'I do not know who put me into the world, nor what the world is, nor what I am myself. I am in a frightful ignorance of all things. I do not know what my body is, what my senses are, what my soul is, and that very part of me which thinks what I am saying, which reflects upon every thing and upon itself, and is no better acquainted with itself than with any thing else. I see these appalling spaces of the universe which enclose me, and I find myself tethered in one corner of this immense expansion without knowing why I am stationed in this place rather than in another, or why this moment of time which is given me to live is assigned me at this point rather than at another of the whole eternity that has preceded me, and of that which is to follow me.

'I see nothing but infinities on every side, which enclose me like an atom, and like a shadow which endures but for an instant, and returns no more.

'All that I know, is that I am soon to die; but what I am most ignorant of, is that very death which I am unable to avoid.

'As I know not whence I came, so I know not whither I go; and I know only, that in leaving this world I fall forever either into nothingness or into the hands of an angry God, without knowing which of these two conditions is to be eternally my lot. Such is my state, — full of misery, of weakness, and of uncertainty.

'And from all this I conclude, that I ought to pass all the

days of my life without a thought of trying to learn what is to befall me hereafter. Perhaps in my doubts I might find some enlightenment; but I am unwilling to take the trouble, or go a single step in search of it; and, treating with contempt those who perplex themselves with such solicitude, my purpose is to go forward without forethought and without fear to try the great event, and passively to approach death in uncertainty of the eternity of my future condition.'

Who would desire to have for a friend a man who discourses in this manner? Who would select such a one for the confidant of his affairs? Who would have recourse to such a one in his afflictions? And, in fine, for what use of life could such a man be destined?

The central thought on which the projected apologetic of Pascal was to revolve as on a pivot, is the contrasted greatness and wretchedness of man, — with Divine Revelation, in its doctrine of a fall on man's part from original nobleness, supplying the needed link, and the only link conceivable, of explanation, to unite the one with the other, the human greatness with the human wretchedness. This contrast of dignity and disgrace should constantly be in the mind of the reader of the "Thoughts" of Pascal. It will often be found to throw a very necessary light upon the meaning of the separate fragments that make up the series.

We now present a brief fragment asserting, with vivid metaphor, at the same time the fragility of man's frame and the majesty of man's nature. This is a very famous Thought: — .

Man is but a reed, the weakest in nature, but he is a thinking reed. It is not necessary that the entire universe arm itself to crush him. An exhalation, a drop of water, suffices to kill him. But were the universe to crush him, man would still be more noble than that which kills him, because he knows that he is dying, and knows the advantage that the universe has over him. The universe knows nothing of it.

Our whole dignity consists, then, in thought.

One is reminded of the memorable saying of a celebrated philosopher: "In the universe there is nothing great but man; in man there is nothing great but mind."

What a sudden, almost ludicrous, reduction in scale, the greatness of Cæsar, as conqueror, is made to suffer when looked at in the way in which Pascal asks you to look at it in the following Thought! (Remember that Cæsar, when he began fighting for universal empire, was fifty-one years of age:) —

Cæsar was too old, it seems to me, to amuse himself with conquering the world. This amusement was well enough for Augustus or Alexander; they were young people, whom it is difficult to stop; but Cæsar ought to have been more mature.

That is as if you should reverse the tube of your telescope, with the result of seeing the object observed made smaller instead of larger.

The following sentence might be a Maxim of La Rochefoucauld. Pascal was, no doubt, a debtor to him as well as to Montaigne: —

I lay it down as a fact, that, if all men knew what others say of them, there would not be four friends in the world.

Here is one of the most current of Pascal's sayings : —

Rivers are highways that move on and bear us whither we wish to go.

The following "Thought" condenses the substance of the book proposed, into three short sentences : —

The knowledge of God without that of our misery produces pride. The knowledge of our misery without that of God gives despair. The knowledge of Jesus Christ is intermediate, because therein we find God and our misery.

The prevalent seeming severity and intellectual coldness of Pascal's "Thoughts" yield to a touch from the heart, and become pathetic, in such utterances as the following, supposed to be addressed by the Saviour to the penitent seeking to be saved : —

Console thyself ; thou wouldst not seek me if thou hadst not found me.

I thought on thee in my agony ; such drops of blood I shed for thee.

It is austerity again, but not unjust austerity, that speaks as follows : —

Religion is a thing so great that those who would not take the pains to seek it if it is obscure, should be deprived of it. What do they complain of, then, if it is such that they could find it by seeking it ?

But we must take our leave of Pascal. His was a suffering as well as an aspiring spirit. He suffered because he aspired. But, at least, he did not suffer long. He aspired himself quickly away. Toward the last he wrought at a problem in his first favorite study, that of mathematics, and left behind him, as a memorial of his later life, a remarkable result of investigation on the curve called the cycloid. During his final illness he pierced himself through with many sorrows, — unnecessary sorrows, sorrows, too, that bore a double edge, hurting not only him, but also his kindred, — in practising, from mistaken religious motives, a hard repression upon his natural instinct to love, and to welcome love. He thought that God should be all, the creature nothing. The thought was half true, but it was half false. God should, indeed, be all. But, in God, the creature also should be something.

In French history, — we may say, in the history of the world, — if there are few brighter, there also are few purer, fames than the fame of Pascal.

IX.

MADAME DE SÉVIGNÉ.

1626-1696.

OF Madame de Sévigné, if it were permitted here
to make a pun and a paradox, one might justly and
descriptively say that she was not a woman of letters,
but only a woman of — letters. For Madame de
Sévigné's addiction to literature was not at all that
of an author by profession. She simply wrote admirable private letters, in great profusion, and
became famous thereby.

Madame de Sévigné's fame is partly her merit,
but it is also partly her good fortune. She was
rightly placed to be what she was. This will appear
from a sketch of her life, and still more from specimens to be exhibited of her own epistolary writing.

Marie de Rabutin-Chantal was her maiden name.
She was born a baroness. She was married, young,
a marchioness. First early left an orphan, she was
afterward early left a widow, — not too early, however, to have become the mother of two children,
a son and a daughter. The daughter grew to be the
life-long idol of the widowed mother's heart. The
letters she wrote to this daughter, married, and living
remote from her, compose the greater part of that
voluminous epistolary production by which Madame

de Sévigné became, without her ever aiming at such a result, or probably ever thinking of it, one of the classics of the French language.

Madame de Sévigné was wealthy as orphan heiress, and she should have been wealthy as widow. But her husband was profligate, and he wasted her substance. She turned out to be a thoroughly capable woman of affairs who managed her property well. During her long and stainless widowhood — her husband fell in a shameful duel when she was but twenty-five years old, and she lived to be seventy — she divided her time between her estate, The Rocks, in Brittany, and her residence in Paris. This period was all embraced within the protracted reign of Louis XIV., perhaps, upon the whole, the most memorable age in the history of France.

Beautiful, and, if not brilliantly beautiful, at least brilliantly witty, Madame de Sévigné was virtuous — in that chief sense of feminine virtue — amid an almost universal empire of profligacy around her. Her social advantages were unsurpassed, and her social success was equal to her advantages. She had the woman courtier's supreme triumph in being once led out to dance by the king — her own junior by a dozen years — no vulgar king, remember, but the "great" Louis XIV. Her cynical cousin, himself a writer of power, who had been repulsed in dishonorable proffers of love by the young marchioness during the lifetime of her husband, — we mean Count Bussy, — says, in a scurrilous work of his, that Ma-

dame de Sévigné remarked, on returning to her seat
after her dancing-bout with the king, that Louis possessed great qualities, and would certainly obscure
the lustre of all his predecessors. "I could not
help laughing in her face," the ungallant cousin
declared, "seeing what had produced this pane-
gyric." Probably, indeed, the young woman was
pleased. But, whatever may have been her faults
or her follies, nothing can rob Madame de Sévigné
of the glory that is hers, in having been strong
enough in womanly and motherly honor to preserve,
against many dazzling temptations, amid general
bad example, and even under malignant aspersions,
a chaste and spotless name. When it is added, that,
besides access to the royal court itself, this gifted
woman enjoyed the familiar acquaintance of La
Rochefoucauld and other high-bred wits, less famous,
not a few, enough will have been said to show
that her position was such as to give her talent its
best possible chance. The French history of the
times of Louis XIV. is hinted in glimpses the most
vivid and the most suggestive, throughout the whole
series of the letters.

We owe it to our readers (and to Madame de
Sévigné no less) first of all to let them see a specimen of the affectionate adulation that this French
woman of rank and of fashion, literally in almost
every letter of hers, effuses on her daughter, — a
daughter who, by the way, seems very languidly to
have responded to such demonstrations : —

THE ROCKS, Sunday, June 28, 1671.

You have amply made up to me my late losses ; I have received two letters from you which have filled me with transports of joy. The pleasure I take in reading them is beyond all imagination. If I have in any way contributed to the improvement of your style I did it in the thought that I was laboring for the pleasure of others, not for my own. But Providence, who has seen fit to separate us so often, and to place us at such immense distances from each other, has repaid me a little for the privation in the charms of your correspondence, and still more in the satisfaction you express in your situation, and the beauty of your castle; you represent it to me with an air of grandeur and magnificence that enchants me. I once saw a similar account of it by the first Madame de Grignan; but I little thought at that time, that all these beauties were one day to be at your command. I am very much obliged to you for having given me so particular an account of it. If I could be tired in reading your letters, it would not only betray a very bad taste in me, but would likewise show that I could have very little love or friendship for you. Divest yourself of the dislike you have taken to circumstantial details. I have often told you, and you ought yourself to feel the truth of this remark, that they are as dear to us from those we love, as they are tedious and disagreeable from others. If they are displeasing to us, it is only from the indifference we feel for those who write them. Admitting this observation to be true, I leave you to judge what pleasure yours afford me. It is a fine thing, truly, to play the great lady, as you do at present.

Conceive the foregoing multiplied by the whole number of the separate letters composing the correspondence, and you will have no exaggerated idea of the display that Madame de Sévigné makes of her regard for her daughter. This regard was a passion, morbid, no doubt, by excess, and, even at that, extravagantly demonstrated ; but it was fundamentally sincere. Madame de Sévigné idealized her absent daughter, and literally " loved but only her." We need not wholly admire such maternal affection. But we should not criticise it too severely.

We choose next a marvellously vivid " instantaneous view," in words, of a court afternoon and evening at Versailles. This letter, too, is addressed to the daughter — Madame de Grignan, by her married name. It bears date, " Paris, Wednesday, 29th July." The year is 1676, and the writer is just fifty : —

I was at Versailles last Saturday with the Villarses. . . . At three the king, the queen, Monsieur [eldest brother to the king], Madame [that brother's wife], Mademoiselle [that brother's eldest unmarried daughter], and every thing else which is royal, together with Madame de Montespan [the celebrated mistress of the king] and train, and all the courtiers, and all the ladies, — all, in short, which constitutes the court of France, is assembled in the beautiful apartment of the king's, which you remember. All is furnished divinely, all is magnificent. Such a thing as heat is unknown ; you pass from one place to another without the slightest pressure. A game at *reversis* [the description is of a gambling scene, in which Dangeau figures as a cool and skilful gamester] gives the company a form and a settlement. The king and Madame de Montespan keep a bank together ; different tables are occupied by Monsieur, the queen, and Madame de Soubise, Dangeau and party, Langlée and party. Everywhere you see heaps of louis d'ors ; they have no other counters. I saw Dangeau play, and thought what fools we all were beside him. He dreams of nothing but what concerns the game ; he wins where others lose ; he neglects nothing, profits by every thing, never has his attention diverted ; in short, his science bids defiance to chance. Two hundred thousand francs in ten days, a hundred thousand crowns in a month, these are the pretty memorandums he puts down in his pocket-book. He was kind enough to say that I was partners with him, so that I got an excellent seat. I made my obeisance to the king, as you told me ; and he returned it as if I had been young and handsome. . . . The duke said a thousand kind things without minding a word he uttered. Marshal de Lorges attacked me in the name of the Chevalier de Grignan ; in short, *tutti quanti* [the whole company]. You know what it is to get a word from everybody you meet. Madame de Montespan talked to me of Bourbon, and asked me how I liked Vichi, and whether the place did me good. She said that Bourbon, instead of curing a pain in one of her knees, injured both. . . . Her size is reduced by a good half, and yet her complexion, her eyes, and her lips, are as fine as ever. She was dressed all in French point, her hair in a thousand ringlets, the two side ones hanging low on her cheeks, black ribbons on her head, pearls (the same that belonged to Madame de l'Hôpital), the loveliest diamond earrings, three or four bodkins — nothing else on the head ; in short, a triumphant beauty, worthy the admiration of all the foreign ambassadors. She was accused of preventing the whole French nation from seeing the king ; she has restored him, you see, to their eyes ; and you cannot conceive the joy it has given all the world, and the splendor it has thrown upon the court. This charming confusion, without confusion, of all which is the most select, continues from three till six. If couriers arrive, the king retires a moment to read the despatches, and returns. There is always some music going on, to which he listens, and which has an excellent effect. He talks with such of the ladies as are accustomed to enjoy that honor. . . . At six the carriages are at the door. The king is in one of them with Madame de Montespan, Monsieur and Madame de Thianges, and honest d'Heudicourt in a fool's paradise on the stool. You know how these open carriages are made ; they do not sit face to face, but all looking the same way. The queen occupies another with the princess ; and the rest come flocking after, as it may happen. There are then gondolas on the canal, and music ; and at ten they come back, and then there is a play ; and twelve strikes, and they go to supper ; and thus rolls round the Saturday. If I were to tell you how often you were asked after, how many questions were put to me without waiting for answers, how often I neglected to answer, how little they cared, and how much less I did, you would see the *iniqua corte* [wicked court] before you in all its perfection. However, it never was so pleasant before, and everybody wishes it may last.

There is your picture. Picture, pure and simple, it is — comment none, least of all, moralizing comment. The wish is sighed by "everybody," that such pleasant things may "last." Well, they did last the writer's time. But meanwhile the French revolution was a-preparing. A hundred years later it will come, with its terrible reprisals.

We have gone away from the usual translations to find the foregoing extract in an article published forty years ago and more, in the "Edinburgh Review." Again we draw from the same source — this time, the description of a visit paid by a company of grand folks, of whom the writer of the letter was one, to an iron-foundery : —

FRIDAY, 1st Oct. (1677).

Yesterday evening at Cone, we descended into a veritable hell, the true forges of Vulcan. Eight or ten Cyclops were at work, forging, not arms for Æneas, but anchors for ships. You never saw strokes redoubled so justly, nor with so admirable a cadence. We stood in the middle of four furnaces ; and the demons came passing about us, all melting in sweat, with pale faces, wild-staring eyes, savage mustaches, and hair long and black, — a sight enough to frighten less well-bred folks than ourselves. As for me, I could not comprehend the possibility of refusing any thing which these gentlemen, in their hell, might have chosen to exact. We got out at last, by the help of a shower of silver, with which we took care to refresh their souls, and facilitate our exit.

Once more : —

PARIS, 29th November (1679).

I have been to the wedding of Madame de Louvois. How shall I describe it ? Magnificence, illuminations, all France, dresses all gold and brocade, jewels, braziers full of fire, and stands full of flowers, confusions of carriages, cries out of doors, lighted torches, pushings back, people run over; in short, a whirlwind, a distraction ; questions without answers, compliments without knowing what is said, civilities without knowing who is spoken to, feet entangled in trains. From the midst of all this, issue inquiries after your health, which not being answered as quick as lightning, the inquirers pass on, contented to remain in the state of ignorance and indifference in which they [the inquiries] were made. O vanity of vanities ! Pretty little De Mouchy has had the small-pox. O vanity, et cætera !

Yet again. The gay writer has been sobered, perhaps hurt, by a friend's frankly writing to her, "You are old." To her daughter : —

So you were struck with the expression of Madame de la Fayette, blended with so much friendship. 'Twas a truth, I own, which I ought to have borne in mind; and yet I must confess it astonished me, for I do not yet perceive in myself any such decay. Nevertheless, I cannot help making many reflections and calculations, and I find the conditions of life hard enough. It seems to me that I have been dragged, against my will, to the fatal period when old age must be endured; I see it; I have come to it; and I would fain, if I could help it, not go any farther; not advance a step more in the road of infirmities, of pains, of losses of memory, of *disfigurements* ready to do me outrage; and I hear a voice which says, "You must go on in spite of yourself; or, if you will not go on, you must die;" and this is another extremity from which nature revolts. Such is the lot, however, of all who advance beyond middle life. What is their resource? To think of the will of God and of universal law, and so restore reason to its place, and be patient. Be you, then, patient accordingly, my dear child, and let not your affection soften into such tears as reason must condemn.

She dates a letter, and recalls that the day was the anniversary of an event in her life : —

PARIS, Friday, Feb. 5, 1672.

This day thousand years I was married.

Here is a passage with power in it. The great war minister of Louis has died. Madame de Sévigné was now sixty-five years old. The letter is to her cousin Coulanges : —

I am so astonished at the news of the sudden death of M. de Louvois, that I am at a loss how to speak of it. Dead, however, he is, this great minister, this potent being, who occupied so great a place; whose me (*le moi*), as M. Nicole says, had so wide a dominion; who was the centre of so many orbs. What affairs had he not to manage! what designs, what projects, what secrets! what interests to unravel, what wars to undertake, what intrigues, what noble games at chess to play and to direct! Ah! my God, grant me a little time; I want to give check to the Duke of Savoy — checkmate to the Prince of Orange. No, no, you shall not have a moment, not a single moment. Are events like these to be talked of? Not they. We must reflect upon them in our closets.

A glimpse of Bourdaloue : —

Ah, that Bourdaloue! his sermon on the Passion was, they say, the most perfect thing of the kind that can be imagined; it was the same he preached last year, but revised and altered with the assistance of some of his friends, that it might be wholly inimitable. How can one love God, if one never hears him properly spoken of? You must really possess a greater portion of grace than others.

A distinguished caterer or steward, a gentleman described as possessing talent enough to have governed a province, commits suicide on a professional point of honor : —

PARIS, Sunday, April 26, 1671.

I have just learned from Moreuil, of what passed at Chantilly with regard to poor Vatel. I wrote to you last Friday that he had stabbed himself — these are the particulars of the affair: The king arrived there on Thursday night; the walk, and the collation, which was served in a place set apart for the purpose, and strewed with jonquils, were just as they should be. Supper was served; but there was no roast meat at one or two of the tables, on account of Vatel's having been obliged to provide several dinners more than were expected. This affected his spirits; and he was heard to say several times, "I have lost my honor! I cannot bear this disgrace!" "My head is quite bewildered," said he to Gourville. "I have not had a wink of sleep these twelve nights; I wish you would assist me in giving orders." Gourville did all he could to comfort and assist him, but the failure of the roast meat (which, however, did not happen at the king's table, but at some of the other twenty-five) was always uppermost with him. Gourville mentioned it to the prince [Condé, the great Condé, the king's host], who went directly to Vatel's apartment, and said to him, "Every thing is extremely well conducted, Vatel; nothing could be more admirable than his Majesty's supper." "Your highness's goodness," replied he, "over-whelms me; I am sensible that there was a deficiency of roast meat at two tables." "Not at all," said the prince; "do not perplex yourself, and all will go well." Midnight came; the fireworks did not succeed; they were covered with a thick cloud; they cost sixteen thousand francs. At four o'clock in the morning Vatel went round and found everybody asleep; he met one of the under-purveyors, who was just come in with only two loads of fish. "What!" said he, "is this all?" "Yes, sir," said the man, not knowing that Vatel had despatched other people to all the seaports around. Vatel waited for some time; the other purveyors did not arrive; his head grew distracted; he thought there was no more fish to be had. He flew to Gourville: "Sir," said he, "I cannot outlive this disgrace." Gourville laughed at him. Vatel, however, went to his apartment, and setting the hilt of his sword against the door, after two ineffectual attempts, succeeded, in the third, in forcing his sword through his heart. At that instant the couriers arrived with the fish; Vatel was inquired after to distribute it. They ran to his apartment, knocked at the door, but received no answer; upon which they broke it open, and found him weltering in his blood. A messenger was immediately despatched to acquaint the prince with what had happened, who was like a man in despair. The Duke wept, *for his Burgundy journey depended upon Vatel.*

The italics here are our own. We felt that we must use them.

Is it not all pathetic? But how exquisitely characteristic of the nation and of the times! "Poor Vatel," is the extent to which Madame de Sévigné allows herself to go in sympathy. Her heart never bleeds very freely — for anybody except her daughter. Madame de Sévigné's heart, indeed, we grieve to fear, was somewhat hard.

In another letter, after a long strain as worldly as any one could wish to see, this lively woman thus touches, with a sincerity as unquestionable as the levity is, on the point of personal religion : —

But, my dear child, the greatest inclination I have at present is to be a little religious. I plague La Mousse about it every day. I belong neither to God nor to the devil. I am quite weary of such a situation; though, between you and me, I look upon it as the most natural one in the world. I am not the devil's, because I fear God, and have at the bottom a principle of religion; then, on the other hand, I am not properly God's, because his law appears hard and irksome to me, and I cannot bring myself to acts of self-denial; so that altogether I am one of those called lukewarm Christians, the great number of which does not in the least surprise me, for I perfectly understand their sentiments, and the reasons that influence them. However, we are told that this is a state highly displeasing to God; if so, we must get out of it. Alas! this is the difficulty. Was ever any thing so mad as I am, to be thus eternally pestering you with my rhapsodies ?

Madame de Sévigné involuntarily becomes a maxim-maker : —

The other day I made a maxim off-hand, without once thinking of it; and I liked it so well that I fancied I had taken it out of M. de la Rochefoucauld's. Pray tell me whether it is so or not, for in that case my memory is more to be praised than my judgment. I said, with all the ease in the world, that "ingratitude begets reproach, as acknowledgment begets new favors." Pray, where did this come from ? Have I read it ? Did I dream it ? Is it my own idea ? Nothing can be truer than the thing itself, nor than that I am totally ignorant how I came by it. I found it properly arranged in my brain, and at the end of my tongue.

The partial mother lets her daughter know whom the maxim was meant for. She says, "It is intended for your brother." This young fellow had, we suspect, been first earning his mother's "reproaches" for spendthrift habits, and then getting more money from her by "acknowledgment."

She hears that son of hers read "some chapters out of Rabelais," "which were enough," she declares, "to make us die with laughing." "I cannot affect," she says, "a prudery which is not natural to me." No, indeed, a prude this woman was not. She had the strong æsthetic stomach of her time. It is queer to have Rabelais rubbing cheek and jowl with Nicole ("We are going to begin a moral treatise of Nicole's"), a severe Port-Royalist, in one and the same letter. But this is French; above all, it is Madame de Sévigné. By the way, she and her friends, first and last, "die" a thousand jolly deaths "with laughing."

A contemporary allusion to "Tartuffe," with more French manners implied : —

The other day La Biglesse played Tartuffe to the life. Being at table, she happened to tell a fib about some trifle or other, which I noticed, and told her of it ; she cast her eyes to the ground, and with a very demure air, "Yes, indeed, madam," said she, "I am the greatest liar in the world ; I am very much obliged to you for telling me of it." We all burst out a-laughing, for it was exactly the tone of Tartuffe, — "Yes, brother, I am a wretch, a vessel of iniquity."

M. de La Rochefoucauld appears often by name in the letters. Here he appears anonymously by his effect : —

"Warm affections are never tranquil" ; a *maxim*.

Not a very sapid bit of gnomic wisdom, certainly. We must immediately make up to our readers, on Madame de Sévigné's behalf, for the insipidity of the foregoing "maxim" of hers, by giving here two or three far more sententious excerpts from the letters, excerpts collected by another : —

There may be so great a weight of obligation that there is no way of being delivered from it but by ingratitude.

Long sicknesses wear out grief, and long hopes wear out joy.

Shadow is never long taken for substance ; you must be, if you would appear to be. The world is not unjust long.

Madame de Sévigné makes a confession, which will comfort readers who may have experienced the same difficulty as that of which she speaks : —

I send you M. de Rochefoucauld's "Maxims," revised and corrected, with additions ; it is a present to you from himself. Some of them I can make shift to guess the meaning of ; but there are others that, to my shame be it spoken, I cannot understand at all. God knows how it will be with you.

What was it changed this woman's mood to serious? She could not have been hearing Massillon's celebrated sermon on the "fewness of the elect," for Massillon was yet only a boy of nine years ; she may have been reading Pascal's "Thoughts," — Pascal had been dead ten years, and the "Thoughts" had been published ; or she may have been listening to one of those sifting, heart-searching discourses of Bourdaloue, — the date of her letter is March 16, 1672, and during the Lent of that year Bourdaloue preached at Versailles, — when she wrote sombrely as follows : —

You ask me if I am as fond of life as ever. I must own to you that I experience mortifications, and severe ones too ; but I am still unhappy at the thoughts of death ; I consider it so great a misfortune to see the termination of all my pursuits, that I should desire nothing better, if it were practicable, than to begin life again. I find myself engaged in a scene of confusion and trouble ; I was embarked in life without my own consent, and know I must leave it again ; this distracts me, for how shall I leave it ? In what manner ? By what door ? At what time ? In what disposition ? Am I to suffer a thousand pains and torments that will make me die in a state of despair ? Shall I lose my senses ? Am I to die by some sudden accident ? How shall I stand with God ? What shall I have to offer to him ? Will fear and necessity make my peace with him ? Shall I have no other sentiment but that of fear ? What have I to hope ? Am I worthy of heaven ? Or have I deserved the torments of hell ? Dreadful alternative ! Alarming uncertainty ! Can there be greater madness than to place our eternal salvation in uncertainty ? Yet what is more natural, or can be more easily accounted for, than the foolish manner in which I have spent my life ? I am frequently buried in thoughts of this nature, and then death appears so dreadful to me that I hate life more for leading me to it, than I do for all the thorns that are strewed in its way. You will ask me, then, if I would wish to live forever ? Far from it ; but, if I had been consulted, I would very gladly have died in my nurse's arms ; it would have spared me many vexations, and would have insured heaven to me at a very easy rate ; but let us talk of something else.

A memorable sarcasm saved for us by Madame de Sévigné, at the very close of one of her letters : —

Guillenagues said yesterday that Pelisson abused the privilege men have of being ugly.

Readers familiar with Dickens's " Tale of Two Cities," will recognize in the following narrative a state of society not unlike that described by the novelist as immediately preceding the French Revolution : —

The Archbishop of Rheims, as he returned yesterday from St. Germain, met with a curious adventure. He drove at his usual rate, like a whirlwind. If he thinks himself a great man, his servants think him still greater. They passed through Nanterre, when they met a man on horseback, and in an insolent tone bid him clear the way. The poor man used his utmost endeavors to avoid the danger that threatened him, but his horse proved unmanageable. To make short of it, the coach-and-six turned them both topsy-turvy; but at the same time the coach, too, was completely overturned. In an instant the horse and the man, instead of amusing themselves with having their limbs broken, rose almost miraculously; the man remounted, and galloped away, and is galloping still, for aught I know; while the servants, the archbishop's coachman, and the archbishop himself at the head of them, cried out, "Stop that villain, stop him! thrash him soundly!" The rage of the archbishop was so great, that afterward, in relating the adventure, he said, if he could have caught the rascal, he would have broke all his bones, and cut off both his ears.

If such things were done by the aristocracy — and the spiritual aristocracy at that! — in the green tree, what might not be expected in the dry? The writer makes no comment — draws no moral. "Adieu, my dear, delightful child. I cannot express my eagerness to see you," are her next words. She rattles along, three short sentences more, and finishes her letter.

We should still not have done with these letters, were we to go on a hundred pages, or two hundred, farther. Readers have already seen truly what Madame de Sévigné is. They have only not seen fully all that she is. And that they would not see short of reading her letters entire. Horace Walpole aspired to do in English for his own time something like what Madame de Sévigné had done in French for hers. In a measure he succeeded. The difference is, that he was imitative and affected, where she was original and genuine.

Lady Mary Wortley Montagu must, of course, also be named, as, by her sex, her social position, her talent, and the devotion of her talent, an English analogue to Madame de Sévigné. But these comparisons, and all comparison, leave the French woman without a true parallel, alone in her rank, the most famous letter-writer in the world.

X.

CORNEILLE.

1606-1684.

THE two great names in French tragedy are Corneille and Racine. French tragedy is a very different affair from either modern tragedy in English or ancient tragedy in Greek. It comes nearer being Roman epic, such as Lucan wrote Roman epic, dramatized.

Drama is everywhere and always, and this from the nature of things, a highly conventional literary form. But the convention under which French tragedy should be judged differs, on the one hand, from that which existed for Greek tragedy, and, on the other hand, from that existing for the English. The atmosphere of real life present in English tragedy is absent in French. The quasi-supernatural religious awe that reigned over Greek tragedy, French tragedy does not affect. You miss also in French tragedy the severe simplicity, the self-restraint, the statuesque repose, belonging to the Greek model. Loftiness, grandeur, a loftiness somewhat strained, a grandeur tending to be tumid, an heroic tone sustained at sacrifice of ease and nature — such is the element in which French tragedy lives and flourishes. You must grant your French tragedists this their conventional privilege, or you will not enjoy them. You must grant them this, or you cannot understand them. Resolve that you will like grandiloquence, requiring only that the grandiloquence be good, and on this condition we can promise that you will be pleased with Corneille and Racine. In fact, our readers, we are sure, will find the grandiloquence of these two tragedy-writers so very good that a little will suffice them.

Voltaire in his time impressed himself strongly enough on his countrymen to get accepted by his own generation as an equal third in tragedy with Corneille and Racine. There was then a French triumvirate of tragedists to be paralleled with the triumvirate of the Greeks. Corneille was Æschylus;

Racine was Sophocles; and, of course, Euripides had his counterpart in Voltaire. Voltaire has since descended from the tragic throne, and that neat symmetry of trine comparison is spoiled. There is, however, some trace of justice in making Corneille as related to Racine resemble Æschylus as related to Sophocles. Corneille was first, more rugged, loftier; Racine was second, more polished, more severe in taste. Racine had, too, in contrast with Corneille, more of the Euripidean sweetness. In fact, La Bruyère's celebrated comparison of the two Frenchmen — made, of course, before Voltaire — yoked them, Corneille with Sophocles, Racine with Euripides.

It was perhaps not without its influence on the style of Corneille, that a youthful labor of his in authorship was to translate, wholly or partially, the "Pharsalia" of Lucan. Corneille always retained his fondness for Lucan. This taste on his part, and the rhymed Alexandrines in which he wrote tragedy, may together help account for the hyper-heroic style which is Corneille's great fault. A lady criticised his tragedy, "The Death of Pompey," by saying: "Very fine, but too many heroes in it." Corneille's tragedies generally have, if not too many heroes, at least too much hero, in them. Concerning the historian Gibbon's habitual pomp of expression, it was once wittily said that nobody could possibly tell the truth in such a style as that. It would be equally near the mark if we should say of Corneille's chosen

mould of verse, that nobody could possibly be simple
and natural in that. Molière's comedy, however,
would almost confute us.

Pierre Corneille was born in Rouen. He studied
law, and he was admitted to practice as an advocate,
like Molière; but, like Molière, he heard and he
heeded an inward voice summoning him away from
the bar to the stage. Corneille did not, however,
like Molière, tread the boards as an actor. He had
a lively sense of personal dignity. He was eminently
the "lofty, grave tragedian," in his own esteem.
"But I am Pierre Corneille notwithstanding," he
self-respectingly said once, when friends were regret-
ting to him some deficiency of grace in his personal
carriage. One can imagine him taking off his hat
to himself with unaffected deference.

But this serious genius began dramatic composition with writing comedy. He made several experiments in this kind with no commanding success;
but at thirty he wrote the tragedy of "The Cid," and
instantly became famous. His subsequent plays
were chiefly on classical subjects. The subject of
"The Cid" was drawn from Spanish literature. This
was emphatically what has been called an "epoch-
making" production. Richelieu's "Academy," at
the instigation, indeed almost under the dictation,
of Richelieu, who was jealous of Corneille, tried to
write it down. They succeeded about as Balaam succeeded in prophesying against Israel. "The Cid"
triumphed over them, and over the great minister.

It established not only Corneille's fame, but his authority. The man of genius taken alone, proved stronger than the men of taste taken together.

For all this, however, our readers would hardly relish "The Cid." Let us go at once to that tragedy of Corneille's which, by the general consent of French critics, is the best work of its author, the "Polyeuctes." The following is the rhetorical climax of praise in which Gaillard, one of the most enlightened of Corneille's eulogists, arranges the different masterpieces of his author: "'The Cid' raised Corneille above his rivals; the 'Horace' and the 'Cinna' above his models; the 'Polyeuctes' above himself." This tragedy will, we doubt not, prove to our readers the most interesting of all the tragedies of Corneille.

"The great Corneille" — to apply the traditionary designation which, besides attributing to our tragedian his conceded general eminence in character and genius, serves also to distinguish him by merit from his younger brother, who wrote very good tragedy — was an illustrious figure at the Hôtel de Rambouillet, that focus of the best literary criticism in France. Corneille reading a play of his to the *coterie* of wits assembled there under the presidency of ladies whose eyes, as in a kind of tournament of letters, rained influence on authors, and judged the prize of genius, is the subject of a striking picture by a French painter. Corneille read "Polyeuctes" at the Hôtel de Rambouillet, and that awful court decided against the play. Corneille, like Michel Angelo, had to a good degree the courage of his own productions; but, in the face of adverse decision so august on his work, he needed encouragement, which happily he did not fail to receive, before he would allow his "Polyeuctes" to be represented. The theatre crowned it with the laurels of victory. It thus fell to Corneille to triumph successively, single-handed, over two great adversary courts of critical appreciation, — the Academy of Richelieu and the not less formidable Hôtel de Rambouillet.

The objection raised by the Hôtel de Rambouillet against the "Polyeuctes" was that it made the stage encroach on the prerogative of the pulpit, and preach instead of simply amusing. And, indeed, never, perhaps, since the Greek tragedy, was the theatre made so much to serve the solemn purposes of religion. (We except the miracle and passion plays and the mysteries of the middle ages, as not belonging within the just bounds of a comparison like that now made.) Corneille's final influence was to elevate and purify the French theatre. In his early works, however, he made surprising concessions to the lewd taste in the drama that he found prevailing when he began to write. With whatever amount of genuine religious scruple affecting his conscience, — on that point we need not judge the poet, — Corneille used, before putting them on the stage, to take his plays to the "Church," — that is, to the priestly hierarchy who constituted the

"Church," — that they might be authoritatively judged as to their possible influence on the cause of Christian truth.

In the "Polyeuctes," the motive is religion. Polyeuctes is an historic or traditional saint of the Roman-Catholic church. His conversion from paganism is the theme of the play. Polyeuctes has a friend Nearchus who is already a Christian convert, and who labors earnestly to make Polyeuctes a proselyte to the faith. Polyeuctes has previously married a noble Roman lady, daughter of Felix, governor of Armenia, in which province the action of the story occurs. (The persecuting Emperor Decius is on the throne of the Roman world.) Paulina is the daughter's name. Paulina married Polyeuctes against her own choice, for she loved Roman Severus better. Her father had put his will upon her, and Paulina had filially obeyed in marrying Polyeuctes. Such are the relations of the different persons of the drama. It will be seen that there is ample room for the play of elevated and tragic passions. Paulina, in fact, is the lofty, the impossible, ideal of wifely and daughterly truth and devotion. Pagan though she is, she is pathetically constant, both to the husband that was forced upon her, and to the father that did the forcing; while still she loves, and cannot but love, the man whom, in spite of her love for him, she, with an act like prolonged suicide, stoically separates from her torn and bleeding heart.

But Severus on his part emulates the nobleness of the woman whom he vainly loves. Learning the true state of the case, he rises to the height of his opportunity for magnanimous behavior, and bids the married pair be happy in a long life together.

A change in the situation occurs, a change due to the changed mood of the father, Felix. Felix learns that Severus is high in imperial favor, and he wishes now that Severus, instead of Polyeuctes, were his son-in-law. A decree of the emperor makes it possible that this preferable alternative may yet be realized. For the emperor has decreed that Christians must be persecuted to the death, and Polyeuctes has been baptized a Christian — though of this Felix will not hear till later.

A solemn sacrifice to the gods is to be celebrated in honor of imperial victories lately won. Felix sends to summon Polyeuctes, his son-in-law. To Felix's horror, Polyeuctes, with his friend Nearchus, coming to the temple, proceeds in a frenzy of enthusiasm to break and dishonor the images of the gods, proclaiming himself a Christian. In obedience to the imperial decree, Nearchus is hurried to execution, in the sight of his friend, while Polyeuctes is thrown into prison to repent and recant.

' Now is my chance,' muses Felix. ' I dare not disobey the emperor, to spare Polyeuctes. Besides, with Polyeuctes once out of the way, Severus and Paulina may be husband and wife.'

Polyeuctes in prison hears that his Paulina is

coming to see him. With a kind of altruistic nobleness which seems contagious in this play, Polyeuctes
resolves that Severus shall come too, and he will
resign his wife, soon to be a widow, to the care of
his own rival, her Roman lover. First, Polyeuctes
and Paulina are alone together — Polyeuctes having,
before she arrived, fortified his soul for the conflict
with her tears, by singing in his solitude a song of
high resolve and of anticipative triumph over his
temptation.

The scene between Paulina, exerting all her power
to detach Polyeuctes from what she believes to be
his folly, and Polyeuctes, on the other hand, rapt
to the pitch of martyrdom, exerting all his power
to resist his wife, and even to convert her — this
scene, we say, is full of noble height and pathos,
as pathos and height were possible in the verse
which Corneille had to write. Neither struggler in
this tragic strife moves the other. Paulina is withdrawing when Severus enters. She addresses her
lover severely, but Polyeuctes intervenes to defend
him. In a short scene, Polyeuctes, by a sort of last
will and testament, bequeaths his wife to his rival,
and retires with his guard. Now, Severus and Paulina are alone together. If there was a trace of the
false heroic in Polyeuctes's resignation of his wife
to Severus, the effect of that is finely counteracted
by the scene which immediately follows between
Paulina and Severus. Severus begins doubtfully,
staggering, as it were, to firm posture, while he

speaks to Paulina. He expresses amazement at the
conduct of Polyeuctes. Christians certainly deport
themselves strangely, he says. He at length finds
himself using the following lover-like language : —

As for me, had my destiny become a little earlier propitious and honored my devotion by marriage with you, I
should have adored only the splendor of your eyes; of them
I should have made my kings; of them I should have made
my gods; sooner would I have been reduced to dust, sooner
would I have been reduced to ashes, than —

But here Paulina interrupts, and Severus is not
permitted to finish his protestation. Her reply is
esteemed, and justly esteemed, one of the noblest
things in French tragedy — a French critic would
be likely to say, the very noblest in tragedy. She
says : —

Let us break off there; I fear listening too long; I fear
lest this warmth, which feels your first fires, force on some
sequel unworthy of us both. [Voltaire, who edited Corneille with a feeling of freedom toward a national idol
comparable to the sturdy independence that animated Johnson in annotating Shakspeare, says of "This warmth which
feels your first fires and which forces on a sequel": "That is
badly written, agreed; but the sentiment gets the better
of the expression, and what follows is of a beauty of
which there had been no example. The Greeks were frigid
declaimers in comparison with this passage of Corneille."]
Severus, learn to know Paulina all in all.

My Polyeuctes touches on his last hour; he has but a
moment to live; you are the cause of this, though innocently
so. I know not if your heart, yielding to your desires, may
have dared build any hope on his destruction; but know

that there is no death so cruel that to it with firm brow I would not bend my steps, that there are in hell no horrors that I would not endure, rather than soil a glory so pure, rather than espouse, after his sad fate, a man that was in any wise the cause of his death; and if you suppose me of a heart so little sound, the love which I had for you would all turn to hate. You are generous; be so even to the end. My father is in a state to yield every thing to you; he fears you; and I further hazard this saying, that, if he destroys my husband, it is to you that he sacrifices him. Save this unhappy man, use your influence in his favor, exert yourself to become his support. I know that this is much that I ask; but the greater the effort, the greater the glory from it. To preserve a rival of whom you are jealous, that is a trait of virtue which appertains only to you. And if your renown is not motive sufficient, it is much that a woman once so well beloved, and the love of whom perhaps is still capable of touching you, will owe to your great heart the dearest possession that she owns; remember, in short, that you are Severus. Adieu. Decide with yourself alone what you ought to do; if you are not such as I dare hope that you are, then, in order that I may continue to esteem you, I wish not to know it.

Voltaire, as editor and commentator of Corneille, is freezingly cold. It is difficult not to feel that at heart he was unfriendly to the great tragedist's fame. His notes often are remorselessly grammatical. "This is not French;" "This is not the right word;" "According to the construction, this should mean so and so — according to the sense, it must mean so and so;" "This is hardly intelligible;" "It is a pity that such or such a fault should mar these fine verses;" "An expression for comedy rather than tragedy,"—are the kind of remarks with which Voltaire chills the enthusiasm of the reader. It is useless, however, to deny that the criticisms thus made are many of them just. Corneille does not belong to the class of the "faultily faultless" writers.

Severus proves equal to Paulina's noble hopes of him. With a great effort of self-sacrifice, he resolves to intercede for Polyeuctes. This is shown in an interview between Severus and his faithful attendant Fabian. Fabian warns him that he appeals for Polyeuctes at his own peril. Severus loftily replies (and here follows one of the most lauded passages in the play) : —

That advice might be good for some common soul. Though he [the Emperor Decius] holds in his hands my life and my fortune, I am yet Severus; and all that mighty power is powerless over my glory, and powerless over my duty. Here honor compels me, and I will satisfy it; whether fate afterward show itself propitious or adverse, perishing glorious I shall perish content.

I will tell thee further, but under confidence, the sect of Christians is not what it is thought to be. They are hated, why I know not; and I see Decius unjust only in this regard. From curiosity I have sought to become acquainted with them. They are regarded as sorcerers taught from hell; and, in this supposition, the punishment of death is visited on secret mysteries which we do not understand. But Eleusinian Ceres and the Good Goddess have their secrets, like those at Rome and in Greece; still we freely tolerate everywhere, their god alone excepted, every kind of god; all the monsters of Egypt have their temples in Rome;

our fathers, at their will, made a god of a man; and, their blood in our veins preserving their errors, we fill heaven with all our emperors; but, to speak without disguise of deifications so numerous, the effect is very doubtful of such metamorphoses.

Christians have but one God, absolute master of all, whose mere will does whatever he resolves; but, if I may venture to say what seems to me true, our gods very often agree ill together; and, though their wrath crush me before your eyes, we have a good many of them for them to be true gods. Finally, among the Christians, morals are pure, vices are hated, virtues flourish; they offer prayers on be-half of us who persecute them; and, during all the time since we have tormented them, have they ever been seen mutinous? Have they ever been seen rebellious? Have our princes ever had more faithful soldiers? Fierce in war, they submit themselves to our executioners; and, lions in combat, they die like lambs. I pity them too much not to defend them. Come, let us find Felix; let us commune with his son-in-law; and let us thus, with one single action, gratify at once Paulina, and my glory, and my com-passion.

Such is the high heroic style in which pagan Severus resolves and speaks. And thus the fourth act ends.

Felix makes a sad contrast with the high-hearted-ness which the other characters, most of them, display. He is base enough to suspect that Severus is base enough to be false and treacherous in his act of intercession for Polyeuctes. He imagines he detects a plot against himself to undermine him with the emperor. Voltaire criticises Corneille for giving this sordid character to Felix. He thinks the tragedist might better have let Felix be actuated by zeal for the pagan gods. The mean selfishness that animates the governor, Voltaire regards as below the right tragic pitch. It is the poet himself, no doubt, with that high Roman fashion of his, who, unconsciously to the critic, taught him to make the criticism.

Felix summons Polyeuctes to an interview, and adjures him to be a prudent man. Felix at length says, "Adore the gods, or die." "I am a Christian," simply replies the martyr. "Impious! Adore them, I bid you, or renounce life." (Here again Voltaire offers one of his refrigerant criticisms: "*Renounce life* does not advance upon the meaning of *die;* when one repeats the thought, the expression should be strengthened.") Paulina meantime has entered to expostulate with Polyeuctes and with her father. Polyeuctes bids her, 'Live with Severus.' He says he has revolved the subject, and he is convinced that another love is the sole remedy for her woe. He proceeds in the calmest manner to point out the advantages of the course recommended. Voltaire remarks, — justly, we are bound to say, — that these maxims are here somewhat revolting; the martyr should have had other things to say. On Felix's final word, "Soldiers, execute the order that I have given," Paulina exclaims, "Whither are you taking him?" "To death," says Felix. "To glory," says Polyeuctes. "Admirable dialogue, and always applauded," is Voltaire's note on this.

The tragedy does not end with the martyrdom of Polyeuctes. Paulina becomes a Christian, but remains pagan enough to call her father " barbarous " in acrimoniously bidding him finish his work by putting his daughter also to death. Severus reproaches Felix for his cruelty, and threatens him with his own enmity. Felix undergoes instantaneous conversion, — a miracle of grace which, under the circumstances provided by Corneille, we may excuse Voltaire for laughing at. Paulina is delighted; and Severus asks, " Who would not be touched by a spectacle so tender?"

The tragedy thus comes near ending happily enough to be called a comedy.

Such as the foregoing exhibits him, is Corneille, the father of French tragedy, where at his best; where at his worst, he is something so different that you would hardly admit him to be the same man. For never was genius more unequal in different manifestations of itself, than Corneille in his different works. Molière is reported to have said that Corneille had a familiar, or a fairy, that came to him at times, and enabled him to write sublimely; but that, when the poet was left to himself, he could write as poorly as another man.

Corneille produced some thirty-three dramatic pieces in all, but of these not more than six or seven retain their place on the French stage.

Besides his plays, there is a translation in verse by him of the "Imitation of Christ;" there are

metrical versions of a considerable number of the
Psalms; there are odes, madrigals, sonnets, stanzas, addresses to the king. Then there are discourses in prose on dramatic poetry, on tragedy,
and on the three unities. Add to these, elaborate
appreciations by himself of a considerable number
of his own plays, prefaces, epistles, arguments to
his pieces, and you have, what with the notes, the
introductions, the eulogies, and other such things
that the faithful French editor knows so well how
to accumulate, matter enough of Corneille to swell
out eleven, or, in one edition, — that issued under
Napoleon as First Consul, — even twelve, handsome
volumes of his works.

Corneille and Bossuet together constitute a kind
of rank by themselves among the *Dii Majores* of
the French literary Olympus.

XI.

RACINE.

1639-1699.

JEAN RACINE was Pierre Corneille reduced to rule.
The younger was to the elder somewhat as Sophocles
or Euripides was to Æschylus, as Virgil was to
Lucretius, as Pope was to Dryden. Nature was

more in Corneille, art was more in Racine. Corneille was a pathfinder in literature. He led the way, even for Molière, still more for Racine. But Racine was as much before Corneille in perfection of art, as Corneille was before Racine in audacity of genius. Racine, accordingly, is much more even and uniform than Corneille. Smoothness, polish, ease, grace, sweetness, — these, and monotony in these, are the mark of Racine. But if there is, in the latter poet, less to admire, there is also less to forgive. His taste and his judgment were surer than the taste and the judgment of Corneille. He enjoyed, moreover, an inestimable advantage in the life-long friendship of the great critic of his time, Boileau. Boileau was a literary conscience to Racine. He kept Racine constantly spurred to his best endeavors in art. Racine was congratulating himself to his friend on the ease with which he produced his verse. " Let me teach you to produce easy verse with difficulty," was the critic's admirable reply. Racine was a docile pupil. He became as painstaking an artist in verse as Boileau would have him.

It will always be a matter of individual taste, and of changing fashion in criticism, to decide which of the two is, on the whole, to be preferred to the other. Racine eclipsed Corneille in vogue during the lifetime of the latter. Corneille's old age was, perhaps, seriously saddened by the consciousness, which he could not but have, of being retired from the place of ascendency once accorded to him over all. His case repeated the fortune of Æschylus in relation to Sophocles. The eighteenth century, taught by Voltaire, established the precedence of Racine. But the nineteenth century has restored the crown to the brow of Corneille. To such mutations is subject the fame of an author.

Jean Racine was early left an orphan. His grandparents put him, after preparatory training at another establishment, to school at Port Royal, where during three years he had the best opportunities of education that the kingdom afforded. His friends wanted to make a clergyman of him; but the preferences of the boy prevailed, and he addicted himself to literature. The Greek tragedists became familiar to him in his youth, and their example in literary art exercised a sovereign influence over Racine's development as author. It pained the good Port-Royalists to see their late gifted pupil, now out of their hands, inclined to write plays. Nicole printed a remonstrance against the theatre, in which Racine discovered something that he took to slant anonymously at himself. He wrote a spirited reply, of which no notice was taken by the Port-Royalists. Somebody, however, on their behalf, rejoined to Racine, whereupon the young author wrote a second letter to the Port-Royalists, which he showed to his friend Boileau. "This may do credit to your head, but it will do none to your heart," was that faithful mentor's comment, in returning the document. Racine suppressed his second letter, and did his best to recall the first. But he went on in his course of writing for the stage.

The "Thebaïd" was Racine's first tragedy, — at least his first that attained to the honor of being represented. Molière brought it out in his theatre, the Palais Royal. His second tragedy, the "Alexander the Great," was also put into the hands of Molière.

This latter play the author took to Corneille to get his judgment on it. Corneille was thirty-three years the senior of Racine, and he was at this time the undisputed master of French tragedy. "You have undoubted talent for poetry — for tragedy, not; try your hand in some other poetical line," was Corneille's sentence on the unrecognized young rival, who was so soon to supplant him in popular favor.

The "Andromache" followed the "Alexander," and then Racine did try his hand in another poetical line; for he wrote a comedy, his only one, "The Suitors," as is loosely translated "Les Plaideurs," a title which has a legal, and not an amorous, meaning. This play, after it had at first failed, Louis XIV. laughed into court favor. It became thenceforward a great success. It still keeps its place on the stage. It is, however, a farce, rather than a comedy.

We pass over now one or two of the subsequent productions of Racine, to mention next a play of

his which had a singular history. It was a fancy of
the brilliant Princess Henriette (that same daughter
of English Charles I., Bossuet's funeral oration on
whom, presently to be spoken of, is so celebrated)
to engage the two great tragedists, Corneille and
Racine, both at once, in labor, without their mutual
knowledge, upon the same subject, — a subject
which she herself, drawing it from the history of
Tacitus, conceived to be eminently fit for tragical
treatment. Corneille produced his "Berenice,"
and Racine his "Titus and Berenice." The princess died before the two plays which she had inspired
were produced; but, when they were produced, Racine's work won the palm. The rivalry created a
bitterness between the two authors, of which, naturally, the defeated one tasted the more deeply. An
ill-considered pleasantry, too, of Racine's, in making,
out of one of Corneille's tragic lines in his "Cid,"
a comic line in "The Suitors," hurt the old man's
pride. That pride suffered a worse hurt still. The
chief Parisian theatre, completely occupied with the
works of his victorious rival, rejected tragedies
offered by Corneille.

Still, Racine did not have things all his own way.
Some good critics considered the rage for this
younger dramatist a mere passing whim of fashion.
These — Madame de Sévigné was of them — stood
by their "old admiration," and were true to Corneille.

A memorable mortification and chagrin for our

poet was now prepared by his enemies — he seems never to have lacked enemies — with lavish and elaborate malice. Racine had produced a play from Euripides, the "Phædra," on which he had unstintingly bestowed his best genius and his best art. It was contrived that another poet, one Pradon, should, at the self-same moment, have a play represented on the self-same subject. At a cost of many thousands of dollars, the best seats at Racine's theatre were all bought by his enemies, and left solidly vacant. The best seats at Pradon's theatre were all bought by the same interested parties, and duly occupied with industrious and zealous applauders. This occurred at six successive representations. The result was the immediate apparent triumph of Pradon over the humiliated Racine. Boileau in vain bade his friend be of good cheer, and await the assured reversal of the verdict. Racine was deeply wounded.

This discomposing experience of the poet's, joined with conscientious misgivings on his part as to the propriety of his course in writing for the stage, led him now, at the early age of thirty-eight, to renounce tragedy altogether. His son Louis, from whose life of Racine we have chiefly drawn our material for the present sketch, conceives this change in his father as a profound and genuine religious conversion. Writers whose spirit inclines them not to relish a condemnation such as seems thus to be reflected on the theatre, take a less charitable view of the change. They account for it as a reaction of mortified pride. Some of them go so far as groundlessly to impute sheer hypocrisy to Racine.

A long interval of silence, on Racine's part, had elapsed, when Madame de Maintenon, the wife of Louis XIV., asked the unemployed poet to prepare a sacred play for the use of the high-born girls educated under her care at St. Cyr. Racine consented, and produced his "Esther." This achieved a prodigious success; for the court took it up, and an exercise written for a girls' school became the admiration of a kingdom. A second similar play followed, the "Athaliah," — the last, and, by general agreement, the most perfect, work of its author. We thus reach that tragedy of Racine's which both its fame and its character dictate to us as the one by eminence to be used here in exhibition of the quality of this Virgil among tragedists.

Our readers may, if they please, refresh their recollection of the history on which the drama is founded by perusing Second Kings, chapter eleven, and Second Chronicles, chapters twenty-two and twenty-three. Athaliah, whose name gives its title to the tragedy, was daughter to the wicked king, Ahab. She reigns as queen at Jerusalem over the kingdom of Judah. To secure her usurped position, she had sought to kill all the descendants of King David, even her own grandchildren. She had succeeded, — but not quite. Young Joash escaped, to be secretly reared in the temple by the high priest. The final disclosure of this hidden prince, and his coronation as king in place of usurping Athaliah, destined to be fearfully overthrown, and put to death in his name, afford the action of the play. Action, however, there is almost none in classic French tragedy. The tragic drama is, with the French, as it was with the Greeks, after whom it was framed, merely a succession of scenes in which speeches are made by the actors. Lofty declamation is always the character of the play. In the "Athaliah," as in the "Esther," Racine introduced the feature of the chorus, a restoration which had all the effect of an innovation. The chorus in "Athaliah" consisted of Hebrew virgins, who, at intervals marking the transitions between the acts, chanted the spirit of the piece in its successive stages of progress toward the final catastrophe. The "Athaliah" is almost proof against technical criticism. It is acknowledged to be, after its kind, a nearly ideal product of art.

There is a curious story about the fortune of this piece with the public, that will interest our readers. The first success of "Athaliah" was not great. In fact, it was almost a flat failure. But a company of wits, playing at forfeits somewhere in the country, severely sentenced one of their number to go by himself, and read the first act of "Athaliah." The victim went, and did not return. Sought at length, he was found just commencing a second perusal of the play entire. He reported of it so enthusiastically, that he was asked to read it before the company, which he did, to their delight. This started a reaction in favor of the condemned play, which soon came to be counted the masterpiece of its author.

First, in specimen of the choral feature of the drama, we content ourselves with giving a single chorus from the "Athaliah." This we turn into rhyme, clinging pretty closely all the way to the form of the original. Attentive readers may, in one place of our rendering, observe an instance of identical rhyme. This, in a piece of verse originally written in English, would, of course, be a fault. In a translation from French, it may pass for a merit; since, to judge from the practice of the national poets, the French ear seems to be even better pleased with such strict identities of sound, at the close of corresponding lines, than it is with those definite mere resemblances to which, in English versification, rhymes are rigidly limited. Suspense between hope and dread, dread preponderating, is the state of feeling represented in the present chorus. Salomith is the leading singer : —

SALOMITH.

The Lord hath deigned to speak,
But what he to his prophet now hath shown —
Who unto us will make it clearly known ?
Arms he himself to save us, poor and weak ?
Arms he himself to have us overthrown ?

THE WHOLE CHORUS.

O promises! O threats! O mystery profound!
　What woe, what weal, are each in turn foretold?
How can so much of wrath be found
　So much of love to enfold?

A VOICE.

Zion shall be no more; a cruel flame
　Will all her ornaments devour.

A SECOND VOICE.

　God shelters Zion; she has shield and tower
In His eternal name.

FIRST VOICE.

I see her splendor all from vision disappear.

SECOND VOICE.

I see on every side her glory shine more clear.

FIRST VOICE.

Into a deep abyss is Zion sunk from sight.

SECOND VOICE.

Zion lifts up her brow amid celestial light.

FIRST VOICE.

What dire despair!

SECOND VOICE.

　　　　What praise from every tongue!

FIRST VOICE.

What cries of grief !

SECOND VOICE.

　　　　What songs of triumph sung!

A Third Voice.
Cease we to vex ourselves; our God, one day,
  Will this great mystery make clear.

All Three Voices.
  Let us his wrath revere,
While on his love, no less, our hopes we stay.

The catastrophe is reached in the coronation of
little Joash as king, and in the destruction of usurping and wicked Athaliah. Little Joash, by the way,
with his rather precocious wisdom of reply, derived
to himself, for the moment, a certain factitious interest, from the resemblance, meant by the poet to
be divined by spectators, between him and the little
Duke of Burgundy, Louis XIV.'s grandson, then
of about the same age with the Hebrew boy, and
of high reputation for mental vivacity.

The scene in which the high priest, Jehoiada, for
the first time discloses to his foster-son, Joash, the
latter's royal descent from David, and his true heir-
ship to the throne of Judah, will serve sufficiently
to exhibit what maturity of modest and pious wisdom the dramatist attributes to this Hebrew boy of
nine or ten years. Nine or ten years of age Racine
makes Joash, instead of seven, as Scripture, interpreted without violence, would make him. The lad
has had his sage curiosity excited by seeing preparations in progress for some important ceremonial.
That ceremonial is his own coronation, but he does
not guess the secret. Nay, he has just touchingly

asked his foster-mother, observed by him to be in tears : —

> What pity touches you? Is it that in a holocaust to be this day offered, I, like Jephtha's daughter in other times, must pacify by my death the anger of the Lord? Alas, a son has nothing that does not belong to his father!

The discreet foster-mother refers the lad to her husband, Jehoiada, now approaching. Joash rushes into the arms of the high priest, exclaiming, "My father!" "Well, my son?" the high-priest replies. "What preparations, then, are these?" asks Joash. The high priest bids him prepare himself to listen and learn, the time being now come for him to pay his debt to God : —

> JOASH. I feel myself ready, if he wishes it, to give to him my life.
> JEHOIADA. You have often heard read the history of our kings. Do you remember, my son, what strict laws a king worthy of the crown ought to impose upon himself?
> JOASH. A wise and good king, so hath God himself declared, puts not his reliance upon riches and gold; he fears the Lord his God, has ever before him his precepts, his laws, his judgments severe, and does not with unjust burdens overwhelm his brethren.

Fénelon had already been two years preceptor to the Duke of Burgundy when this tragedy was written. It is impossible not to feel that Racine must have had that prince in mind when he put into the mouth of young Joash sentiments so likely to have been instilled into the heart of his royal pupil, the great king's grandson, by such a preceptor as Fénelon.   How could the selfish old monarch of France contrive to avoid recognizing his own portrait, suggested by contrast in that description of the good king from the lips of little Joash?   Racine was here treading on treacherous ground.   He will presently find his footing quite give way under him, to let him down into the " horrible pit" of disgrace with his king.   This not, however, in the present play.

The tragedist has generously bestowed upon wicked Queen Athaliah a certain loftiness of spirit which, in its display in the final catastrophe, almost redeems her to admiration, if not to sympathy.   There is nothing in the play more nearly sublime in declamation than the final speech in which Athaliah greets her own doom, and blasphemously forecasts, for young King Joash, a future of apostasy from God. With this admirable piece of rhetoric, resembling a burst of blasphemy from Satan in " Paradise Lost," so far as French poetry may be allowed to resemble English, we conclude our representation of Racine. Athaliah has now just heard the announcement of things that assure her of the overthrow of her usurpation.   She expresses herself in a speech, the first words of which were, no doubt, designed by the poet to recall the celebrated traditional exclamation of Julian the Apostate, uttered at a moment of irretrievable disaster to his impious hopes, — " O Galilean, thou hast conquered!" as follows : —

God of the Jews, 'tis thou that dost prevail!
Ay, it is Joash; all without avail
Seek I to cheat myself with other thought:
I know the wound my weapon on him wrought;
I see his father Ahaziah's face;
Naught but brings back to me that hated race.
David doth triumph, Ahab only fall, —
Unpitying God, thou only hast done all!
'Tis thou that flattering me to hope in vain
For easy vengeance, o'er and o'er again
Hast with myself myself embroiled anew,
Now pangs of conscience rousing, not a few,
Now dazzling me with thy rich treasures rare,
Which I to burn or pillage did not dare.
Let him, then, reign, this son, thy care, thy toil,
And, so to signalize his new-got spoil,
Let him into my bosom plunge the knife,
And take with filial hand his mother's life.
Hearken what wish for him she dying breathes —
Wish? nay, what hope, assured hope, bequeaths, —
That, disobedient, proud, rebellious, he,
Faithful to Ahab's blood received from me,
To his grandfather, to his father, like,
Abhorrent heir of David, down may strike
Thy worship and thy fane, avenger fell
Of Athaliah, Ahab, Jezebel!

With words thus rendered into such English verse as we could command for the purpose, Athaliah disappears from the stage. Her execution follows immediately. This is not exhibited, but is announced with brief, solemn comment from Jehoiada. And so the tragedy ends.

The interest of the piece, to the modern reader, is by no means equal to its fame. One reproaches one's self, but one yawns in conscientiously perusing it. Still, one feels the work of the author to be irreproachably, nay, consummately, good. But fashions in taste change; and we cannot hold ourselves responsible for admiring, or, at any rate, for enjoying, according to the judgment of other races and of former generations. It is — so, with grave concurrence, we say — It is a great classic, worthy of the praise that it receives. We are glad that we have read it; and, let us be candid, equally glad that we have not to read it again.

As has already been intimated, Racine, after "Athaliah," wrote tragedy no more. He ceased to interest himself in the fortune of his plays. His son Louis, in his Life of his father, testifies that he never heard his father speak in the family of the dramas that he had written. His theatrical triumphs seemed to afford him no pleasure. He repented of them rather than gloried in them.

While one need not doubt that this regret of Racine's for the devotion of his powers to the production of tragedy, was a sincere regret of his conscience, one may properly wish that the regret had been more heroic. The fact is, Racine was somewhat feminine in character as well as in genius. He could not beat up with stout heart undismayed against an adverse wind. And the wind blew adverse at length to Racine, from the principal quarter, the court of Versailles. From being a chief favorite with his sovereign, Racine fell into the position of an exile from the royal presence. The immediate occasion was one honorable rather than otherwise to the poet.

In conversation with Madame de Maintenon, Racine had expressed views on the state of France and on the duties of a king to his subjects, which so impressed her mind that she desired him to reduce his observations to writing, and confide them to her, she promising to keep them profoundly secret from Louis. But Louis surprised her with the manuscript in her hand. Taking it from her, he read in it, and demanded to know the author. Madame de Maintenon could not finally refuse to tell. "Does M. Racine, because he is a great poet, think that he knows every thing?" the despot angrily asked. Louis never spoke to Racine again. The distressed and infatuated poet still made some paltry request of the king, to experience the humiliation that he invoked. His request was not granted. Racine wilted, like a tender plant, under the sultry frown of his monarch. He could not rally. He soon after died, literally killed by the mere displeasure of one man. Such was the measureless power wielded by Louis XIV.; such was the want of virile stuff in Racine. A spirit partly kindred to the tragedist, Archbishop Fénelon, will presently be shown to have had at about the same time a partly similar experience.

XII.

BOSSUET: 1627–1704; BOURDALOUE: 1632–1704; MASSILLON: 1663–1742.

WE group three names in one title, Bossuet, Bourdaloue, Massillon, to represent the pulpit orators of France. There are other great names, — as Fléchier, with Claude and Saurin, the last two, Protestants both, — but the names we choose are the greatest.

Bossuet's individual distinction is, that he was a great man as well as a great orator; Bourdaloue's, that he was priest-and-preacher simply; Massillon's, that his sermons, regarded quite independently of their subject, their matter, their occasion, regarded merely as masterpieces of pure and classic style, became at once, and permanently became, a part of French literature.

The greatness of Bossuet is an article in the French national creed. No Frenchman disputes it; no Frenchman, indeed, but proclaims it. Protestant agrees with Catholic, infidel with Christian, at least in this. Bossuet, twinned here with Corneille, is to the Frenchman, as Milton is to the Englishman, his synonym for sublimity. Eloquence, somehow, seems a thing too near the common human level to answer fully the need that Frenchmen feel in speaking of Bossuet. Bossuet is not eloquent, he is sublime.

That in French it is in equal part oratory, while in English it is poetry almost alone, that supplies in literature its satisfaction to the sentiment of the sublime, very well represents the difference in genius between the two races. The French idea of poetry is eloquence; and it is eloquence carried to its height, whether in verse or in prose, that constitutes for the Frenchman sublimity. The difference is a difference of blood. English blood is Teutonic in base, and the imagination of the Teuton is poetic. French blood, in base, is Celtic; and the imagination of the Celt is oratoric.

Jacques Bénigne Bossuet was of good *bourgeois*, or middle-class, stock. He passed a well-ordered and virtuous youth, as if in prophetic consistency with what was to be his subsequent career. He was brought forward while a young man in the Hôtel de Rambouillet, where, on a certain occasion, he preached a kind of show sermon, under the auspices of his admiring patron. In due time he attracted wide public attention, not merely as an eloquent orator, but as a profound student and as a powerful controversialist. His character and influence became in their maturity such, that La Bruyère aptly called him a "Father of the Church." "The Corneille of the pulpit," was Henri Martin's characterization and praise. A third phrase, "the eagle of Meaux," has passed into almost an alternative name for Bossuet. He soared like an eagle in his eloquence, and he was bishop of Meaux.

Bossuet and Louis XIV. were exactly suited to each other, in the mutual relation of subject and sovereign. Bossuet preached sincerely — as everybody knows Louis sincerely practised — the doctrine of the divine right of kings to rule absolutely. But the proud prelate compromised neither his own dignity nor the dignity of the Church in the presence of the absolute monarch.

Bossuet threw himself with great zeal, and to prodigious effect, into the controversy against Protestantism. His "History of the Variations of the Protestant Churches," in two good volumes, was one of the mightiest pamphlets ever written. As tutor to the Dauphin (the king's eldest son), he produced, with other works, his celebrated "Discourse on Universal History."

In proceeding now to give, from the three great preachers named in our title, a few specimen passages of the most famous pulpit oratory in the world, we need to prepare our readers against a natural disappointment. That which they are about to see has nothing in it of what will at first strike them as brilliant. The pulpit eloquence of the Augustan age of France was distinctly "classic," and not at all "romantic," in style. Its character is not ornate, but severe. There is little rhetorical figure in it, little of that "illustration" which our own different national taste is accustomed to demand from the pulpit. There is plenty of white light, "dry light" and white, for the reason; but there is almost no bright color for the fancy, and, it must be added, not a great deal of melting warmth for the heart.

The funeral orations of Bossuet are generally esteemed the masterpieces of this orator's eloquence. He had great occasions, and he was great to match them. Still, readers might easily be disappointed in perusing a funeral oration of Bossuet's. The discourse will generally be found to deal in commonplaces of description, of reflection, and of sentiment. Those commonplaces, however, are often made very impressive by the lofty, the magisterial, the imperial, manner of the preacher in treating them. We exhibit a specimen, a single specimen only, and a brief one, in the majestic exordium to the funeral oration on the Princess Henrietta of England.

This princess was the last one left of the children of King Charles I. of England. Her mother's death — her mother was of the French house of Bourbon — had occurred but a short time before, and Bossuet had on that occasion pronounced the eulogy. The daughter, scarcely returned to France from a secret mission of state to England, the success of which made her an object of distinguished regard at Versailles, suddenly fell ill and died. Bossuet was summoned to preach at her funeral. (We have not been able to find an English translation of Bossuet, and we accordingly make the present transfer from French ourselves. We do the same, for the same reason, in the case of Massillon. In the case of Bourdaloue, we succeeded in obtaining a printed translation which we could modify to suit our purpose.)   Bossuet : —

It was then reserved for my lot to pay this funereal tribute to the high and potent princess, Henrietta of England, Duchess of Orleans. She whom I had seen so attentive while I was discharging a like office for the queen her mother, was so soon after to be the subject of a similar discourse, and my sad voice was predestined to this melancholy service. O vanity! O nothingness! O mortals! ignorant of their destiny! Ten months ago, would she have believed it ? And you, my hearers, would you have thought, while she was shedding so many tears in this place, that she was so soon to assemble you here to deplore her own loss ? O princess! the worthy object of the admiration of two great kingdoms, was it not enough that England should deplore your absence, without being yet further compelled to deplore your death ? France, who with so much joy beheld you again, surrounded with a new brilliancy, had she not in reserve other pomps and other triumphs for you, returned from that famous voyage whence you had brought hither so much glory, and hopes so fair ? "Vanity of vanities; all is vanity." Nothing is left for me to say but that; that is the only sentiment which, in presence of so strange a casualty, grief so well-grounded and so poignant, permits me to indulge. Nor have I explored the Holy Scriptures in order to find therein some text which I might apply to this princess; I have taken, without premeditation and without choice, the first expression presented to me by the Preacher, with whom vanity, although it has been so often named, is yet, to my mind, not named often enough to suit the purpose that I have in view. I wish, in a single misfortune, to lament all the calamities of the human race, and in a single death to exhibit the death and the nothingness of all human greatness. This text, which suits all the circumstances and all the occurrences of our life, becomes, by a special adaptedness, appropriate to my mournful theme; since never were the vanities of the earth either so clearly disclosed or so openly confounded. No, after what we have just seen, health is but a name, life is but a dream, glory is but a shadow, charms and pleasures are but a dangerous diversion. Every thing is vain within us, except the sincere acknowledgment made before God of our vanity, and the fixed judgment of the mind, leading us to despise all that we are.

But did I speak the truth? Man, whom God made in his own image, is he but a shadow? That which Jesus Christ came from heaven to earth to seek, that which he deemed that he could, without degrading himself, ransom with his own blood, is that a mere nothing? Let us acknowledge our mistake; surely this sad spectacle of the vanity of things human was leading us astray, and public hope, baffled suddenly by the death of this princess, was urging us too far. It must not be permitted to man to despise himself entirely, lest he, supposing, in common with the wicked, that our life is but a game in which chance reigns, take his way without rule and without self-control, at the pleasure of his own blind wishes. It is for this reason that the Preacher, after having commenced his inspired production by the expressions which I have cited, after having filled all its pages with contempt for things human, is pleased at last to show man something more substantial, by saying to him, " Fear God, and keep his commandments; for this is the whole duty of man. For God shall bring every work into judgment, with every secret thing, whether it be good, or whether it be evil.'' Thus every thing is vain in man, if we regard what he gives to the world; but, on the contrary, every thing is important, if we consider what he owes to God. Once again, every thing is vain in man, if we regard the course of his mortal life; but every thing is of value, every thing is important, if we contemplate the goal where it ends, and the account of it which he must render. Let us, therefore, meditate to-day, in presence of this altar and of this tomb, the first and the last utterance of the Preacher; of which the one shows the nothingness of man, the other establishes his greatness. Let this tomb convince us of our nothingness, provided that this altar, where is daily offered for us a Victim of price so great, teach us at the same time our dignity. The princess whom we weep shall be a faithful witness, both of the one and of the other. Let us survey that which a sudden death has taken away from her; let us survey that which a holy death has bestowed upon her. Thus shall we learn to despise that which she quitted without regret, in order to attach all our regard to that which she embraced with so much ardor, — when her soul, purified from all earthly sentiments, full of the heaven on whose border she touched, saw the light completely revealed. Such are the truths which I have to treat, and which I have deemed worthy to be proposed to so great a prince, and to the most illustrious assembly in the world.

It will be felt how removed is the foregoing from any thing like an effort, on the preacher's part, to startle his audience with the far-fetched and unexpected. It must, however, be admitted that Bossuet was not always — as, of our Webster, it has well been said that he always was — superior to the temptation to exaggerate an occasion by pomps of rhetoric. Bossuet was a great man, but he was not quite great enough to be wholly free from pride of self-consciousness in matching himself as orator against "the most illustrious assembly in the world."

The ordinary sermons of Bossuet are less read, and they less deserve perhaps to be read, than those of Bourdaloue and Massillon.

BOURDALOUE was a voice. He was the voice of one crying, not in the wilderness, but amid the homes and haunts of men, and, by eminence, in the court of the most powerful and most splendid of earthly monarchs. He was a Jesuit, one of the most devoted and most accomplished of an order filled with devoted and accomplished men. It belonged to his Jesuit character and Jesuit training, that Bourdaloue should hold the place that he did as ever-successful courtier at Versailles, all the while that, as preacher, he was using the " holy freedom of the pulpit " to launch those blank fulminations of his at sin in high places, at sin even in the highest, and all the briefer while that, as confessor to Madame de Maintenon, he was influencing the policy of Louis XIV.

No scandal of any sort attaches to the reputation of Louis Bourdaloue. He was a man of spotless fame, — unless it be a spot on his fame that he could please the most selfish of sinful monarchs well enough to be that monarch's chosen preacher during a longer time than any other pulpit orator whatever was tolerated at Versailles. He is described by all who knew him as a man of gracious spirit. If he did not reprobate and denounce the revocation of the Edict of Nantes, that was rather of the age than of Bourdaloue.

Sainte-Beuve, in a remarkably sympathetic appreciation of Bourdaloue, — free, contrary to the critic's wont, from hostile insinuation even, — regards it as part of the merit of this preacher that there is, and

that there can be, no biography of him. His public
life is summed up in simply saying that he was a
preacher. During thirty-four laborious and fruitful
years he preached the doctrines of the Church;
and this is the sole account to be given of him,
except, indeed, that in the confessional he was,
all that time, learning those secrets of the human
heart which he used to such effect in composing his
sermons. He had very suave and winning ways
as confessor, though he enjoined great strictness as
preacher. This led a witty woman of his time to
say of him : " Father Bourdaloue charges high in
the pulpit, but he sells cheap in the confessional."
How much laxity he allowed as confessor, it is, of
course, impossible to say. But his sermons remain
to show that, though indeed he was severe and high
in requirement as preacher, he did not fail to soften
asperity by insisting on the goodness, while he
insisted on the awfulness, of God. Still, it cannot
be denied, that somehow the elaborate compliments
which, as an established convention of his pulpit,
he not infrequently delivered to Louis XIV., tended
powerfully to make it appear that his stern denun-
ciation of sin, which at first blush might seem
directly levelled at the king, had in reality no application at all, or but the very gentlest application, to
the particular case of his Most Christian Majesty.

We begin our citations from Bourdaloue with an
extract from a sermon of his on " A Perverted
Conscience." The whole discourse is one well

worth the study of any reader. It is a piece of searching psychological analysis, and pungent application to conscience. Bourdaloue, in his sermons, has always the air of a man seriously intent on producing practical results. There are no false motions. Every swaying of the preacher's weapon is a blow, and every blow is a hit. There is hardly another example in homiletic literature of such compactness, such solidity, such logical consecutiveness, such cogency, such freedom from surplusage. Tare and tret are excluded. Every thing counts. You meet with two or three adjectives, and you at first naturally assume, that, after the usual manner of homilists, Bourdaloue has thrown these in without rigorously definite purpose, simply to heighten a general effect. Not at all. There follows a development of the preacher's thought, constituting virtually a distinct justification of each adjective employed. You soon learn that there is no random, no waste, in this man's words. But here is the promised extract from the sermon on "A Perverted Conscience." In it Bourdaloue depresses his gun, and discharges it point-blank at the audience before him. You can almost imagine you see the ranks of "the great" laid low. Alas! one fears that, instead of biting the dust, those courtiers, with the king in the midst of them to set the example, only cried bravo in their hearts at the skill of the gunner : —

I have said more particularly that in the world in which you live, — I mean the court, — the disease of a perverted conscience is far more common, and far more difficult to be avoided; and I am sure that in this you will agree with me. For it is at the court that the passions bear sway, that desires are more ardent, that self-interest is keener, and that, by infallible consequence, self-blinding is more easy, and consciences, even the most enlightened and the most upright, become gradually perverted. It is at the court that the goddess of the world, I mean fortune, exercises over the minds of men, and in consequence over their consciences, a more absolute dominion. It is at the court that the aim to maintain one's self, the impatience to raise one's self, the frenzy to push one's self, the fear of displeasing, the desire of making one's self agreeable, produce consciences, which anywhere else would pass for monstrous, but which, finding themselves there authorized by custom, seem to have acquired a right of possession and of prescription. People, from living at court, and from no other cause than having lived there, are filled with these errors. Whatever uprightness of conscience they may have brought thither, by breathing its air and by hearing its language, they are habituated to iniquity, they come to have less horror of vice, and, after having long blamed it, a thousand times condemned it, they at last behold it with a more favorable eye, tolerate it, excuse it; that is to say, without observing what is happening, they make over their consciences, and, by insensible steps, from Christian, which they were, by little and little become quite worldly, and not far from pagan.

What could surpass the adaptedness of such preaching as that to the need of the moment for which it was prepared? And how did the libertine French monarch contrive to escape the force of truth like the following, with which the preacher immediately proceeds? —

You would say, and it really seems, that for the court, there are other principles of religion than for the rest of the world, and that the courtier has a right to make for himself a conscience different in kind and in quality from that of other men; for such is the prevailing idea of the matter, — an idea well sustained, or rather unfortunately justified, by experience. . . . Nevertheless, my dear hearers, St. Paul assures us, that there is but one God and one faith; and woe to the man who dividing Him, this one God, shall represent Him as at court less an enemy to human transgressions than He is outside of the court; or, severing this one faith, shall suppose it in the case of one class more indulgent than in the case of another.

Bourdaloue, as Jesuit, could not but feel the power of Pascal in his "Provincial Letters," constantly undermining the authority of his order. His preaching, as Sainte-Beuve well says, may be considered to have been, in the preacher's intention, one prolonged confutation of Pascal's immortal indictment. We borrow of Sainte-Beuve a short extract from Bourdaloue's sermon on slander, which may serve as an instance to show with what adroitness the Jesuit retorted anonymously upon the Jansenist : —

Behold one of the abuses of our time. Means have been found to consecrate slander, to change it into a virtue, and even into one of the holiest virtues — that means is, zeal for the glory of God. . . . We must humble those people, is the cry; and it is for the good of the Church to tarnish their reputation and to diminish their credit. That idea becomes, as it were, a principle; the conscience is fashioned accordingly, and there is nothing that is not permissible to a motive so noble. You fabricate, you exaggerate, you give things a poisonous taint, you tell but half the truth; you make your prejudices stand for indisputable facts; you spread abroad a hundred falsehoods; you confound what is individual with what is general; what one man has said that is bad, you pretend that all have said; and what many have said that is good, you pretend that nobody has said; and all that, once again, for the glory of God. For such direction of the intention justifies all that. Such direction of the intention will not suffice to justify a prevarication, but it is more than sufficient to justify calumny, provided only you are convinced that you are serving God thereby.

In conclusion, we give a passage or two of Bourdaloue's sermon on " An Eternity of Woe." Stanch orthodoxy the reader will find here. President Edwards's discourse, " Sinners in the Hands of an Angry God," is not more unflinching. But what a relief of contrasted sweetness does Bourdaloue interpose in the first part of the ensuing extract, to set off the grim and grisly horror of that which is to follow! We draw, for this case, from a translation, issued in Dublin under Roman-Catholic auspices, of select sermons by Bourdaloue. The translator, throughout his volume, has been highly loyal in spirit toward the great French preacher; but this has not prevented much enfeebling by him of the style of his original : —

There are some just, fervent, perfect souls, who, like children in the house of the Heavenly Father, strive to please and possess him. in order only to possess and to love him; and who, incessantly animated by this unselfish motive, inviolably adhere to his divine precepts, and lay it down as a rigorous and unalterable rule, to obey the least intimation of his will. They serve him with an affection entirely filial. But there are also dastards, worldlings, sinners, terrestrial and sensual men, who are scarcely susceptible of any other impressions than those of the judgments and vengeance of God. Talk to them of his greatness, of his perfections, of his benefits, or even of his rewards, and they will hardly listen to you; and, if they are prevailed upon to pay some attention and respect to your words, they will sound in their ears, but not reach their hearts. . . . Therefore, to move them, to stir them up, to awaken them from the lethargic sleep with which they are overwhelmed, the thunder of divine wrath and the decree that condemns them to eternal flames must be dinned into their ears: "Depart from me, ye accursed, into everlasting fire" (Matt. xxv.). Make them consider attentively, and represent to them with all the force of grace, the consequences and horror of this word "eternal." . . .

It is not imagination, it is pure reason and intelligence, that now in Bourdaloue goes about the business of impressing the thought of the dreadfulness of an eternity of woe. The effect produced is not that of the lightning-flash suddenly revealing the jaws agape of an unfathomable abyss directly before you. It is rather that of steady, intolerable pressure gradually applied to crush, to annihilate, the soul : —

. . . Struck with horror at so doleful a destiny, I apply to this eternity all the powers of my mind; I examine and scrutinize it in all its parts; and I survey, as it were, its whole dimensions. Moreover, to express it in more lively colors, and to represent it in my mind more conformably to the senses and the human understanding, I borrow comparisons from the Fathers of the Church, and I make, if I may so speak, the same computations. I figure to myself all the stars of the firmament; to this innumerable multitude I add all the drops of water in the bosom of the ocean; and if this be not enough, I reckon, or at least endeavor to reckon, all the grains of sand on its shore. Then I interrogate myself, I reason with myself, and I put to myself the question — If I had for as many ages, and a thousand times as many, undergone torments in that glowing fire which is kindled by the breath of the Lord in his anger to take eternal vengeance, would eternity be at an end? No; and why? Because it is eternity, and eternity is endless. To number up the stars that shine in the heavens, to count the drops of water that compose the sea, to tell the grains of sand that lie upon the shore, is not absolutely impossible; but to measure in eternity the number of days, of years, of ages, is what cannot be compassed, because the days, the years, and the ages are without number; or, to speak more properly, because in eternity there are neither days, nor years, nor ages, but a single, endless, infinite duration.

To this thought I devote my mind. I imagine I see and rove through this same eternity, and discover no end, but find it to be always a boundless tract. I imagine the wide prospect lies open on all sides, and encompasseth me around; that if I rise up, or if I sink down, or what way soever I turn my eyes, this eternity meets them; and that after a thousand efforts to get forward, I have made no progress, but find it still eternity. I imagine that after long revolutions of time, I behold in the midst of this eternity a damned soul, in the same state, in the same affliction, in the same misery still; and putting myself mentally in the place of this soul, I imagine that in this eternal punishment I feel myself continually devoured by that fire which nothing extinguishes; that I continually shed those floods of tears which nothing can dry up; that I am continually gnawed by the worm of conscience, which never dies; that I continually express my despair and anguish by that gnashing of teeth, and those lamentable cries, which never can move the compassion of God. This idea of myself, this representation, amazes and terrifies me. My whole body shudders, I tremble with fear, I am filled with horror, I have the same feelings as the royal prophet, when he cried, "Pierce thou my flesh with thy fear, for I am afraid of thy judgments."

That was a touching tribute from the elder to the younger — tribute touching, whether wrung, perforce, from a proudly humble, or freely offered by a simply magnanimous, heart — when, like John the Baptist speaking of Jesus, Bourdaloue, growing old, said of Massillon, enjoying his swiftly crescent renown: "He must increase, and I must decrease." It was a true presentiment of the comparative fortune of fame that impended for these two men. It was not, however, in the same path, but in a different, that Massillon outran Bourdaloue. In his own sphere, that of unimpassioned appeal to reason and to conscience, Bourdaloue is still without a rival. No one else, certainly, ever earned, so well as he, the double title which his epigrammatic countrymen were once fond of bestowing upon him, — "The king of preachers, and the preacher of kings."

JEAN BAPTISTE MASSILLON became priest by his own internal sense of vocation to the office, against the preference of his family that he should become, like his father, a notary. He seems to have been by nature sincerely modest in spirit. He had to be forced into the publicity of a preaching career at Paris. His ecclesiastical superior peremptorily required at his hands the sacrifice of his wish to be obscure. He at once filled Paris with his fame. The inevitable consequence followed. He was summoned to preach before the king at Versailles. Here he received, as probably he deserved, that celebrated compliment in epigram, from Louis XIV.: "In hearing some preachers, I feel pleased with them; in hearing you, I feel displeased with myself."

It must not, however, be supposed that Massillon preached like a prophet Nathan saying to King David, "Thou art the man;" or like a John the Baptist saying to King Herod, "It is not lawful for *thee* to have *her;*" or like a John Knox denouncing Queen Mary. Massillon, if he was stern, was suavely stern. He complimented the king. The sword with which he wounded was wreathed deep with flowers. It is difficult not to feel that some unspoken understanding subsisted between the preacher and the king, which permitted the king to separate the preacher from the man when Massillon used that great plainness of speech to his sovereign. The king did not, however, often invite this master of eloquence to make the royal conscience displacent with itself. Bourdaloue was ostensibly as outspoken as Massillon; but somehow that Jesuit preacher contented the king to be his hearer during as many as ten annual seasons, against the one or two only that Massillon preached at court before Louis.

The work of Massillon generally judged, though according to Sainte-Beuve not wisely judged, to be his choicest, is contained in that volume of his which goes by the name of " Le Petit Carême," — literally, " The Little Lent," — a collection of sermons preached during a Lent before the king's great-grandson and successor, youthful Louis XV. These sermons especially have given to their author a fame that is his by a title perhaps absolutely unique in literature. We know no other instance of a writer, limited in his production strictly to sermons, who holds his place in the first rank of authorship simply by virtue of supreme mastership in literary style.

Still, from the text of his printed discourses, — admirable, exquisite, ideal compositions in point of form as these are, — it will be found impossible to conceive adequately the living eloquence of Massillon. There are interesting traditions of the effects produced by particular passages of particular sermons of his. When Louis XIV. died, Massillon preached his funeral sermon. He began with that celebrated single sentence of exordium which, it is said, brought his whole audience, by instantaneous, simultaneous impulse, in a body to their feet. The modern reader will experience some difficulty in comprehending at once why that perfectly common-place-seeming expression of the preacher should have produced an effect so powerful. The element of the opportune, the apposite, the fit, is always great part of the secret of eloquence. Nothing more absolutely appropriate can be conceived than was the sentiment, the exclamation, with which Massillon opened that funeral sermon. The image and symbol of earthly greatness, in the person of Louis XIV., had been shattered under the touch of iconoclast death. "God only is great!" said the preacher; and all was said. Those four short words had uttered completely, and with a simplicity incapable of being surpassed, the thought that usurped every breast. It is not the surprise of some striking new thought that is the most eloquent thing. The most eloquent thing is the surprise of that one word, suddenly spoken, which completely expresses some thought, present already and uppermost, but silent till now, awaiting expression, in a multitude of minds. This most eloquent thing it was which, from Massillon's lips that day, moved his susceptible audience to rise, like one man, and bow in mute act of submission to the truth of his words. The inventive and curious reader may exercise his ingenuity at leisure. He will strive in vain to conceive any other exordium than Massillon's that would have matched the occasion presented.

There is an admirable anecdote of the pulpit, which — though since often otherwise applied — had, perhaps, its first application to Massillon. Some one congratulating the orator, as he came down from his pulpit, on the eloquence of the sermon just preached, that wise self-knower fenced by replying, " Ah, the devil has already apprised me of that ! " The recluse celibate preacher was one day asked whence he derived that marvellous knowledge which he displayed of the passions, the weaknesses, the follies, the sins, of human nature. " From my own heart," was his reply. Source sufficient, perhaps ; but from the confessional, too, one may confidently add.

There is probably no better brief, quotable passage to represent Massillon at his imaginative highest in eloquence, than that most celebrated one of all, occurring toward the close of his memorable sermon on the " Fewness of the Elect." The effect attending the delivery of this passage, on both of the two recorded occasions on which the sermon was preached, is reported to have been remarkable. The manner of the orator — downcast, as with the inward oppression of the same solemnity that he, in speaking, cast like a spell on the audience — indefinitely heightened the magical power of the awful conception excited. Not Bourdaloue himself, with that preternatural skill of his to probe the conscience of man to its innermost secret, could have exceeded the heart-searching rigor with which, in the earlier part of the discourse, Massillon had put to the rack the quivering consciences of his hearers. The terrors of the Lord, the shadows of the world to come, were thus already on all hearts. So much as this,

Bourdaloue, too, with his incomparable dialectic, could have accomplished. But there immediately follows a culmination in power, such as was distinctly beyond the height of Bourdaloue. Genius must be superadded to talent if you would have the supreme, either in poetry or in eloquence. There was an extreme point in Massillon's discourse at which mere reason, having done, and done terribly, its utmost, was fain to confess that it could not go a single step farther. At that extreme point, suddenly, inexhaustible imagination took up the part of exhausted reason. Reason had made men afraid; imagination now appalled them. Massillon said: —

I confine myself to you, my brethren, who are gathered here. I speak no longer of the rest of mankind. I look at you as if you were the only ones on the earth; and here is the thought that seizes me, and that terrifies me. I make the supposition that this is your last hour, and the end of the world; that the heavens are about to open above your heads, that Jesus Christ is to appear in his glory in the midst of this sanctuary, and that you are gathered here only to wait for him, and as trembling criminals on whom is to be pronounced either a sentence of grace or a decree of eternal death. For, vainly do you flatter yourselves; you will die such in character as you are to-day. All those impulses toward change with which you amuse yourselves, you will amuse yourselves with them down to the bed of death. Such is the experience of all generations. The only thing new you will then find in yourselves will be, perhaps, a reckoning a trifle larger than that which you would to-day have to render; and according to what you would be if you were this moment to be judged, you may almost determine what will befall you at the termination of your life.

Now I ask you, and I ask it smitten with terror, not separating in this matter my lot from yours, and putting myself into the same frame of mind into which I desire you to come, — I ask you, then, If Jesus Christ were to appear in this sanctuary, in the midst of this assembly, the most illustrious in the world, to pass judgment on us, to draw the dread line of distinction between the goats and the sheep, do you believe that the majority of all of us who are here would be set on his right hand? Do you believe that things would even be equal? Nay, do you believe there would be found so many as the ten righteous men whom anciently the Lord could not find in five whole cities? I put the question to you, but you know not; I know not myself. Thou only, O my God, knowest those that belong to thee! But if we know not those who belong to him, at least we know that sinners do not belong to him. Now, of what classes of persons do the professing Christians in this assembly consist? Titles and dignities must be counted for naught; of these you shall be stripped before Jesus Christ. Who make up this assembly? Sinners, in great number, who do not wish to be converted; in still greater number, sinners who would like it, but who put off their conversion; many others who would be converted, only to relapse into sin; finally, a multitude who think they have no need of conversion. You have thus made up the company of the reprobate. Cut off these four classes of sinners from this sacred assembly, for they will be cut off from it at the great day! Stand forth now, ye righteous! where are you? Remnant of Israel, pass to the right hand! True wheat of Jesus Christ, disengage yourselves from this chaff, doomed to the fire! O God! where are thine elect? and what remains there for thy portion?

Brethren, our perdition is well-nigh assured, and we do not give it a thought. Even if in that dread separation which one day shall be made, there were to be but a single sinner out of this assembly found on the side of the reprobate, and if a voice from heaven should come to give us

assurance of the fact in this sanctuary, without pointing out
the person intended, who among us would not fear that he
might himself be the wretch? Who among us would not
at once recoil upon his conscience, to inquire whether his
sins had not deserved that penalty? Who among us would
not, seized with dismay, ask of Jesus Christ, as did once the
apostles, "Lord, is it I?"

What is there wanting in such eloquence as the
foregoing? Wherein lies its deficiency of power to
penetrate and subdue? Voltaire avowed that he
found the sermons of Massillon to be among "the
most agreeable books we have in our language. I
love," he went on, "to have them read to me at
table." There are things in Massillon that Voltaire
should not have delighted to read, or to hear read, —
things that should have made him wince and revolt,
if they did not make him yield and be converted.
Was there fault in the preacher? Did he preach
with professional, rather than with personal, zeal?
Did his hearers feel themselves secretly acquitted
by the man, at the self-same moment at which they
were openly condemned by the preacher? It is impossible to say. But Massillon's virtue was not
lofty and regal; however it may have been free from
just reproach. He was somewhat too capable of
compliance. He was made bishop of Clermont, and
his promotion cost him the anguish of having to
help consecrate a scandalously unfit candidate as
archbishop of Cambray. Massillon's, however, is
a fair, if not an absolutely spotless, fame. Hierarch

as he was, and orthodox Catholic, this most elegant
of eloquent orators had a liberal strain in his blood
which allied him politically with the " philosophers "
of the time succeeding. He, with Fénelon, and
perhaps with Racine, makes seem less abrupt the
transition in France from the age of absolutism to
the age of revolt and final revolution. There is
distinct advance in Massillon, and advance more
than is accounted for by his somewhat later time,
toward the easier modern spirit in church and in
state, from the high, unbending austerity of that
antique pontiff and minister, Bossuet.

XIII.

FÉNELON.

1651-1715.

IF Bossuet is to Frenchmen a synonym for sublimity, no less to them is Fénelon a synonym for
saintliness. From the French point of view, one
might say, " the sublime Bossuet," " the saintly
Fénelon," somewhat as one says, " the learned Sel-
den," " the judicious Hooker." It is as much a
French delight to idealize Fénelon an archangel
Raphael, affable and mild, as it is to glorify Bossuet
a Michael in majesty and power.

But saintliness of character was in Fénelon commended to the world by equal charm of person and of genius. The words of Milton describing Eve might be applied, with no change but that of gender, to Fénelon, both the exterior and the interior man : —

> Grace was in all his steps, heaven in his eye,
> In every gesture dignity and love.

The consent is general among those who saw Fénelon, and have left behind them their testimony, that alike in person, in character, and in genius, he was such as we thus describe him.

Twice, in his youth, he was smitten to the heart with a feeling of vocation to be a missionary. Both times he was thwarted by the intervention of friends. The second time, he wrote disclosing his half-romantic aspiration in a glowing letter of confidence and friendship to Bossuet, his senior by many years, but not yet become famous. Young Fénelon's friend Bossuet was destined later to prove a bitter antagonist, almost a personal foe.

Until he was forty-two years old, François Fénelon lived in comparative retirement, nourishing his genius with study, with contemplation, with choice society. He experimented in writing verse. Not succeeding to his mind, he turned to prose composition, and leading the way, in a new species of literature, for Rousseau, for Chateaubriand, for Lamartine, and for many others, to follow, went on writing what, in ceasing to be verse, did not cease to be poetry.

The great world will presently involve Fénelon in the currents of history. Louis XIV., grown old, and become as selfishly greedy now of personal salvation as all his life he has been selfishly greedy of personal glory, seeks that object of his soul by serving the church in the wholesale conversion of Protestants. He revokes the Edict of Nantes, which had secured religious toleration for the realm, and proceeds to dragoon the Huguenots into conformity with the Roman-Catholic church. The reaction in public sentiment against such rigors grew a cry that had to be silenced. Fénelon was selected to visit the heretic provinces, and win them to willing submission. He stipulated that every form of coercion should cease, and went to conquer all with love. His success was remarkable. But not even Fénelon quite escaped the infection of violent zeal for the Church. It seems not to be given to any man to rise wholly superior to the spirit of the world in which he lives.

The lustre of Fénelon's name, luminous from the triumphs of his mission among the Protestants, was sufficient to justify the choice of this man, a man both by nature and by culture so ideally formed for the office as was he, to be tutor to the heir prospective of the French monarchy. The Duke of Burgundy, grandson to Louis XIV., was accordingly put under the charge of Fénelon to be trained for future kingship.   Never, probably, in the history of mankind, has there occurred a case in which the victory of a teacher could be more illustrious than actually was the victory of Fénelon as teacher to this scion of the house of Bourbon.   We shall be giving our readers a relishable taste of St. Simon, the celebrated memoir-writer of the age of Louis XIV., if out of the portrait in words, drawn by him from the life, of Fénelon's princely pupil, we transfer here a few strong lines to our pages.   St. Simon says : —

In the first place, it must be said that Monseigneur the Duke of Burgundy had by nature a most formidable disposition.   He was passionate to the extent of wishing to dash to pieces his clocks when they struck the hour which called him to what he did not like, and of flying into the utmost rage against the rain if it interfered with what he wanted to do.   Resistance threw him into paroxysms of fury.   I speak of what I have often witnessed in his early youth.   Moreover, an ungovernable impulse drove him into whatever indulgence, bodily or mental, was forbidden him.   His sarcasm was so much the more cruel as it was witty and piquant, and as it seized with precision upon every point open to ridicule.   All this was sharpened by a vivacity of body and of mind that proceeded to the degree of impetuosity, and that during his early days never permitted him to learn any thing except by doing two things at once.   Every form of pleasure he loved with a violent avidity, and all this with a pride and a haughtiness impossible to describe; dangerously wise, moreover, to judge of men and things, and to detect the weak point in a train of reasoning, and to reason himself more cogently and more profoundly than his teachers.   But at the same time, as soon as his passion was spent, reason resumed her sway; he felt his faults, he acknowledged them, and sometimes with such chagrin that his rage was rekindled. A mind lively, alert, penetrating, stiffening itself against obstacles, excelling literally in every thing. The prodigy is, that in a very short time piety and grace made of him a different being, and transformed faults so numerous and so formidable into virtues exactly opposite.

St. Simon attributes to Fénelon "every virtue under heaven;" but his way was to give to God rather than to man the praise of the remarkable change which, during Fénelon's charge of the Duke of Burgundy, came over the character of the prince.

The grandfather survived the grandson; and it was never put to the stern proof of historical experiment, whether Fénelon had indeed turned out one Bourbon entirely different from all the other members, earlier or later, of that royal line.

Before, however, the Duke of Burgundy was thus snatched away from the perilous prospect of a throne, his beloved teacher was parted from him, not indeed by death, but by what, to the archbishop's susceptible and suffering spirit, was worse than death, — by "disgrace." The disgrace was such as has ever since engaged for its subject the interest, the sympathy, and the admiration, of mankind. Fénelon lost the royal favor. That was all, — for the present, — but that was much. He was banished from court, and he ceased to be preceptor to the Duke of Burgundy. The king, in signal severity, used his own hand to strike Fénelon's name from the list of the household of his grandson and heir. The archbishop — for Fénelon had previously been made archbishop of Cambray — returned into his diocese as into an exile. But his cup of humiliation was by no means full. Bossuet will stain his own glory by following his exiled former pupil and friend, with hostile pontifical rage, to crush him in his retreat.

The occasion was a woman, a woman with the charm of genius and of exalted character, a Christian, a saint, but a mystic — it was Madame Guyon. Madame Guyon taught that it was possible to love God for himself alone, purely and disinterestedly. Fénelon received the doctrine, and Madame Guyon was patronized by Madame de Maintenon. Bossuet scented heresy. He was too much a " natural man " to understand Madame Guyon. The king was like the prelate, his minister, in spirit, and in consequent incapacity. It was resolved that Fénelon must condemn Madame Guyon. But Fénelon would not. He was very gentle, very conciliatory, but in fine he would not. Controversy ensued, haughty, magisterial, domineering, on the part of Bossuet; on the part of Fénelon, meek, docile, suasive. The world wondered, and watched the duel. Fénelon finally did what king James's translators misleadingly make Job wish that his adversary had done, — he wrote a book, " The Maxims of the Saints." In this book, he sought to show that the accepted, and even canonized, teachers of the Church had taught the doctrine for which, in his own case and in the case of Madame Guyon, condemnation was now invoked. Bossuet was pope at Paris; and he, in full presence, denounced to the monarch the heresy of Fénelon. At this moment of crisis for Fénelon, it happened that news was brought him of the burning of his mansion at Cambray with all his books and manuscripts. It will always be remembered that Fénelon only said: "It is better so than if it had been the cottage of a poor laboring-man."

Madame de Maintenon, till now his friend, with perfectly frigid facility separated herself from the side of the accused. The controversy was carried to Rome, where at length Fénelon's book was condemned, — condemned mildly, but condemned. The pope is said to have made the remark that Fénelon erred by loving God too much, and Fénelon's antagonists by loving their fellow-man too little. Fénelon bowed to the authority of the Church, and meekly in his own cathedral confessed his error. It was a logical thing for him, as loyal Catholic, to do; and he did it with a beautiful grace of humility. The Protestant spirit, however, rebels on his behalf, and finds it difficult even to admire the manner in which was done by him a thing that seems so unfit to have been done by him at all. Bossuet did not long survive his inglorious triumph over so much sanctity of personal character, over so much difficult and beautiful height of doctrinal and practical instruction to virtue. Fénelon seems to have been reported as preaching a funeral sermon on the dead prelate. "I have wept and prayed," he wrote to a friend, "for this old instructor of my youth; but it is not true that I celebrated his obsequies in my cathedral, and preached his funeral sermon. Such affectation, you know, is foreign to my nature." The iron must have gone deep, to wring from that gentle bosom even so much cry as this of wounded feeling.

It is hard to tell what might now have befallen Fénelon, in the way of good fortune, — he might even have been recalled to court, and re-installed in his office of tutor to the prince, — had not a sinister incident, not to have been looked for, at an inopportune moment occurred. The "Telemachus" appeared in print, and kindled a sudden flame of popular feeling which instantly spread in universal conflagration over the face of Europe. This composition of Fénelon's the author had written to convey, under a form of quasi-poetical fiction, lessons of wisdom in government to the mind of his royal pupil. The existence of the manuscript book would seem to have been intended to be a secret from the king, — indeed, from almost every one, except the pupil himself for whose use it was made. But a copyist proved false to his trust, and furnished a copy of "Telemachus" to a printer in Holland, who lost no time in publishing a book so likely to sell. But the sale of the book surpassed all expectation. Holland not only, but Belgium, Germany,

France, and England multiplied copies, as fast as they could ; still, Europe could not get copies as fast as it wanted them.

The secret of such popularity did not lie simply in the literary merits of "Telemachus." It lay more in a certain interpretation that the book was supposed to bear. "Telemachus" was understood to be a covert criticism of Louis XIV., and of the principle of absolute monarchy embodied in him. This imputed intention of the book could not fail to become known at Versailles. The result, of course, was fatal, and finally fatal, to the prospects, whatever these may have been, of Fénelon's restoration to favor at court. The archbishop thenceforward was left to do in comparative obscurity the duties of his episcopal office in his diocese of Cambray. He devoted himself, with exemplary and touching fidelity, to the interests of his flock, loving them and loved by them, till he died. It was an entirely worthy and adequate employment of his powers. The only abatement needful from the praise to be bestowed upon his behavior in this pastoral relation is, that he suffered himself sometimes to think of his position as one of "disgrace." His reputation meantime for holy character and conduct was European. His palace at Cambray, hospitably open ever to the resort of suffering need, indeed almost his whole diocese, lying on the frontier of France, was, by mutual consent of contending armies, treated in war as a kind of mutual inviolable ground, invested with privilege of sanctuary. It was an instructive example of the serene and beautiful ascendency sometimes divinely accorded to illustrious personal goodness.

There had been a moment, even subsequently to the affair of the "Telemachus" publication, when it looked as if, after long delay, a complete worldly triumph for Fénelon was assured, and was near. The father of the Duke of Burgundy died, and nothing then seemed to stand between Fénelon's late pupil and the throne, — nothing but the precarious life of an aged monarch, visibly approaching the end. The Duke of Burgundy, through all changes, had remained unchangingly fast in his affectionate loyalty to Fénelon. Sternly forbidden, by the jealous and watchful king, his grandfather, to communicate with his old teacher, he yet had found means to send to Fénelon, from time to time, reassuring signals of his trust and his love. Fénelon was now, in all eyes, the predestined prime minister of a new reign about to commence. Through devoted friends of his own, near to the person of the prince at court, Fénelon sent minutes of advice to his pupil, which outlined a whole beneficent policy of liberal monarchical rule. A new day seemed dawning for France. The horrible reaction of the Regency and of Louis XV. might, perhaps, have been averted, and, with that spared to France, the Revolution itself might have been accomplished without the Revolution. But it was not to be. The Duke of Burgundy first buried his wife, and then, within a few days, followed her himself to the grave. He died sincerely rejoicing that God had taken him away from the dread responsibility of reigning.

"All my ties are broken," mourned Fénelon; "there is no longer any thing to bind me to the earth." In truth, the teacher survived his pupil but two or three years. When he died, his sovereign, gloomy with well-grounded apprehension for the future of his realm, said, with tardy revival of recognition for the virtue that had perished in Fénelon : "Here was a man who could have served us well under the disasters by which my kingdom is about to be assailed!"

Fénelon's literary productions are various; but they all have the common character of being works written for the sake of life, rather than for the sake of literature. They were inspired each by a practical purpose, and adapted each to a particular occasion. His treatise on the "Education of Girls" was written for the use of a mother who desired instruction on the topic from Fénelon. His argument on the "Being of a God" was prepared as a duty of his preceptorship to the prince. But the one book of Fénelon which was an historical event when it appeared, and which stands an indestructible classic in literature, is the "Telemachus." It remains for us briefly to give some idea of this book.

The first thing to be said is, that those are mistaken who suppose themselves to have obtained a

true idea of "Telemachus" from having partly
read it at school, as an exercise in French. The
essence of the work lies beyond those few opening
pages to which the exploration of school-boys and
school-girls is generally limited. This masterpiece
of Fénelon is much more than a charming piece of
romantic and sentimental poetry in prose. It is
a kind of epic, indeed, like the "Odyssey," only
written in rhythmical prose instead of rhythmical
verse ; but, unlike the "Odyssey," it is an idyllic
epic written with an ulterior purpose of moral and
political didactics. It was designed as a manual of
instruction, — instruction made delightful to a prince,
— to inculcate the duties incumbent on a sovereign.

Telemachus, our readers will remember, was the
son of Ulysses. Fénelon's story relates the adventures encountered by Telemachus, in search for his
father, so long delayed on his return from Troy to
Ithaca. Telemachus is imagined by Fénelon to be
attended by Minerva, the goddess of wisdom, masked
from his recognition, as well as from the recognition of others, under the form of an old man.
Minerva, of course, constantly imparts the wisest
counsel to young Telemachus, who has his weaknesses, as had the young Duke of Burgundy, but
who is essentially well-disposed, as Fénelon hoped
his royal pupil would finally turn out to be. Nothing
can exceed the urbanity and grace with which the
delicate business is conducted by Fénelon, of teach-
ing a bad prince, with a very bad example set him

by his grandfather, to be a good king. The style in which the story is told, and in which the advice is insinuated, is exquisite, is beyond praise. The "soft delicious" stream of sound runs on, as from a fountain, and like "linked sweetness long drawn out." Never had prose a flow of melody more luscious. It is perpetual ravishment to the ear. The invention, too, of incident is fruitful, while the landscape and coloring are magical for beauty. We give a few extracts, to be read with that application to Louis XIV., and the state of France, in mind, which, when the book was first printed, gave it such an exciting interest in the eyes of Europe. Telemachus, after the manner of Æneas to Queen Dido, is relating to the goddess Calypso, into whose island he has come, the adventures that have previously befallen him. He says that he, with Mentor (Minerva in disguise), found himself in Crete. Mentor had been there before, and was ready to tell Telemachus all about the country. Telemachus was naturally interested to learn respecting the Cretan monarchy. Mentor, he says, informed him as follows : —

The king's authority over the subject is absolute, but the authority of the law is absolute over him. His power to do good is unlimited, but he is restrained from doing evil. The laws have put the people into his hands, as the most valuable deposit, upon condition that he shall treat them as his children. It is the intent of the law that the wisdom and equity of one man shall be the happiness of many, and not that the wretchedness and slavery of many should gratify the pride

and luxury of one. The king ought to possess nothing more
than the subject, except what is necessary to alleviate the
fatigue of his station, and impress upon the minds of the
people a reverence of that authority by which the laws are
executed. Moreover, the king should indulge himself less,
as well in ease as in pleasure, and should be less disposed to
the pomp and the pride of life than any other man. He
ought not to be distinguished from the rest of mankind
by the greatness of his wealth, or the vanity of his enjoyments, but by superior wisdom, more heroic virtue, and more
splendid glory. Abroad he ought to be the defender of his
country, by commanding her armies; and at home the judge
of his people, distributing justice among them, improving
their morals, and increasing their felicity. It is not for himself that the gods have intrusted him with royalty. He is
exalted above individuals, only that he may be the servant
of the people. To the public he owes all his time, all his
attention, and all his love; he deserves dignity only in proportion as he gives up private enjoyments for the public
good.

Pretty sound doctrine, the foregoing, on the subject of the duties devolving on a king. The
" paternal " idea, to be sure, of government is in it;
but there is the idea, too, of limited or constitutional
monarchy. The spirit of just and liberal political
thought had, it seems, not been wholly extinguished,
even at the court, by that oppression of mind — an
oppression seldom, if ever, in human history exceeded — which was enforced under the unmitigated
absolutism of Louis XIV. The literature that, with
Montesquieu, Voltaire, Rousseau, the Encyclopædists, prepared the Revolution, had already begun
virtually to be written when Fénelon wrote his

"Telemachus." It is easy to see why the fame of Fénelon should by exception have been dear even to the hottest infidel haters of that ecclesiastical hierarchy to which the archbishop of Cambray himself belonged. This lover of liberty, this gentle rebuker of kings, was of the free-thinkers, at least in the sympathy of political thought. Nay, the Revolution itself is foreshown in a remarkable glimpse of conjectural prophecy which occurs in the "Telemachus." Idomeneus is a headstrong king, whom Mentor is made by the author to reprove and instruct, for the Duke of Burgundy's benefit. To Idomeneus — a character taken, and not unplausibly taken, to have been suggested to Fénelon by the example of Louis XIV. — to this imaginary counterpart of the reigning monarch of France, Mentor holds the following language. How could the sequel of Bourbon despotism in France — a sequel suspended now for a time, but two or three generations later to be dreadfully visited on the heirs of Louis XIV. — have been more truly foreshadowed? The "Telemachus:" —

Remember, that the sovereign who is most absolute is always least powerful; he seizes upon all, and his grasp is ruin. He is, indeed, the sole proprietor of whatever his state contains; but, for that reason, his state contains nothing of value: the fields are uncultivated, and almost a desert; the towns lose some of their few inhabitants every day; and trade every day declines. The king, who must cease to be a king when he ceases to have subjects, and who is great only in virtue of his people, is himself insensibly losing his character and his power, as the number of his people, from whom alone both are derived, insensibly diminishes. His dominions are at length exhausted of money and of men: the loss of men is the greatest and the most irreparable he can sustain. Absolute power degrades every subject to a slave. The tyrant is flattered, even to an appearance of adoration, and every one trembles at the glance of his eye; but, at the least revolt, this enormous power perishes by its own excess. It derived no strength from the love of the people; it wearied and provoked all that it could reach, and rendered every individual of the state impatient of its continuance. At the first stroke of opposition, the idol is overturned, broken to pieces, and trodden under foot. Contempt, hatred, fear, resentment, distrust, and every other passion of the soul, unite against so hateful a despotism. The king who, in his vain prosperity, found no man bold enough to tell him the truth, in his adversity finds no man kind enough to excuse his faults, or to defend him against his enemies.

So much is perhaps enough to indicate the political drift of the " Telemachus." That drift is, indeed, observable everywhere throughout the book.

We conclude our exhibition of this fine classic, by letting Fénelon appear more purely now in his character as dreamer and poet. Young Prince Telemachus has, Ulysses-like, and Æneas-like, his descent into Hades. This incident affords Fénelon opportunity to exercise his best powers of awful and of lovely imagining and describing. Christian ideas are, in this episode of the " Telemachus," superinduced upon pagan, after a manner hard, perhaps, to reconcile with the verisimilitude required by art, but at least productive of very noble and very beautiful

results.   First, one glimpse of Tartarus as conceived
by Fénelon.   It is the spectacle of kings who on
earth abused their power, that Telemachus is be-
holding : —

Telemachus observed the countenance of these criminals
to be pale and ghastly, strongly expressive of the torment
they suffered at the heart.   They looked inward with a self-
abhorrence, now inseparable from their existence.   Their
crimes themselves had become their punishment, and it
was not necessary that greater should be inflicted.   They
haunted them like hideous spectres, and continually started
up before them in all their enormity.   They wished for a
second death, that might separate them from these ministers of vengeance, as the first had separated their spirits
from the body, — a death that might at once extinguish all
consciousness and sensibility.   They called upon the depths
of hell to hide them from the persecuting beams of truth, in
impenetrable darkness ; but they are reserved for the cup of
vengeance, which, though they drink of it forever, shall be
ever full.   The truth, from which they fled, has overtaken
them, an invincible and unrelenting enemy.   The ray which
once might have illuminated them, like the mild radiance
of the day, now pierces them like lightning, — a fierce and
fatal fire, that, without injury to the external parts, infixes
a burning torment at the heart.   By truth, now an avenging
flame, the very soul is melted like metal in a furnace; it
dissolves all, but destroys nothing; it disunites the first
elements of life, yet the sufferer can never die.   He is, as it
were, divided against himself, without rest and without
comfort; animated by no vital principle, but the rage that
kindles at his own misconduct, and the dreadful madness
that results from despair.

If the " perpetual feast of nectared sweets " that
the " Telemachus " affords, is felt at times to be

almost cloying, it is not, as our readers have now seen, for want of occasional contrasts of a bitterness sufficiently mordant and drastic. But the didactic purpose is never lost sight of by the author. Here is an aspect of the Elysium found by Telemachus. How could any thing be more delectably conceived and described? The translator, Dr. Hawkesworth, is animated to an English style that befits the sweetness of his original. The " Telemachus : " —

In this place resided all the good kings who had wisely governed mankind from the beginning of time. They were separated from the rest of the just; for, as wicked princes suffer more dreadful punishment than other offenders in Tartarus, so good kings enjoy infinitely greater felicity than other lovers of virtue, in the fields of Elysium.

Telemachus advanced towards these kings, whom he found in groves of delightful fragrance, reclining upon the downy turf, where the flowers and herbage were perpetually renewed. A thousand rills wandered through these scenes of delight, and refreshed the soil with a gentle and unpolluted wave; the song of innumerable birds echoed in the groves. Spring strewed the ground with her flowers, while at the same time autumn loaded the trees with her fruit. In this place the burning heat of the dog-star was never felt, and the stormy north was forbidden to scatter over it the frosts of winter. Neither War that thirsts for blood, nor Envy that bites with an envenomed tooth, like the vipers that are wreathed around her arms, and fostered in her bosom, nor Jealousy, nor Distrust, nor Fears, nor vain Desires, invade these sacred domains of peace. The day is here without end, and the shades of night are unknown. Here the bodies of the blessed are clothed with a pure and lambent light, as with a garment. This light does not resemble that vouch-safed to mortals upon earth, which is rather darkness visible; it is rather a celestial glory than a light — an emanation that penetrates the grossest body with more subtilety than the rays of the sun penetrate the purest crystal, which rather strengthens than dazzles the sight, and diffuses through the soul a serenity which no language can express. By this ethereal essence the blessed are sustained in everlasting life; it pervades them; it is incorporated with them, as food with the mortal body; they see it, they feel it, they breathe it, and it produces in them an inexhaustible source of serenity and joy. It is a fountain of delight, in which they are absorbed as fishes are absorbed in the sea; they wish for nothing, and, having nothing, they possess all things. This celestial light satiates the hunger of the soul; every desire is precluded; and they have a fulness of joy which sets them above all that mortals seek with such restless ardor, to fill the vacuity that aches forever in their breast. All the delightful objects that surround them are disregarded; for their felicity springs up within, and, being perfect, can derive nothing from without. So the gods, satiated with nectar and ambrosia, disdain, as gross and impure, all the dainties of the most luxurious table upon earth. From these seats of tranquillity all evils fly far away; death, disease, poverty, pain, regret, remorse, fear, even hope, — which is sometimes not less painful than fear itself, — animosity, disgust, and resentment can never enter there.

The leaden good sense of Louis XIV. pronounced Fénelon the "most chimerical" man in France. The Founder of the kingdom of heaven would have been a dreamer, to this most worldly-minded of "Most Christian" monarchs. Bossuet, who, about to die, read something of Fénelon's "Telemachus," said it was a book hardly serious enough for a clergyman to write. A more serious book, whether its purpose be regarded, or its undoubted actual influence in moulding the character of a prospective ruler of France, was not written by any clergyman of Fénelon's or Bossuet's time.

Fénelon was an eloquent preacher as well as an elegant writer. His influence exerted in both the two functions, that of the writer and that of the preacher, was powerfully felt in favor of the freedom of nature in style as against the conventionality of culture and art. He insensibly helped on that reform from a too rigid classicism which in our day we have seen pushed to its extreme in the exaggerations of romanticism. Few wiser words have ever been spoken on the subject of oratory, than are to be found in his "Dialogues on Eloquence."

French literature, unfortunately, is on the whole such in character as to need all that it can show, to be cast into the scale of moral elevation and purity. Fénelon alone is, in quantity as in quality, enough, not indeed to overcome, but to go far toward overcoming, the perverse inclination of the balance.

XIV.

MONTESQUIEU.

1689-1755.

To Montesquieu belongs the glory of being the founder, or inventor, of the philosophy of history. Bossuet might dispute this palm with him; but Bossuet, in his "Discourse on Universal History," only exemplified the principle which it was left to Montesquieu afterward more consciously to develop.

Three books, still living, are associated with the name of Montesquieu, — "The Persian Letters," "The Greatness and the Decline of the Romans," and "The Spirit of Laws." "The Persian Letters" are a series of epistles purporting to be written by a Persian sojourning in Paris and observing the manners and morals of the people around him. The idea is ingenious; though the ingenuity, we suppose, was not original with Montesquieu. Such letters afford the writer of them an admirable advantage for telling satire on contemporary follies. This production of Montesquieu became the suggestive example to Goldsmith for his "Citizen of the World; or, Letters of a Chinese Philosopher." We shall have here no room for illustrative citations from Montesquieu's "Persian Letters."

The second work, that on the "Greatness and the Decline of the Romans," is less a history than a series of essays on the history of Rome. It is brilliant, striking, suggestive. It aims to be philosophical rather than historical. It deals in bold generalizations. The spirit of it is, perhaps, too constantly and too profoundly hostile to the Romans. Something of the ancient Gallic enmity — as if a derivation from that last and noblest of the Gauls, Vercingetorix — seems to animate the Frenchman in discussing the character and the career of the great conquering nation of antiquity. The critical element is the element chiefly wanting to make Montesquieu's work equal to the demands of modern historical scholarship. Montesquieu was, however, a full worthy forerunner of the philosophical historians of to-day. We give a single extract in illustration, — an extract condensed from the chapter in which the author analyzes and expounds the foreign policy of the Romans. The generalizations are bold and brilliant, — too bold, probably, for strict critical truth. (We use, for our extract, the recent translation by Mr. Jehu Baker, who enriches his volume with original notes of no little interest and value.) Montesquieu : —

This body [the Roman Senate] erected itself into a tribunal for the judgment of all peoples, and at the end of every war it decided upon the punishments and the recompenses which it conceived each to be entitled to. It took away parts of the lands of the conquered states, in order to bestow them upon the allies of Rome, thus accomplishing two objects at once, — attaching to Rome those kings of whom she had little to fear and much to hope, and weakening those of whom she had little to hope and all to fear.

Allies were employed to make war upon an enemy, but the destroyers were at once destroyed in their turn. Philip was beaten with the half of the Ætolians, who were immediately afterwards annihilated for having joined themselves to Antiochus. Antiochus was beaten with the help of the Rhodians, who, after having received signal rewards, were humiliated forever, under the pretext that they had requested that peace might be made with Perseus.

When they had many enemies on hand at the same time, they accorded a truce to the weakest, which considered itself happy in obtaining such a respite, counting it for much to be able to secure a postponement of its ruin.

When they were engaged in a great war, the senate affected to ignore all sorts of injuries, and silently awaited the arrival of the proper time for punishment; when, if it saw that only some individuals were culpable, it refused to punish them, choosing rather to hold the entire nation as criminal, and thus reserve to itself a useful vengeance.

As they inflicted inconceivable evils upon their enemies, there were not many leagues formed against them; for those who were most distant from danger were not willing to draw nearer to it. The consequence of this was, that they were rarely attacked; whilst, on the other hand, they constantly made war at such time, in such manner, and against such peoples, as suited their convenience; and, among the many nations which they assailed, there were very few that would not have submitted to every species of injury at their hands if they had been willing to leave them in peace.

It being their custom to speak always as masters, the ambassadors whom they sent to nations which had not yet felt their power were certain to be insulted; and this was an infallible pretext for a new war.

As they never made peace in good faith, and as, with the design of universal conquest, their treaties were, properly speaking, only suspensions of war, they always put conditions in them which began the ruin of the states which accepted them. They either provided that the garrisons of strong places should be withdrawn, or that the number of troops should be limited, or that the horses or the elephants of the vanquished party should be delivered over to themselves; and if the defeated people was powerful on sea, they compelled it to burn its vessels, and sometimes to remove, and occupy a place of habitation farther inland.

After having destroyed the armies of a prince, they ruined his finances by excessive taxes, or by the imposition of a tribute under pretext of requiring him to pay the expenses of the war, — a new species of tyranny, which forced the vanquished sovereign to oppress his own subjects, and thus to alienate their affection.

When they granted peace to a king, they took some of his brothers or children as hostages. This gave them the means of troubling his kingdom at their pleasure. If they held the nearest heir, they intimidated the possessor; if only a prince of a remote degree, they used him to stir up revolts against the legitimate ruler.

Whenever any people or prince withdrew their obedience from their sovereign, they immediately accorded to them the title of allies of the Roman people, and thus rendered them sacred and inviolable; so that there was no king, however great he might be, who could for a moment be sure of his subjects, or even of his family.

Although the title of Roman ally was a species of servitude, it was, nevertheless, very much sought after; for the possession of this title made it certain that the recipients of it would receive injuries from the Romans only, and there was ground for the hope that this class of injuries would be rendered less grievous than they would otherwise be.

Thus, there was no service which nations and kings were

not ready to perform, nor any humiliation which they did not submit to, in order to obtain this distinction. . . .

These customs were not merely some particular facts which happened at hazard. They were permanently established principles, as may be readily seen; for the maxims which the Rómans acted upon against the greatest powers were precisely those which they had employed in the beginning of their career against the small cities which surrounded them. . . .

But nothing served Rome more effectually than the respect which she inspired among all nations. She immediately reduced kings to silence, and rendered them as dumb. With the latter, it was not a mere question of the degree of their power: their very persons were attacked. To risk a war with Rome was to expose themselves to captivity, to death, and to the infamy of a triumph. Thus it was that kings, who lived in pomp and luxury, did not dare to look with steady eyes upon the Roman people, and, losing courage, they hoped, by their patience and their obsequiousness, to obtain some postponement of the calamities with which they were menaced.

The "Spirit of Laws" is probably to be considered the masterpiece of Montesquieu. It is our duty, however, to say, that this work is quite differently estimated by different authorities. By some, it is praised in terms of the highest admiration, as a great achievement in wide and wise political or juridical philosophy. By others, it is dismissed very lightly, as the ambitious, or, rather, pretentious, effort of a superficial man, a showy mere sciolist. It acquired great contemporary fame, both at home and abroad. It was promptly translated into English, the translator earning the merited compli-

ment of the author's own hearty approval of his
work.   Horace Walpole, who was something of a
Gallomaniac, makes repeated allusion to Montesquieu's "Spirit of Laws," in letters of his written
at about the time of the appearance of the book.
But Walpole's admiring allusions themselves contain
evidence that admiration equal to his own of the
work that he praised, was by no means universal in
England.

The general aspect of the book is that of a composition meant to be luminously analyzed and arranged.   Divisions and titles abound. There are
thirty-one "books"; and each book contains, on the
average, perhaps about the same number of chapters.
The library edition, in English, consists of two volumes, comprising together some eight hundred open
pages, in good-sized type.   The books and chapters
are therefore not formidably long.   The look of the
work is as if it were readable ; and its character, on
the whole, corresponds.   It would hardly be French,
if such were not the case.   Except that Montesquieu's "Spirit of Laws" is, as we have indicated,
a highly organized, even an over-organized, book,
which, by emphasis, Montaigne's "Essays" is not,
these two works may be said, in their contents,
somewhat to resemble each other.   Montesquieu is
nearly as discursive as Montaigne.   He wishes to
be philosophical, but he is not above supplying his
reader with interesting historical instances.

We shall not do better, in giving our readers a

comprehensive idea of Montesquieu's "Spirit of Laws," than to begin by showing them the titles of a number of the books : —

Book I. Of Laws in General. Book II. Of Laws Directly Derived from the Nature of Government. Book III. Of the Principles of the Three Kinds of Government. Book IV. That the Laws of Education ought to be Relative to the Principles of Government. Book V. That the Laws given by the Legislator ought to be Relative to the Principle of Government. Book VI. Consequences of the Principles of Different Governments with Respect to the Simplicity of Civil and Criminal Laws, the Form of Judgments, and the Inflicting of Punishments. Book VII. Consequences of the Different Principles of the Three Governments with Respect to Sumptuary Laws, Luxury, and the Condition of Women. Book VIII. Of the Corruption of the Principles of the Three Governments. Book XIV. Of Laws as Relative to the Nature of the Climate.

The philosophical aim and ambition of the author at once appear in the inquiry which he institutes for the three several animating *principles* of the three several forms of government respectively distinguished by him ; namely, democracy (or republicanism), monarchy, and despotism. What these three principles are, will be seen from the following statement : " As *virtue* is necessary in a republic, and in monarchy, *honor*, so *fear* is necessary in a despotic government." The meaning is, that in republics, virtue possessed by the citizens is the spring of national prosperity ; that under a monarchy, the desire of preferment at the hands of the sovereign is what quickens men to perform services to the state; that despotism thrives by fear inspired in the breasts of those subject to its sway.

To illustrate the freely discursive character of the work, we give the whole of chapter sixteen — there are chapters still shorter — in Book VII. : —

AN EXCELLENT CUSTOM OF THE SAMNITES.

The Samnites had a custom which in so small a republic, and especially in their situation, must have been productive of admirable effects. The young people were all convened in one place, and their conduct was examined. He that was declared the best of the whole assembly, had leave given him to take which girl he pleased for his wife; the second best chose after him, and so on. Admirable institution! The only recommendation that young men could have on this occasion, was their virtue, and the service done their country. He who had the greatest share of these endowments, chose which girl he liked out of the whole nation. Love, beauty, chastity, virtue, birth, and even wealth itself, were all, in some measure, the dowry of virtue. A nobler and grander recompense, less chargeable to a petty state, and more capable of influencing both sexes, could scarce be imagined.

The Samnites were descended from the Lacedæmonians; and Plato, whose institutes are only an improvement of those of Lycurgus, enacted nearly the same law.

The relation of the foregoing chapter to the subject indicated in the title of the book, is sufficiently obscure and remote, for a work like this purporting to be philosophical. What relation exists, seems to be found in the fact that the Samnite custom described tends to produce that popular virtue by which republics flourish. But the information, at all events, is curious and interesting.

The following paragraphs, taken from the second chapter of Book XIV., contain in germ nearly the whole of the philosophy underlying M. Taine's essays on the history of literature : —

OF THE DIFFERENCE OF MEN IN DIFFERENT CLIMATES.

A cold air constringes the extremities of the external fibres of the body; this increases their elasticity, and favors the return of the blood from the extreme parts to the heart. It contracts those very fibres; consequently it increases also their force. On the contrary, a warm air relaxes and lengthens the extremes of the fibres; of course it diminishes their force and elasticity.

People are therefore more vigorous in cold climates. Here the action of the heart and the reaction of the extremities of the fibres are better performed, the temperature of the humors is greater, the blood moves freer towards the heart, and reciprocally the heart has more power. This superiority of strength must produce various effects; for instance, a greater boldness, — that is, more courage; a greater sense of superiority, — that is, less desire of revenge; a greater opinion of security, — that is, more frankness, less suspicion, policy and cunning. In short, this must be productive of very different tempers. Put a man into a close, warm place, and, for the reasons above given, he will feel a great faintness. If under this circumstance you propose a bold enterprise to him, I believe you will find him very little disposed towards it; his present weakness will throw him into a despondency; he will be afraid of every thing, being in a state of total incapacity. The inhabitants of warm countries are, like old men, timorous; the people in cold countries are, like young men, brave.

In the following extract, from chapter five, Book
XXIV., the climatic theory is again applied, this
time to the matter of religion, in a style that makes
one think of Buckle's " History of Civilization : "—

When the Christian religion, two centuries ago, became
unhappily divided into Catholic and Protestant, the people
of the north embraced the Protestant, and those south ad-
hered still to the Catholic.

The reason is plain: the people of the north have, and
will forever have, a spirit of liberty and independence, which
the people of the south have not; and therefore, a religion
which has no visible head, is more agreeable to the inde-
pendency of the climate, than that which has one.

Climate is a " great matter " with Montesquieu.
In treating of the subject of a state changing its
religion, he says : —

The ancient religion is connected with the constitution of
the kingdom, and the new one is not; the former *agrees
with the climate,* and very often the new one is opposite
to it.

For the Christian religion, Montesquieu professes
profound respect, — rather as a pagan political philosopher might do, than as one intimately acquainted
with it by a personal experience of his own.   His
spirit, however, is humane and liberal.   It is the
spirit of Montaigne, it is the spirit of Voltaire,
speaking in the idiom of this different man, and of
this different man as influenced by his different circumstances.   Montesquieu had had practical proof

of the importance to himself of not offending the dominant hierarchy.

The latter part of "The Spirit of Laws" contains discussions exhibiting no little research on the part of the author. There is, for one example, a discussion of the course of commerce in different ages of the world, and of the influences that have wrought from time to time to bring about the changes occurring. For another example, there is a discussion of the feudal system.

Montesquieu was an admirer of the English constitution. His work, perhaps, contains no extended chapters more likely to instruct the general reader and to furnish a good idea of the writer's genius and method, than the two chapters — chapter six, Book XI., and chapter twenty-seven, Book XIX. — in which the English nation and the English form of government are sympathetically described. We simply indicate, for we have no room to exhibit, these chapters. Voltaire, too, expressed Montesquieu's admiration of English liberty and English law.

On the whole, concerning Montesquieu it may justly be said, that of all political philosophers, he, if not the profoundest, is at least one of the most interesting; if not the most accurate and critical, at least one of the most brilliant and suggestive.

As to Montesquieu the man, it is perhaps sufficient to say that he seems to have been a very good type of the French gentleman of quality. An interesting story told by Sainte-Beuve reveals, if true, a side at once attractive and repellent of his personal character. Montesquieu at Marseilles employed a young boatman, whose manner and speech indicated more cultivation than was to have been looked for in one plying his vocation. The philosopher learned his history. The youth's father was at the time a captive in one of the Barbary States, and this son of his was now working to earn money for his ransom. The stranger listened apparently unmoved, and went his way. Some months later, home came the father, released he knew not how, to his surprised and overjoyed family. The son guessed the secret, and, meeting Montesquieu a year or so after in Marseilles, threw himself in grateful tears at his feet, begged the generous benefactor to reveal his name and to come and see the family he had blessed. Montesquieu, calmly expressing himself ignorant of the whole business, actually shook the young fellow off, and turned away without betraying the least emotion. It was not till after the cold-blooded philanthropist's death that the fact came out.

A tranquil, happy temperament was Montesquieu's. He would seem to have come as near as any one ever did to being the natural master of his part in life. But the world was too much for him, as it is for all — at last. Witness the contrast of these two different sets of expressions from his pen. In earlier manhood he says : —

Study has been for me the sovereign remedy for all the dissatisfactions of life, having never had a sense of chagrin that an hour's reading would not dissipate. I wake in the morning with a secret joy to behold the light. I behold the light with a kind of ravishment, and all the rest of the day I am happy.

Within a few years of his death, the brave, cheerful tone had declined to this: —

I am broken down with fatigue; I must repose for the rest of my life.

Then further to this: —

I have expected to kill myself for the last three months, finishing an addition to my work on the origin and changes of the French civil law. It will take only three hours to read it; but, I assure you, it has been such a labor to me, that my hair has turned white under it all.

Finally it touches nadir: —

It [his work] has almost cost me my life; I must rest; I can work no more.

My candles are all burned out; I have set off all my cartridges.

When Montesquieu died, only Diderot, among Parisian men of letters, followed him to his tomb.

XV.

VOLTAIRE.

1694-1778.

By the volume and the variety, joined to the unfailing brilliancy, of his production; by his prodigious effectiveness; and by his universal fame,—Voltaire is undoubtedly entitled to rank first, with no fellow, among the eighteenth-century literary men, not merely of France, but of the world. He was not a great man,—he produced no single great work,—but he must nevertheless be pronounced a great writer. There is hardly any species of composition to which, in the long course of his activity, he did not turn his talent. It cannot be said that he succeeded splendidly in all; but in some he succeeded splendidly, and he failed abjectly in none. There is not a great thought, and there is not a flat expression, in the whole bulk of his multitudinous and multifarious works. Read him wherever you will, in the ninety-seven volumes (equivalent, probably, in the aggregate, to three hundred volumes like the present) which, in one leading edition, collect his productions,—you may often find him superficial, you may often find him untrustworthy, you will certainly often find him flippant, but not less certainly you will never find him obscure, and you will never find him dull. The clearness, the vivacity, of this man's mind were something almost preternatural. So, too, were his readiness, his versatility, his audacity. He had no distrust of himself, no awe of his fellow-men, no reverence for God, to deter him from any attempt with his pen, however presuming. If a state ode were required, it should be ready to order at twelve to-morrow ; if an epic poem — to be classed with the "Iliad" and the "Æneid" — the "Henriade" was promptly forthcoming, to answer the demand. He did not shrink from flouting a national idol, by freely finding fault with Corneille ; and he lightly undertook to extinguish a venerable form of Christianity, simply with pricks, innumerably repeated, of his tormenting pen.

A very large part of the volume of Voltaire's production consists of letters, written by him to correspondents perhaps more numerous, and more various in rank, from kings on the throne down to scribblers in the garret, than ever, in any other case, exchanged such communications with a literary man. Another considerable proportion of his work in literature took the form of pamphlets, either anonymously or pseudonymously published, in which this master-spirit of intellectual disturbance and ferment found it convenient, or advantageous, or safe, to promulge and propagate his ideas. A shower of such publications was incessantly escaping from Voltaire's pen. More formal and regular, more confessedly ambitious, literary essays of his, were poems in every kind, — heroic, mock-heroic, lyric, elegiac, comic, tragic, satiric, — historical and biographical monographs, and tales or novels of a peculiar class.

Voltaire's poetry does not count for very much now. Still, its first success was so great that it will always remain an important topic in literary history. Besides this, it really is, in some of its kinds, remarkable work. Voltaire's epic verse is almost an exception, needful to be made, from our assertion that this author is nowhere dull. "The Henriade" comes dangerously near that mark. It is a tasteless reproduction of Lucan's faults, with little reproduction of Lucan's virtues. Voltaire's comedies are bright and witty, but they are not laughter-provoking; and they do not possess the elemental and creative character of Shakspeare's or Molière's work. His tragedies are better; but they do not avoid that cast of mechanical which seems necessarily to belong to poetry produced by talent, however consummate, unaccompanied with genius. Voltaire's histories are luminous and readable narratives, but they cannot claim either the merit of critical accuracy or of philosophic breadth and insight. His letters would have to be read in considerable volume in order to furnish a full satisfactory idea of the author. His tales, finally, afford the most available, and, on the whole, likewise, the best, means of coming shortly and easily at a knowledge of Voltaire.

Among Voltaire's tales, doubtless the one most eligible for use, to serve our present purpose, is his "Candide." This is a nondescript piece of fiction, the design of which is, by means of a narrative of travel and adventure, constructed without much regard to the probability of particular incidents, to set forth, in the characteristic mocking vein of Voltaire, the vanity and misery of mankind. The author's invention is often whimsical enough; but it is constantly so ready, so reckless, and so abundant, that the reader never tires, as he is hurried ceaselessly forward from change to change of scene and circumstance. The play of wit is incessant. The style is limpidity itself. Your sympathies are never painfully engaged, even in recitals of experience that ought to be the most heart-rending. There is never a touch of noble moral sentiment, to relieve the monotony of mockery that lightly laughs at you, and tantalizes you, page after page, from the beginning to the end of the book. The banter is not good-natured; though, on the other hand, it cannot justly be pronounced ill-natured; and it is, in final effect upon the reader's mind, bewildering and depressing in the extreme. Vanity of vanities, all is vanity, — such is the comfortless doctrine of the book. The apples are the apples of Sodom, everywhere in the world. There is no virtue anywhere, no good, no happiness. Life is a cheat, the love of life is a cruelty, and beyond life there is nothing. At least, there is no glimpse given of any compensating future reserved for men, a future to redress the balance of good and ill experienced here and now. Faith and hope, those two eyes of the soul, are smilingly quenched in their sockets; and you are left blind, in a whirling world of darkness, with a whirling world of darkness before you.

Such is "Candide." We select a single passage for specimen. The passage we select is more nearly free than almost any other passage as long, in this extraordinary romance, would probably be found, from impure implications. It is, besides, more nearly serious in apparent motive, than is the general tenor of the production. Here, however, as elsewhere, the writer keeps carefully down his mocking-mask. At least, you are left tantalizingly uncertain all the time how much the grin you face is the grin of the man, and how much the grin of a visor that he wears.

Candide, the hero, is a young fellow of ingenuous character, brought successively under the lead of several different persons wise in the ways of the world, who act toward him, each in his turn, the part of "guide, philosopher, and friend." Candide, with such a mentor bearing the name Martin, has now arrived at Venice. Candide speaks : —

"I have heard great talk of the Senator Pococuranté, who lives in that fine house at the Brenta, where they say he entertains foreigners in the most polite manner. They pretend this man is a perfect stranger to uneasiness." — "I should be glad to see so extraordinary a being," said Martin.

Candide thereupon sent a messenger to Signor Pococuranté, desiring permission to wait on him the next day.

Candide and his friend Martin went into a gondola on the Brenta, and arrived at the palace of the noble Pococuranté: the gardens were laid out in elegant taste, and adorned with fine marble statues; his palace was built after the most approved rules of architecture. The master of the house, who was a man of sixty, and very rich, received our two travellers with great politeness, but without much ceremony, which somewhat disconcerted Candide, but was not at all displeasing to Martin.

As soon as they were seated, two very pretty girls, neatly dressed, brought in chocolate, which was extremely well frothed. Candide could not help making encomiums upon their beauty and graceful carriage. "The creatures are well enough," said the senator. "I make them my companions, for I am heartily tired of the ladies of the town, their coquetry, their jealousy, their quarrels, their humors, their meannesses, their pride, and their folly. I am weary of making sonnets, or of paying for sonnets to be made, on them; but, after all, these two girls begin to grow very indifferent to me."

After having refreshed himself, Candide walked into a large gallery, where he was struck with the sight of a fine collection of paintings. "Pray," said Candide, "by what master are the two first of these?" — "They are Raphael's," answered the senator. "I gave a great deal of money for them seven years ago, purely out of curiosity, as they were said to be the finest pieces in Italy: but I cannot say they please me; the coloring is dark and heavy; the figures do not swell nor come out enough; and the drapery is very bad. In short, notwithstanding the encomiums lavished upon them, they are not, in my opinion, a true representation of nature. I approve of no paintings but where I think I behold Nature herself; and there are very few, if any, of that kind to be met with. I have what is called a fine collection, but I take no manner of delight in them."

While dinner was getting ready, Pococuranté ordered a concert. Candide praised the music to the skies. "This noise," said the noble Venetian, "may amuse one for a little time; but if it was to last above half an hour, it would grow tiresome to everybody, though perhaps no one would care to own it. Music is become the art of executing what is difficult; now, whatever is difficult cannot be long pleasing.

"I believe I might take more pleasure in an opera, if they had not made such a monster of that species of dramatic entertainment as perfectly shocks me; and I am amazed how people can bear to see wretched tragedies set to music, where the scenes are contrived for no other purpose than to lug in, as it were by the ears, three or four ridiculous songs, to give a favorite actress an opportunity of exhibiting her pipe. Let who will or can die away in raptures at the trills of a eunuch quavering the majestic part of Cæsar or Cato, and strutting in a foolish manner upon the stage. For my part, I have long ago renounced these paltry entertainments, which constitute the glory of modern Italy, and are so dearly purchased by crowned heads." Candide opposed these sentiments, but he did it in a discreet manner. As for Martin, he was entirely of the old senator's opinion.

Dinner being served up, they sat down to table, and after a very hearty repast, returned to the library. Candide, observing Homer richly bound, commended the noble Venetian's taste. "This," said he, "is a book that was once the delight of the great Pangloss, the best philosopher in Germany." — "Homer is no favorite of mine," answered Pococuranté very coolly. "I was made to believe once that I took a pleasure in reading him; but his continual repetitions of battles must have all such a resemblance with each other; his gods that are forever in a hurry and bustle, without ever doing any thing; his Helen, that is the cause of the war, and yet hardly acts in the whole performance; his Troy, that holds out so long without being taken; in short, all these things together make the poem very insipid to me. I have asked some learned men whether they are not in reality as much tired as myself with reading this poet. Those who spoke ingenuously assured me that he had made them fall asleep, and yet that they could not well avoid giving him a place in their libraries; but that it was merely as they would do an antique, or those rusty medals which are kept only for curiosity, and are of no manner of use in commerce."

"But your excellency does not surely form the same opinion of Virgil?" said Candide. "Why, I grant," replied Pococuranté, "that the second, third, fourth, and sixth books of his ' Æneid' are excellent; but as for his pious Æneas, his strong Cloanthus, his friendly Achates, his boy Ascanius, his silly King Latinus, his ill-bred Amata, his insipid Lavinia, and some other characters much in the same strain, I think there cannot in nature be any thing more flat and disagreeable. I must confess I prefer Tasso far beyond him; nay, even that sleepy tale-teller Ariosto."

"May I take the liberty to ask if you do not receive great pleasure from reading Horace?" said Candide. "There are maxims in this writer," replied Pococuranté, "from whence a man of the world may reap some benefit; and the short measure of the verse makes them more easily to be retained in the memory. But I see nothing extraordinary in his journey to Brundusium, and his account of his bad dinner; nor in his dirty, low quarrel between one Rupilius, whose words, as he expresses it, were full of poisonous filth; and another, whose language was dipped in vinegar. His indelicate verses against old women and witches have frequently given me great offence; nor can I discover the great merit of his telling his friend Mæcenas, that, if he will but rank him in the class of lyric poets, his lofty head shall touch the stars. Ignorant readers are apt to advance every thing by the lump in a writer of reputation. For my part, I read only to please myself. I like nothing but what makes for my purpose." Candide, who had been brought up with a notion of never making use of his own judgment, was astonished at what he heard; but Martin found there was a good deal of reason in the senator's remarks.

"Oh, here is a Tully!" said Candide; "this great man, I fancy, you are never tired of reading." — "Indeed, I never read him at all," replied Pococuranté. "What a deuce is it to me whether he pleads for Rabirius or Cluentius? I try causes enough myself. I had once some liking to his philosophical works; but when I found he doubted of every thing, I thought I knew as much as himself, and had no need of a guide to learn ignorance."

"Ha!" cried Martin, "here are fourscore volumes of the 'Memoirs of the Academy of Sciences;' perhaps there may be something curious and valuable in this collection." — "Yes," answered Pococuranté; "so there might, if any one of these compilers of this rubbish had only invented the art of pin-making. But all these volumes are filled with mere chimerical systems, without one single article conducive to real utility."

"I see a prodigious number of plays," said Candide, "in Italian, Spanish, and French." — "Yes," replied the Venetian; "there are, I think, three thousand, and not three dozen of them good for any thing. As to those huge volumes of divinity, and those enormous collections of sermons, they are not all together worth one single page of Seneca; and I fancy you will readily believe that neither myself nor any one else ever looks into them."

Martin, perceiving some shelves filled with English books, said to the senator, "I fancy that a republican must be highly delighted with those books, which are most of them written with a noble spirit of freedom." — "It is noble to write as we think," said Pococuranté; "it is the privilege of humanity. Throughout Italy we write only what we do not think; and the present inhabitants of the country of the Cæsars and Antoninuses dare not acquire a single idea without the permission of a father Dominican. I should be enamoured of the spirit of the English nation did it not utterly frustrate the good effects it would produce by passion and the spirit of party."

Candide, seeing a Milton, asked the senator if he did not think that author a great man. "Who!" said Pococuranté sharply. "That barbarian, who writes a tedious commentary, in ten books of rambling verse, on the first chapter of Genesis! That slovenly imitator of the Greeks, who disfigures the creation by making the Messiah take a pair of compasses from heaven's armory to plan the world; whereas Moses represented the Deity as producing the whole universe by his fiat! Can I think you have any esteem for a writer who has spoiled Tasso's hell and the devil; who transforms Lucifer, sometimes into a toad, and at others into a pygmy; who makes him say the same thing over again a hundred times; who metamorphoses him into a school-divine; and who, by an absurdly serious imitation of Ariosto's comic invention of fire-arms, represents the devils and angels cannonading each other in heaven! Neither I, nor any other Italian, can possibly take pleasure in such melancholy reveries. But the marriage of Sin and Death, and snakes issuing from the womb of the former, are enough to make any person sick that is not lost to all sense of delicacy. This obscene, whimsical, and disagreeable poem met with the neglect that it deserved at its first publication; and I only treat the author now as he was treated in his own country by his contemporaries."

Candide was sensibly grieved at this speech, as he had a great respect for Homer, and was very fond of Milton. "Alas!" said he softly to Martin, "I am afraid this man holds our German poets in great contempt." — "There would be no such great harm in that," said Martin. — "Oh, what a surprising man!" said Candide to himself. "What a prodigious genius is this Pococuranté! Nothing can please him."

After finishing their survey of the library they went down into the garden, when Candide commended the several beauties that offered themselves to his view. "I know nothing upon earth laid out in such bad taste," said Pococuranté; "every thing about it is childish and trifling; but I shall have another laid out to-morrow upon a nobler plan."

As soon as our two travellers had taken leave of his excellency, "Well," said Candide to Martin, "I hope you will own that this man is the happiest of all mortals, for he is above every thing he possesses." — "But do you not see," answered Martin, "that he likewise dislikes every thing he possesses ? It was an observation of Plato long since, that those are not the best stomachs that reject, without distinction, all sorts of aliments." — "True," said Candide; "but still, there must certainly be a pleasure in criticising every thing, and in perceiving faults where others think they see beauties." — "That is," replied Martin, "there is a pleasure in having no pleasure." — "Well, well," said Candide, "I find that I shall be the only happy man at last, when I am blessed with the sight of my dear Cunegund." — "It is good to hope," said Martin.

The single citation preceding sufficiently exemplifies, at their best, though at their worst, not, the style and the spirit of Voltaire's "Candide;" as his "Candide" sufficiently exemplifies the style and the spirit of the most characteristic of Voltaire's writings in general. "Pococurantism" is a word, now not uncommon in English, contributed by Voltaire to the vocabulary of literature. To readers of the foregoing extract, the sense of the term will not need to be explained. We respectfully suggest to our dictionary-makers, that the fact stated of its origin in the "Candide" of Voltaire would be interesting and instructive to many. Voltaire coined the name, to suit the character of his Venetian gentleman, from two Italian words which mean together "little-caring." Signor Pococuranté is the immortal type of men that have worn out their capacity of fresh sensation and enjoyment.

It was a happy editorial thought of Mr. Henry Morley, in his cheap library, now issuing, of standard books for the people, to bind up Johnson's "Rasselas" in one volume with Voltaire's "Candide." The two stories, nearly contemporaneous in their production, offer a stimulating contrast in treatment, at the hands of two sharply contrasted writers, of much the same subject, — the unsatisfactoriness of the world.

Mr. John Morley, a very different writer and a very different man from his namesake just mentioned, has an elaborate monograph on Voltaire in a volume perhaps twice as large as the present. This work claims the attention of all students desirous of exhaustive acquaintance with its subject. Mr. John Morley writes in sympathy with Voltaire, so far as Voltaire was an enemy of the Christian religion; but in antipathy to him, so far as Voltaire fell short of being an atheist. A similar sympathy, limited by a similar antipathy, is observable in the same author's still more extended monograph on Rousseau. It is only in his two volumes on "Diderot and the Encyclopædists," that Mr. Morley finds himself able to write without reserve in full moral accord with the men whom he describes. Of course, in all these books the biographer and critic feels, as Englishman, obliged to concede much to his English audience, in the way of condemning impurities in his authors. The concession thus made is made with great adroitness of manner, the writer's aim evidently being to imply that his infidels and atheists, if they are somewhat vicious in taste, had the countenance of good Christian example or parallel for all the lapses they show. Mr. Morley wishes to be fair, but his atheist zeal overcomes him. This is especially evident in his work on " Diderot and the Encyclopædists," where his propagandist desire to clear the character of his hero bribes him once and again to unconscious false dealing. In his " Voltaire," and in his " Rousseau," Mr. Morley is so lofty in tone, expressing himself against the moral obliquities of the men with whom he is dealing, that often you feel the ethic atmosphere of the books to be pure and bracing, almost beyond the standard of biblical and Christian. But in his " Diderot and the Encyclopædists," such fine severity is conspicuously absent. Mr. Morley is so deeply convinced that atheism is what we all most need just now, that when he has — not halting mere infidels, like Voltaire and Rousseau — but good thorough-going atheists, like Diderot and his fellows, to exhibit, he can hardly bring himself to injure their exemplary influence with his readers, by allowing to exist any damaging flaws in their character.

Even in Voltaire and Rousseau, but particularly in Voltaire, Mr. Morley, though his sympathy with these writers is, as we have said, not complete, finds far more to praise than to blame. To this eager apostle of atheism, Voltaire was at least on the right road, although he did, unfortunately, stop short of the goal. His influence was potent against Christianity, and potent it certainly was not against atheism. Voltaire might freely be lauded as on the whole a mighty and a beneficent liberalizer of thought.

And we, we who are neither atheists nor deists — let us not deny to Voltaire his just meed of praise. There were streaks of gold in the base alloy of that character of his. He burned with magnanimous heat against the hideous doctrine and practice of ecclesiastical persecution. Carlyle says of Voltaire, that he "spent his best efforts, and as many still think, successfully, in assaulting the Christian religion." This, true though it be, is liable to be falsely understood. It was not against the Christian religion, as the Christian religion really is, but rather against the Christian religion as the Roman hierarchy misrepresented it, that Voltaire ostensibly directed his efforts. "You are right," wrote he to his henchman D'Alembert, in 1762, "in assuming that I speak of superstition only; for as to the Christian religion, I respect it and love it, as you do." This distinction of Voltaire's, with whatever degree of simple sincerity on his part made, ought to be remembered in his favor, when his memorable motto, "*Écrasez l'Infâme*," is interpreted and applied. He did not mean Jesus Christ by *l'Infâme;* he did not mean the Christian religion by it; he did not even mean the Christian Church by it; he meant the oppressive despotism and the crass obscurantism of the Roman-Catholic hierarchy. At least, this is what he would have said that he meant, what in fact he substantially did say that he meant, when incessantly reiterating, in its various forms, his watchword, "*Écrasez l'Infâme*," "*Écrasons l'Infâme*,"— "Crush the wretch!" "Let us crush the wretch!" His blows were aimed, perhaps, at "superstition;" but they really fell, in the full half of their effect, on Christianity itself. Whether Voltaire regretted this, whether he would in his heart have had it otherwise, may well, in spite of any protestation from him of love for Christianity, be doubted. Still, it is never, in judgment of Voltaire, to be forgotten that the organized Christianity which he confronted, was in large part a system justly hateful to the true and wise lover whether of God or of man. That system he did well in fighting. Carnal indeed were the weapons with which he fought it; and his victory over it was a carnal victory, bringing, on the whole, but slender net advantage, if any such advantage at all, to the cause of final truth and light. The French Revolution, with its excesses and its horrors, was perhaps the proper, the legitimate, the necessary, fruit of resistance such as was Voltaire's, in fundamental spirit, to the evils in church and in state against which he conducted so gallantly his life-long campaign.

But though we thus bring in doubt the work of Voltaire, both as to the purity of its motive, and as to the value of its fruit, we should wrong our sense of justice to ourselves if we permitted our readers to suppose us blind to the generous things that this arch-infidel did on behalf of the suffering and the oppressed. Voltaire more than once wielded that pen of his, the most dreaded weapon in Europe, like a knight sworn to take on himself the championship of the forlornest of causes. There is the historic case of Jean Calas at Toulouse, Protestant, an old man of near seventy, broken on the wheel, as suspected, without evidence, and against accumulated impossibilities, of murdering his own son, a young man of about thirty, by hanging him. Voltaire took up the case, and pleaded it to the common sense, and to the human feeling, of France, with immense effectiveness. It is, in truth, Voltaire's advocacy of righteousness, in this instance of incredible wrong, that has made the instance itself immortal. His part in the case of Calas, though the most signal, is not the only, example of Voltaire's literary knighthood. He hated oppression, and he loved liberty, for himself and for all men, with a passion as deep and as constant as any passion of which nature had made Voltaire capable. If the liberty that he loved was fundamentally liberty

as against God no less than as against men, and if
the oppression that he hated was fundamentally the
oppression of being put under obligation to obey
Christ as lord of life and of thought, this was something of which, probably, Voltaire never had a
clear consciousness.

We have now indicated what was most admirable
in Voltaire's personal character. On the whole, he
was far from being an admirable man. He was
vain, he was shallow, he was frivolous, he was de-
ceitful, he was voluptuous, he fawned on the great,
he abased himself before them, he licked the dust
on which they stood. *" Trajan, est-il content?"*
(" Is Trajan satisfied?") — this, asked, in nauseous
adulation, and nauseous self-abasement, by Voltaire of Louis XV., so little like Trajan in character — is monumental. The occasion was the production of a piece of Voltaire's written at the instance
of Louis XV.'s mistress, the infamous Madame de
Pompadour. The king, for answer, simply gorgon-
ized the poet with a stony Bourbon stare.

But, taken altogether, Voltaire's life was a great
success. He got on in the world, was rich, was
fortunate, was famous, was gay, if he was not
happy. He had his friendship with the great
Frederick of Prussia, who filled for his false French
flatterer a return cup of sweetness, cunningly mixed
with exceeding bitterness. His death was an appropriate *coup de théâtre*, a felicity of finish to such a
life, quite beyond the reach of art. He came back

to Paris, whence he had been an exile, welcomed with a triumph transcending the triumph of a conqueror. They made a great feast for him, a feast of flattery, in the theatre. The old man was drunk with delight. The delight was too much for him. It literally killed him. It was as if a favorite actress should be quite smothered to death on the stage, under flowers thrown in excessive profusion at her feet.

Let Carlyle's sentence be our epigraph on Voltaire : —

"No great Man. . . . Found always at the top, less by power in swimming than by lightness in floating."

XVI.

ROUSSEAU.

1712-1778.

THERE are two Rousseaus in French literature. At least, there was a first, until the second effaced him, and became the only.

We speak, of course, in comparison, and hyperbolically. J. B. Rousseau is still named as a lyric poet of the time of Louis XIV. But when Rousseau, without initials, is spoken of, it is always Jean Jacques Rousseau that is meant.

Jean Jacques Rousseau is perhaps the most squalid, as it certainly is one of the most splendid, among French literary names. The squalor belongs chiefly to the man, but the splendor is wholly the writer's. There is hardly another example in the world's literature of a union so striking of these opposites.

Rousseau's life he has himself told, in the best, the worst, and the most imperishable, of his books, the "Confessions." This book is one to which the adjective charming attaches, in a peculiarly literal sense of the word. The spell, however, is repellent as well as attractive. But the attraction of the style asserts and pronounces itself only the more, in triumph over the much there is in the matter to disgust and revolt. It is quite the most offensive, and it is well-nigh the most fascinating, book that we know.

The "Confessions" begin as follows : —

I purpose an undertaking that never had an example, and whose execution never will have an imitator. I would exhibit to my fellows a man in all the truth of nature, and that man — myself.

Myself alone. I know my own heart, and I am acquainted with men. I am made unlike any one I have ever seen, — I dare believe unlike any living being. If no better than, I am at least different from, others. Whether nature did well or ill in breaking the mould wherein I was cast, can be determined only after having read me.

Let the last trumpet sound when it will, I will come, with this book in my hand, and present myself before the Sovereign Judge. I will boldly proclaim: Thus have I acted, thus have I thought, such was I. With equal frankness have I disclosed the good and the evil. I have omitted nothing bad, added nothing good; and if I have happened to make use of some unimportant ornament, it has, in every case, been simply for the purpose of filling up a void occasioned by my lack of memory. I may have taken for granted as true what I knew to be possible, never what I knew to be false. Such as I was, I have exhibited myself, — despicable and vile, when so; virtuous, generous, sublime, when so. I have unveiled my interior being, such as Thou, Eternal Existence, hast beheld it. Assemble around me the numberless throng of my fellow-mortals; let them listen to my confessions, let them blush at my depravities, let them shrink appalled at my miseries. Let each of them, in his turn, with equal sincerity, lay bare his heart at the foot of thy throne, and then let a single one tell thee, if he dare, *I was better than that man.*

Notwithstanding our autobiographer's disavowal of debt to example for the idea of his "Confessions," it seems clear that Montaigne here was at least inspiration, if not pattern, to Rousseau. But Rousseau resolved to do what Montaigne had done, more ingenuously and more courageously than Montaigne had done it. This writer will make himself his subject, and then treat his subject with greater frankness than any man before him ever used about himself, or than any man after him would ever use. He undoubtedly succeeded in his attempt. His frankness, in fact, is so forward and eager, that it is probably even inventive of things disgraceful to himself. Montaigne makes great pretence of telling his

own faults, but you observe that he generally chooses
rather amiable faults of his own to tell.   Rousseau's
morbid vulgarity leads him to disclose traits in
himself, of character or of behavior, that, despite
whatever contrary wishes on your part, compel your
contempt of the man.   And it is for the man who
confesses, almost more than for the man who is
guilty, that you feel the contempt.

The " Confessions " proceed : —

I was born at Geneva, in 1712, of Isaac Rousseau and
Susannah Bernard, citizens. . . . I came into the world
weak and sickly.   I cost my mother her life, and my birth
was the first of my misfortunes.

I never learned how my father supported his loss, but I
know that he remained ever after inconsolable. . . . When
he used to say to me, " Jean Jacques, let us speak of your
mother," my usual reply was, " Well, father, we'll cry,
then," a reply which would instantly bring the tears to his
eyes.   "Ah!" he would exclaim with agitation, "give me
her back, console me for her loss, fill up the void she has left
in my soul.   Could I love thee thus wert thou but *my* son?"
Forty years after having lost her he expired in the arms of
a second wife, but with the name of the first on his lips,
and her image engraven on his heart.

Such were the authors of my being.   Of all the gifts
Heaven had allotted them, a feeling heart was the only one
I had inherited.   While, however, this had been the source
of their happiness, it became the spring of all my misfortunes.

" A feeling heart ! "   That expression tells the
literary secret of Rousseau.   It is hardly too much
to say that Rousseau was the first French writer to

write with his heart; but heart's blood was the ink in which almost every word of Rousseau's was written. This was the spring of his marvellous power. Rousseau: —

My mother had left a number of romances. These father and I betook us to reading during the evenings. At first the sole object was, by means of entertaining books, to improve me in reading; but, ere long, the charm became so potent, that we read turn about without intermission, and passed whole nights in this employment. Never could we break up till the end of the volume. At times my father, hearing the swallows of a morning, would exclaim, quite ashamed of himself, "Come, let's to bed; I'm more of a child than you are!"

The elder Rousseau was right respecting himself. And such a father would almost necessarily have such a child. Jean Jacques Rousseau is to be judged tenderly for his faults. What birth and what breeding were his! The "Confessions" go on: —

I soon acquired, by this dangerous course, not only an extreme facility in reading and understanding, but, for my age, a quite unprecedented acquaintance with the passions. I had not the slightest conception of things themselves, at a time when the whole round of sentiments was already perfectly familiar to me. I had apprehended nothing — I had felt all.

Some hint now of other books read by the boy: —

With the summer of 1719 the romance-reading termi-
nated. . . . "The History of the Church and Empire" by
Lesueur, Bossuet's "Dissertation on Universal History,"
Plutarch's "Lives," Nani's "History of Venice," Ovid's
"Metamorphoses," "La Bruyère," Fontenelle's "Worlds,"
his "Dialogues of the Dead," and a few volumes of Molière,
were transported into my father's shop; and I read them to
him every day during his work. For this employment I
acquired a rare, and, for my age, perhaps unprecedented,
taste. Plutarch especially became my favorite reading. The
pleasure which I found in incessantly reperusing him, cured
me in some measure of the romance madness; and I soon
came to prefer Agesilaus, Brutus, and Aristides, to Oronda-
tes, Artemenes, and Juba. From these interesting studies,
joined to the conversations to which they gave rise with my
father, resulted that free, republican spirit, that haughty
and untamable character, fretful of restraint or subjection,
which has tormented me my life long, and that in situations
the least suitable for giving it play. Incessantly occupied
with Rome and Athens, living, so to speak, with their great
men, born myself the citizen of a republic [Geneva], the son
of a father with whom patriotism was the ruling passion, I
caught the flame from him — I imagined myself a Greek
or a Roman, and became the personage whose life I was
reading.

On such food of reading and of reverie, young
Rousseau's imagination and sentiment battened,
while his reason and his practical sense starved
and died within him. Unconsciously thus in part
was formed the dreamer of the "Émile" and of
"The Social Contract." Another glimpse of the
home-life — if home-life such experience can be
called — of this half-orphan, homeless Genevan
boy : —

I had a brother, my elder by seven years. . . . He fell into the ways of debauchery, even before he was old enough to be really a libertine. . . . I remember once when my father was chastising him severely and in anger, that I impetuously threw myself between them, clasping him tightly. I thus covered him with my body, receiving the blows that were aimed at him; and I held out so persistently in this position, that whether softened by my cries and tears, or fearing that I should get the worst of it, my father was forced to forgive him. In the end my brother turned out so bad that he ran away and disappeared altogether.

It is pathetic — Rousseau's attempted contrast following, between the paternal neglect of his older brother and the paternal indulgence of himself : —

If this poor lad was carelessly brought up, it was quite otherwise with his brother. . . . My desires were so little excited, and so little crossed, that it never came into my head to have any. I can solemnly aver, that, till the time when I was bound to a master, I never knew what it was to have a whim.

Poor lad ! "Never knew what it was to have a whim !" It well might be, however — his boy's life all one whim uncrossed, unchecked ; no contrast of saving restraint, to make him know that he was living by whim alone ! The "Confessions" truly say : —

Thus commenced the formation or the manifestation in me of that heart at once so haughty and so tender, of that effeminate and yet unconquerable character which, ever vacillating between courage and weakness, between virtue and yielding to temptation, has all along set me in contradiction to myself, and has resulted in my failing both of abstinence and enjoyment, both of prudence and pleasure.

The half-orphan becomes orphan entire, not by the death, but by the withdrawing, of the father. That father, having been accused of a misdemeanor, "preferred," Rousseau somewhat vaguely says, "to quit Geneva for the remainder of his life, rather than give up a point wherein honor and liberty appeared to him compromised." Jean Jacques was sent to board with a parson, who taught him Latin, and, along with Latin, supplied, Rousseau scornfully says, "all the accompanying mass of paltry rubbish styled education." He adds : —

The country was so entirely new to me, that I could never grow weary in my enjoyment of it; and I acquired so strong a liking for it, that it has never become extinguished.

Young Jean Jacques was at length apprenticed to an engraver. He describes the contrast of his new situation and the effect of the contrast upon his own character and career : —

I learned to covet in silence, to dissemble, to dissimulate, to lie, and at last to steal, — a propensity for which I had never hitherto had the slightest inclination, and of which I have never since been able quite to cure myself. . . .

My first theft was the result of complaisance, but it opened the door to others which had not so laudable a motive.

My master had a journeyman named M. Verrat. . . . [He] took it into his head to rob his mother of some of her early asparagus and sell it, converting the proceeds into some extra good breakfasts. As he did not wish to expose himself, and not being very nimble, he selected me for this expedition. . . . Long did I stickle, but he persisted. I never could resist kindness, so I consented. I went every morning to the garden, gathered the best of the asparagus, and took it to "the Molard," where some good creature, perceiving that I had just been stealing it, would insinuate that little fact, so as to get it the cheaper. In my terror I took whatever she chose to give me, and carried it to M. Verrat.

This little domestic arrangement continued for several days before it came into my head to rob the robber, and tithe M. Verrat for the proceeds of the asparagus. . . . I thus learned that to steal was, after all, not so very terrible a thing as I had conceived; and ere long I turned this discovery to so good an account, that nothing I had an inclination for could safely be left within my reach. . . .

And now, before giving myself over to the fatality of my destiny, let me, for a moment, contemplate what would naturally have been my lot had I fallen into the hands of a better master. Nothing was more agreeable to my tastes, nor better calculated to render me happy, than the calm and obscure condition of a good artisan, more especially in certain lines, such as that of an engraver at Geneva. . . . In my native country, in the bosom of my religion, of my family, and my friends, I should have led a life gentle and uncheckered as became my character, in the uniformity of a pleasing occupation and among connections dear to my heart. I should have been a good Christian, a good citizen, a good father, a good friend, a good artisan, and a good man in every respect. I should have loved my station; it may be I should have been an honor to it: and after having passed an obscure and simple, though even and happy, life,

I should peacefully have departed in the bosom of my kindred. Soon, it may be, forgotten, I should at least have been regretted as long as the remembrance of me survived.

Instead of this . . . what a picture am I about to draw!

Thus ends the first book of the "Confessions."

The picture Rousseau is "about to draw" has in it a certain Madame de Warens for a principal figure. (Apprentice Jean Jacques has left his master, and entered on a vagabond life.) This lady is a character very difficult for us Protestant Americans in our contrasted society to conceive as real or as possible. She kept a house of, what shall we call it? detention, for souls doubtfully in the way of being reclaimed from Protestant error into the bosom of the Roman-Catholic Church. She was herself a Roman-Catholic convert from Protestantism. She had forsaken a husband, not loved, and was living on a bounty from King Victor Amadeus of Sardinia. For Annecy, the home of Madame de Warens, our young Jean Jacques, sent thither by a Roman-Catholic curate, sets out on foot. The distance was but one day's walk; which one day's walk, however, the humor of the wanderer stretched into a saunter of three days. The man of fifty-four, become the biographer of his own youth, finds no loathness of self-respect to prevent his detailing the absurd adventures with which he diverted himself on the way. For example: —

Not a country-seat could I see, either to the right or left, without going after the adventure which I was certain awaited me. I could not muster courage to enter the mansion, nor even to knock, for I was excessively timid; but I sang beneath the most inviting window, very much astonished to find, after wasting my breath, that neither lady nor miss made her appearance, attracted by the beauty of my voice, or the spice of my songs, — seeing that I knew some capital ones that my comrades had taught me, and which I sang in the most admirable manner.

Rousseau describes the emotions he experienced in his first meeting with Madame de Warens : —

I had pictured to myself a grim old devotee — M. de Pontverre's "worthy lady" could, in my opinion, be none other. But lo, a countenance beaming with charms, beautiful, mild blue eyes, a complexion of dazzling fairness, the outline of an enchanting neck ! Nothing escaped the rapid glance of the young proselyte; for that instant I was hers, sure that a religion preached by such missionaries could not fail to lead to paradise!

This abnormally susceptible youth had remarkable experiences, all within his own soul, during his sojourn, of a few days only, on the present occasion, under Madame de Warens's hospitable roof. These experiences, the autobiographer, old enough to call himself "old dotard," has, nevertheless, not grown wise enough to be ashamed to be very detailed and psychological in recounting. It was a case of precocious love at first sight. One could afford to laugh at it as ridiculous, but that it had a sequel full of sin and of sorrow. Jean Jacques was now forwarded to Turin, to become inmate of a sort of charity school for the instruction of catechumens. The very day after he started on foot, his father, with a friend of his, reached Annecy on horseback, in pursuit of the truant boy. They might easily have overtaken him, but they let him go his way. Rousseau explains the case on behalf of his father as follows : —

My father was not only an honorable man, but a person of the most reliable probity, and endowed with one of those powerful minds that perform deeds of loftiest heroism. I may add, he was a good father, especially to me. Tenderly did he love me, but he loved his pleasures also; and, since our living apart, other ties had, in a measure, weakened his paternal affection. He had married again, at Nyon; and though his wife was no longer of an age to present me with brothers, yet she had connections; another family-circle was thus formed, other objects engrossed his attention, and the new domestic relations no longer so frequently brought back the remembrance of me. My father was growing old, and had nothing on which to rely for the support of his declining years. My brother and I had something coming to us from my mother's fortune; the interest of this my father was to receive during our absence. This consideration did not present itself to him directly, nor did it stand in the way of his doing his duty; it had, however, a silent, and to himself imperceptible, influence, and at times slackened his zeal, which, unacted upon by this, would have been carried much farther. This, I think, was the reason, that, having traced me as far as Annecy, he did not follow me to Chamberi, where he was morally certain of overtaking me. This will also explain why, in visiting him many times after my flight, I received from him on every occasion a father's kindness, though unaccompanied by any very pressing efforts to retain me.

Rousseau's filial regard for his father was pecul-iar. It did not lead him to hide, it only led him to account for, his father's sordidness. The son generalized and inferred a moral maxim for the conduct of life from this behavior of the father's, — a maxim, which, as he thought, had done him great good. He says : —

This conduct on the part of a father of whose affection and virtue I have had so many proofs, has given rise within me to reflections on my own character which have not a little contributed to maintain my heart uncorrupted. I have derived therefrom this great maxim of morality, perhaps the only one of any use in practice; namely, to avoid such situations as put our duty in antagonism with our interest, or disclose our own advantage in the misfortunes of another, certain that in such circumstances, however sincere the love of virtue we bring with us, it will sooner or later, and whether we perceive it or not, become weakened, and we shall come to be unjust and culpable in our acts without having ceased to be upright and blameless in our intentions.

The fruitful maxim thus deduced by Rousseau, he thinks he tried faithfully to put in practice. With apparent perfect assurance concerning himself, he says : —

I have sincerely desired to do what was right. I have, with all the energy of my character, shunned situations which set my interest in opposition to the interest of another, thus inspiring me with a secret though involuntary desire prejudicial to that man.

Jean Jacques at Turin made speed to convert himself, by the abjurations required, into a pretty good Catholic. He was hereon free to seek his fortune in the Sardinian capital. This he did by getting successively various situations in service. In one of these he stole, so he tells us, a piece of ribbon, which was soon found in his possession. He said a maid-servant, naming her, gave it to him. The two were confronted with each other. In spite of the poor girl's solemn appeal, Jean Jacques persisted in his lie against her. Both servants were discharged. The autobiographer protests that he has suffered much remorse for this lie of his to the harm of the innocent maid. He expresses confident hope that his suffering sorrow, already experienced on this behalf, will stand him in stead of punishment that might be his due in a future state. Remorse is a note in Rousseau that distinguishes him from Montaigne. Montaigne reviews his own life to live over his sins, not to repent of them.

The end of several vicissitudes is, that young Rousseau gets back to Madame de Warens. She welcomes him kindly. He says : —

From the first day, the most affectionate familiarity sprang up between us, and that to the same degree in which it continued during all the rest of her life. *Petit*—Child — was my name, *Maman*—Mamma — hers; and *Petit* and *Maman* we remained, even when the course of time had all but effaced the difference of our ages. These two names seem to me marvellously well to express our tone towards each other, the simplicity of our manners, and, more than all, the relation of our hearts. She was to me the tenderest of mothers, never seeking her own pleasure, but ever my welfare; and if the senses had any thing to do with my attachment for her, it was not to change its nature, but only to render it more exquisite, and intoxicate me with the charm of having a young and pretty mamma whom it was delightful for me to caress. I say quite literally, to caress; for it never entered into her head to deny me the tenderest maternal kisses and endearments, nor into my heart to abuse them. Some may say that, in the end, quite other relations subsisted between us. I grant it; but have patience, — I cannot tell every thing at once.

With Madame de Warens, Rousseau's relations, as is intimated above, became licentious. This continued until, after an interval of years (nine years, with breaks), in a fit of jealousy he forsook her. Rousseau's whole life was a series of self-indulgences, grovelling, sometimes, beyond what is conceivable to any one not learning of it all in detail from the man's own pen. The reader is fain at last to seek the only relief possible from the sickening story, by flying to the conclusion that Jean Jacques Rousseau, with all his genius, was wanting in that mental sanity which is a condition of complete moral responsibility.

We shall, of course, not follow the "Confessions" through their disgusting recitals of sin and shame. We should do wrong, however, to the literary, and even to the moral, character of the work, were we not to point out that there are frequent oases of sweetness and beauty set in the wastes of incredible foulness which overspread so widely the pages of Rousseau's "Confessions." Here, for example, is an idyll of vagabondage that might almost make one willing to play tramp one's self, if one by so doing might have such an experience : —

I remember, particularly, having passed a delicious night without the city on a road that skirted the Rhone or the Saône, for I cannot remember which. On the other side were terraced gardens. It had been a very warm day; the evening was charming; the dew moistened the faded grass; a calm night, without a breeze; the air was cool without being cold; the sun in setting had left crimson vapors in the sky, which tinged the water with its roseate hue, while the trees along the terrace were filled with nightingales gushing out melodious answers to each other's song. I walked along in a species of ecstasy, giving up heart and senses to the enjoyment of the scene, only slightly sighing with regret at enjoying it alone. Absorbed in my sweet reverie, I prolonged my walk far into the night, without perceiving that I was wearied out. At length I discovered it. I lay voluptuously down on the tablet of a sort of niche or false door sunk in the terrace wall. The canopy of my couch was formed by the over-arching boughs of the trees; a nightingale sat exactly above me; its song lulled me to sleep; my slumber was sweet, and my awaking still more so. It was broad day; my eyes, on opening, fell on the water, the verdure, and the admirable landscape spread out before me. I arose and shook off dull sleep; and, growing hungry, I gayly directed my steps towards the city, bent on transforming two *pieces de six blancs* that I had left, into a good breakfast. I was so cheerful that I went singing along the whole way.

This happy-go-lucky, vagabond, grown-up child, this sentimentalist of genius, had now and then different experiences, — experiences to which the reflection of the man grown old attributes important influence on the formation of his most controlling beliefs : —

One day, among others, having purposely turned aside to get a closer view of a spot that appeared worthy of all admiration, I grew so delighted with it, and wandered round it so often, that I at length lost myself completely. After several hours of useless walking, weary and faint with hunger and thirst, I entered a peasant's hut which did not present a very promising appearance, but it was the only one I saw around. I conceived it to be here as at Geneva and throughout Switzerland, where all the inhabitants in easy circumstances are in the situation to exercise hospitality. I entreated the man to get me some dinner, offering to pay for it. He presented me with some skimmed milk and coarse barley bread, observing that that was all he had. I drank the milk with delight, and ate the bread, chaff and all; but this was not very restorative to a man exhausted with fatigue. The peasant, who was watching me narrowly, judged of the truth of my story by the sincerity of my appetite. All of a sudden, after having said that he saw perfectly well that I was a good and true young fellow that did not come to betray him, he opened a little trap-door by the side of his kitchen, went down and returned a moment afterwards with a good brown loaf of pure wheat, the remains of a toothsome ham, and a bottle of wine, the sight of which rejoiced my heart more than all the rest. To these he added a good thick omelette, and I made such a dinner as none but a walker ever enjoyed. When it came to pay, lo! his disquietude and fears again seized him; he would none of my money, and rejected it with extraordinary manifestations of disquiet. The funniest part of the matter was, that I could not conceive what he was afraid of. At length, with fear and trembling, he pronounced those terrible words, *Commissioners* and *Cellar-rats.* He gave me to understand that he concealed his wine because of the excise, and his bread on account of the tax, and that he was a lost man if they got the slightest inkling that he was not dying of hunger. Every thing he said to me touching this matter, whereof, indeed, I had not the slightest idea, produced an impression on me that can never be effaced. It became the germ of that inextinguishable hatred that afterwards sprang up in my heart against the vexations to which these poor people are subject, and against their oppressors. This man, though in easy circumstances, dared not eat the bread he had gained by the sweat of his brow, and could escape ruin only by presenting the appearance of the same misery that reigned around him.

A hideously false world, that world of French society was, in Rousseau's time. The falseness was full ripe to be laid bare by some one; and Rousseau's experience of life, as well as his temperament and his genius, fitted him to do the work of exposure that he did. What we emphatically call character was sadly wanting in Rousseau — how sadly, witness such an acted piece of mad folly as the following : —

I, without knowing aught of the matter, . . . gave myself out for a [musical] composer. Nor was this all: having been presented to M. de Freytorens, law-professor, who loved music, and gave concerts at his house, nothing would do but I must give him a sample of my talent; so I set about composing a piece for his concert quite as boldly as though I had really been an adept in the science. I had the constancy to work for fifteen days on this fine affair, to copy it fair, write out the different parts, and distribute them with as much assurance as though it had been a masterpiece of harmony. Then, what will scarcely be believed, but which yet is gospel truth, worthily to crown this sublime production, I tacked to the end thereof a pretty minuet which was then having a run on the streets. . . . I gave it as my own just as resolutely as though I had been speaking to inhabitants of the moon.

They assembled to perform my piece. I explain to each the nature of the movement, the style of execution, and the relations of the parts — I was very full of business. For five or six minutes they were tuning; to me each minute seemed an age. At length, all being ready, I rap with a handsome paper *bâton* on the leader's desk the five or six beats of the "*Make ready.*" Silence is made — I gravely set to beating time — they commence! No, never since French operas began, was there such a *charivari* heard. Whatever they might have thought of my pretended talent, the effect was worse than they could possibly have imagined. The musicians choked with laughter; the auditors opened their eyes, and would fain have closed their ears. But that was an impossibility. My tormenting set of symphonists, who seemed rather to enjoy the fun, scraped away with a din sufficient to crack the tympanum of one born deaf. I had the firmness to go right ahead, however, sweating, it is true, at every pore, but held back by shame; not daring to retreat, and glued to the spot. For my consolation I heard the company whispering to each other, quite loud enough for it to reach my ear: "It is not bearable!" said one. "What music gone mad!" cried another. "What a devilish din!" added a third. Poor Jean Jacques, little dreamed you, in that cruel moment, that one day before the King of France and all the court, thy sounds would excite murmurs of surprise and applause, and that in all the boxes around thee the loveliest ladies would burst forth with, "What charming sounds! what enchanting music! every strain reaches the heart!"

But what restored every one to good humor was the minuet. Scarcely had they played a few measures than I heard bursts of laughter break out on all hands. Every one congratulated me on my fine musical taste; they assured me that this minuet would make me spoken about, and that I merited the loudest praises. I need not attempt depicting my agony, nor own that I well deserved it.

Readers have now had an opportunity to judge for themselves, by specimen, of the style, both of the writer and of the man Jean Jacques Rousseau. The writer's style they must have felt, even through the medium of imperfect anonymous translation, to be a charming one. If they have felt the style of the man to be contrasted, as squalor is contrasted with splendor, that they must not suppose to be a contrast of which Jean Jacques himself, the confessor, was in the least displacently conscious. Far from it. In a later part of his "Confessions," a part that deals with the author as one already now acknowledged a power in the world of letters, though with all his chief works still to write, Rousseau speaks thus of himself (he was considering at the time the ways and means available to him of obtaining a livelihood) : —

I felt that writing for bread would soon have extinguished my genius, and destroyed my talents, which were less in my pen than in my heart, and solely proceeded from an elevated and noble manner of thinking. . . . It is too difficult to think nobly when we think for a livelihood.

Is not that finely said? And one need not doubt that it was said with perfect sincerity. For our own part, paradoxical though it be to declare it, we are wholly willing to insist that Rousseau did think on a lofty plane. The trouble with him was, not that he thus thought with his heart, rather than with his head, — which, however, he did, — but that he thought with his heart alone, and not at all with his conscience and his will. In a word, his thought was sentiment rather than thought. He was a sentimentalist instead of a thinker. One illustration of the divorce that he decreed for himself, or rather — for we have used too positive a form of expression — that he allowed to subsist, between sentiment and conduct, will suffice. It was presently to be his fortune, as author of a tract on education (the " Émile "), to change the habit of a nation in the matter of nurture for babes. French mothers of the higher social class in Rousseau's time almost universally gave up their infants to be nursed at alien bosoms. Rousseau so eloquently denounced the unnaturalness of this, that from his time it became the fashion for French mothers to suckle their children themselves. Meantime, the preacher himself of this beautiful humanity, living in unwedded union with a woman (not Madame de Warens, but a woman of the laboring class, found after Madame de Warens was abandoned), sent his illegitimate children, against the mother's remonstrance, one after another, to the number of five, to be brought up unknown at the hospital for foundlings! He tells the story himself in his " Confessions." This course on his own part he subsequently laments with many tears and many self-upbraidings. But these, alas, he intermingles with self-justifications, nearly as many, — so that at last it is hard to say whether the balance of his judgment inclines for or against himself in the matter. A paradox of inconsistencies and self-contradictions, this man, — a problem in human character, of which the supposition of partial insanity in him, long working subtly in the blood, seems the only solution. The occupation finally adopted by Rousseau for obtaining subsistence, was the copying of music. It extorts from one a measure of involuntary respect for Rousseau, to see patiently toiling at this slavish work, to earn its owner bread, the same pen that had lately set all Europe in ferment with the " Émile " and " The Social Contract."

From Rousseau's " Confessions," we have not room to purvey further. It is a melancholy book, — written under monomaniac suspicion on the part of the author that he was the object of a wide-spread conspiracy against his reputation, his peace of mind, and even his life. The poor, shattered, self-consumed sensualist and sentimentalist paid dear in the agonies of his closing years for the indulgences of an unregulated life. The tender-hearted, really affectionate and loyal, friend came at length to live in a world of his own imagination, full of treachery to himself. David Hume, the Scotchman, tried to befriend him ; but the monomaniac was incapable of being befriended. Nothing could be more pitiful than were the decline and the extinction that occurred of so much brilliant genius, and so much lovable character. It is even doubtful whether Rousseau did not at last take his own life. The voice of accusation is silenced, in the presence of an earthly retribution so dreadful. One may not indeed approve, but one may at least be free to pity, more than he blames, in judging Rousseau.

Accompanying, and in some sort complementing, the "Confessions," are often published several detached pieces called "Reveries," or "Walks." These are very peculiar compositions, and very characteristic of the author. They are dreamy meditations or reveries, sad, even sombre, in spirit, but "beautiful exceedingly," in form of expression. Such works as the "Réné" of Chateaubriand, works but too abundant since in French literature, must all trace their pedigree to Rousseau's "Walks." We introduce two specimen extracts. The shadow of Rousseau's monomania will be felt thick upon them : —

It is now fifteen years since I have been in this strange situation, which yet appears to me like a dream; ever imagining that, disturbed by indigestion, I sleep uneasily, but shall soon awake, freed from my troubles, but surrounded by my friends. . . .

How could I possibly foresee the destiny that awaited me ? . . . Could I, if in my right senses, suppose that one day, the man I was, and yet remain, should be taken, without any kind of doubt, for a monster, a poisoner, an assassin, the horror of the human race, the sport of the rabble, my only salutation to be spit upon, and that a whole generation would unanimously amuse themselves in burying me alive ? When this strange revolution first happened, taken by unawares, I was overwhelmed with astonishment; my agitation, my indignation, plunged me into a delirium, which ten years have scarcely been able to calm : during this interval, falling from error to error, from fault to fault, and folly to folly, I have, by my imprudence, furnished the contrivers of my fate with instruments, which they have artfully employed to fix it without resource. . . .

Every future occurrence will be immaterial to me ; I have in the world neither relative, friend, nor brother ; I am on the earth as if I had fallen into some unknown planet ; if I contemplate any thing around me, it is only distressing, heart-rending objects ; every thing I cast my eyes on conveys some new subject either of indignation or affliction ; I will endeavor henceforward to banish from my mind all painful ideas which unavailingly distress me. Alone for the rest of my life, I must only look for consolation, hope, or peace in my own breast; and neither ought nor will, henceforward, think of any thing but myself. It is in this state that I return to the continuation of that severe and just examination which formerly I called my Confessions ; I consecrate my latter days to the study of myself, and to the preparation of that account which I must shortly render up of my actions. I resign my thoughts entirely to the pleasure of conversing with my own soul ; that being the only consolation that man cannot deprive me of. If by dint of reflection on my internal propensities, I can attain to putting them in better order, and correcting the evil that remains in me, these meditations will not be utterly useless ; and though I am accounted worthless on earth, shall not cast away my latter days. The leisure of my daily walks has frequently been filled with charming contemplations, which I regret having forgot ; but I will write down those that occur in future ; then, every time I read them over, I shall forget my misfortunes, disgraces, and persecutors, in recollecting and contemplating the integrity of my own heart.

Rousseau's books in general are now little read. They worked their work, and ceased. But there are in some of them passages that continue to live. Of these, perhaps quite the most famous is the "Savoyard Curate's Confession of Faith," a document of some length, incorporated into the "Émile." This, taken as a whole, is the most seductively eloquent argument against Christianity that perhaps ever was written. It contains, however, concessions to the sublime elevation of Scripture and to the unique virtue and majesty of Jesus, which are often quoted, and which will bear quoting here. The Savoyard Curate is represented speaking to a young friend as follows : —

I will confess to you further, that the majesty of the Scriptures strikes me with admiration, as the purity of the gospel hath its influence on my heart. Peruse the works of our philosophers with all their pomp of diction ; how mean, how contemptible, are they, compared with the Scripture ! Is it possible that a book at once so simple and sublime should be merely the work of man ? Is it possible that the Sacred Personage, whose history it contains, should be himself a mere man ? Do we find that he assumed the tone of an enthusiast or ambitious sectary ? What sweetness, what purity, in his manners ! What an affecting gracefulness in his delivery ! What sublimity in his maxims ! What profound wisdom in his discourses ! What presence of mind, what subtilty, what truth, in his replies ! How great the command over his passions ! Where is the man, where the philosopher, who could so live and die, without weakness and without ostentation ? When Plato described his imaginary good man loaded with all the shame of guilt, yet meriting the highest reward of virtue, he described exactly the character of Jesus Christ : the resemblance was so striking that all the Fathers perceived it.

What prepossession, what blindness, must it be to compare the son of Sophroniscus to the Son of Mary ! What an infinite disproportion there is between them ! Socrates, dying without pain or ignominy, easily supported his character to the last ; and if his death, however easy, had not crowned his life, it might have been doubted whether Socrates, with all his wisdom, was any thing more than a vain sophist. He invented, it is said, the theory of morals. Others, however, had before put them in practice ; he had only to say what they had done, and reduce their examples to precepts. Aristides had been *just* before Socrates defined justice ; Leonidas gave up his life for his country before Socrates declared patriotism to be a duty ; the Spartans were a sober people before Socrates recommended sobriety ; before he had even defined virtue, Greece abounded in virtuous men. But where could Jesus learn, among his compatriots, that pure and sublime morality of which he only has given us both precept and example ? The greatest wisdom was made known amidst the most bigoted fanaticism, and the simplicity of the most heroic virtues did honor to the vilest people on the earth. The death of Socrates, peaceably philosophizing with his friends, appears the most agreeable that could be wished for ; that of Jesus, expiring in the midst of agonizing pains, abused, insulted, cursed by a whole nation, is the most horrible that could be feared. Socrates, in receiving the cup of poison, blessed indeed the weeping executioner who administered it ; but Jesus, in the midst of excruciating tortures, prayed for his merciless tormentors. Yes, if the life and death of Socrates are those of a sage, the life and death of Jesus are those of a God. Shall we suppose the evangelic history a mere fiction? Indeed, my friend, it bears not the marks of fiction ; on the contrary, the history of Socrates, which nobody presumes to doubt, is not so well attested as that of Jesus Christ. Such a supposition, in fact, only shifts the difficulty without removing it ; it is more inconceivable that a number of persons should agree to write such a history, than that one only should furnish the subject of it. The Jewish authors were incapable of the diction, and strangers to the morality contained in the gospel, the marks of whose truth are so striking and inimitable that the inventor would be a more astonishing character than the hero.

So far in eloquent ascription of incomparable excellence to the Bible and to the Founder of Christianity. But then immediately Rousseau's Curate proceeds : —

And yet, with all this, the same gospel abounds with incredible relations, with circumstances repugnant to reason, and which it is impossible for a man of sense either to conceive or admit.

The compliment to Christianity almost convinces you, — until suddenly you are apprised that the author of the compliment was not convinced himself !

Jean Jacques Rousseau, in the preface to his "Confessions," appealed from the judgment of men to the judgment of God. This judgment it was his habit, to the end of his days, thanks to the effect of his early Genevan education, always to think of as certainly impending. Let us adjourn our final sentence upon him, until we hear that Omniscient award.

XVII.

THE ENCYCLOPÆDISTS.

A CENOTAPH is a monument erected to the memory of one dead, but not marking the spot in which his remains rest. The present chapter is a cenotaph to the French Encyclopædists. It is in the nature of a memorial of their literary work, but it will be found to contain no specimen extracts from their writings.

Everybody has heard of the Encyclopædists of France. Who are they? They are a group of men who, during the eighteenth century, associated themselves together for the production of a great work to be the repository of all human knowledge, — in one word, of an encyclopædia. The project was a laudable one; and the motive to it was laudable — in part. For there was mixture of motive in the case. In part, the motive was simple desire to advance the cause of human enlightenment; in part, however, the motive was desire to undermine Christianity. This latter end the encyclopædist collaborators may have thought to be an indispensable means subsidiary to the former end. They probably did think so — with such imperfect sincerity as is possible to those who set themselves, consciously or unconsciously, against God. The fact is, that the Encyclopædists came at length to be nearly as much occupied in extinguishing Christianity, as in promoting public enlightenment. They went about this their task of destroying, in a way as effective as has ever been devised for accomplishing a similar work. They gave a vicious turn of insinuation against Christianity to as many articles as possible. In the most unexpected places, throughout the entire work, pitfalls were laid of anti-Christian implication, awaiting the unwary feet of the reader. You were nowhere sure of your ground. The world has never before seen, it has never seen since, an example of propagandism altogether so adroit and so alert. It is not too much to say further, that history can supply few instances of propagandism so successful. The Encyclopædists might almost be said to have given the human mind a fresh start and a new orbit. The fresh start is, perhaps, spent; the new orbit has at length, to a great extent, returned upon the old; but it holds true, nevertheless, that the Encyclopædists of France were for a time, and that not a short time, a prodigious force of impulsion and direction to the Occidental mind. It ought to be added that the aim of the Encyclopædists was political also, not less than religious. In truth, religion and politics, Church and State, in their day, and in France, were much the same thing. The "Encyclopædia" was as revolutionary in politics as it was atheistic in religion.

The leader in this movement of insurrectionary thought was Denis Diderot. Diderot (1713–1784) was born to be an encyclopædist, and a captain of encyclopædists.   Force inexhaustible, and inexhaustible willingness to give out force; unappeasable curiosity to know; irresistible impulse to impart knowledge; versatile capacity to do every thing, carried to the verge, if not carried beyond the verge, of incapacity to do any thing thoroughly well; quenchless zeal and quenchless hope; levity enough of temper to keep its subject free from those depressions of spirit and those cares of conscience which weigh and wear on the over-earnest man; abundant physical health, — gifts such as these made up the manifold equipment of Diderot for rowing and steering the gigantic enterprise of the "Encyclopædia" triumphantly to the port of final completion, through many and many a zone of stormy adverse wind and sea, traversed on the way.   Diderot produced no signal independent and original work of his own; probably he could not have produced such a work. On the other hand, it is simply just to say that hardly anybody but Diderot could have achieved the "Encyclopædia."   That, indeed, may be considered an achievement not more to the glory, than to the shame, of its author; but whatever its true moral character, in whatever proportion shameful or glorious, it is inalienably and peculiarly Diderot's achievement; at least in this sense, that without Diderot the "Encyclopædia" would never have been achieved.

We have already, in discussing Voltaire, adverted sufficiently to Mr. John Morley's volumes in honor of Diderot and his compeers. Diderot is therein ably presented in the best possible light to the reader; and we are bound to say, that, despite Mr. Morley's friendly endeavors, Diderot therein appears very ill. He married a young woman, whose simple and touching self-sacrifice on her husband's behalf, he presently requited by giving himself away, body and soul, to a rival. In his writings, he is so easily insincere, that not unfrequently it is a problem, even for his biographer, to decide when he is expressing his sentiments truly and when not; insomuch that, once and again, Mr. Morley himself is obliged to say, "This is probably hypocritical on Diderot's part," or something to that effect. As for filthy communication out of his mouth and from his pen, — not, of course, habitual, but occasional, — the subject will not bear more than this mention. These be thy gods, O Atheism! one, in reading Mr. Morley on Diderot, is tempted again and again to exclaim. To offset such lowness of character in the man, it must in justice be added that Diderot was, notwith-standing, of a generous, uncalculating turn of mind, not grudging, especially in intellectual relations, to give of his best to others, expecting nothing again. Diderot, too, as well as Voltaire, had his royal or imperial friends, in the notorious Empress Catherine of Russia, and in King Stanislaus of Poland. He visited Catherine once in her capital, and was there munificently entertained by her. She was regally pleased to humor this gentleman of France, permitting him to bring down his fist in gesture violently on the redoubtable royal knee, according to a pleasant way Diderot had of emphasizing a point in familiar conversation. His truest claim to praise for intellectual superiority is, perhaps, that he was a prolific begetter of wit in other men.

D'Alembert (Jean le Rond, 1717–1783) was an eminent mathematician. He wrote especially, though not at first exclusively, on mathematical subjects, for the "Encyclopædia." He was, indeed, at the outset, published as mathematical editor of the work. His European reputation in science made his name a tower of strength to the "Encyclopædia," — even after he ceased to be an editorial coadjutor in the enterprise. For there came a time when D'Alembert abdicated responsibility as editor, and left the undertaking to fall heavily on the single shoulder, Atlantean shoulder it proved to be, of Diderot. The celebrated "Preliminary Discourse," prefixed to the "Encyclopædia," proceeded from the hand of D'Alembert. This has always been esteemed a masterpiece of comprehensive grasp and lucid exposition. A less creditable contribution of D'Alembert's to the "Encyclopædia" was his article on "Geneva," in the course of which, at the instance of Voltaire, who wanted a chance to have his plays represented in that city, he went out of his way to recommend to the Genevans that they establish for themselves a theatre. This brought out Rousseau in an eloquent harangue against the theatre as exerting influence to debauch public morals. D'Alembert, in the contest, did not carry off the honors of the day. D'Alembert's "Éloges," so called, a series of characterizations and appreciations written by the author in his old age, of members of the French Academy, enjoy deserved reputation for sagacious intellectual estimate, and for clear, though not supremely elegant, style of composition.

Diderot and D'Alembert are the only men whose names appear on the titlepage of the "Encyclopædia;" but Voltaire, Rousseau, Turgot, Helvétius, Duclos, Condillac, Buffon, Grimm, D'Holbach, with many others whom we must not stay even to mention, contributed to the work.

The influence of the "Encyclopædia," great during its day, is by no means yet exhausted. But it is an influence indirectly exerted, for the "Encyclopædia" itself has long been an obsolete work.

There is a legal maxim that the laws are silent, when a state of war exists. Certainly, amid the madness of a Revolution such as, during the closing years of the eighteenth century, the influence of Voltaire, Rousseau, and the Encyclopædists, with Beaumarchais, reacting against the accumulated political and ecclesiastical oppressions of ages, precipitated upon France, it might safely be assumed that letters would be silent. But the nation meantime was portentously preparing material for a literature which many wondering centuries to follow would occupy themselves with writing.

XVIII.

EPILOGUE.

In looking backward over the preceding pages, we think of many things which we should like still to say. Of these many things, we limit ourselves to saying here, as briefly as we can, some four or five only.

To begin with, in nearly every successive case, we have found ourselves lamenting afresh that, from the authors to be represented, the representative extracts must needs be so few and so short. We have, therefore, sincerely begrudged to ourselves every line of room that we felt obliged to occupy with matter, preparatory, explanatory, or critical, of our own. Whatever success we may have achieved in fulfilling our purpose, our purpose has been to say ourselves barely so much as was indispensable in order finally to convey, upon the whole, to our readers, within the allotted space, the justest and the fullest impression of the selected authors, through the medium of their own quoted words.

In the second place, it was with great regret that we yielded to the necessity of omitting entirely, or dismissing with scant mention, such literary names, for example, as Boileau, of the age of Louis Quatorze, and, a little later than he, Fontenelle, spanning with his century of years the space from 1657 to 1757, — these, and, belonging to the period that ushered in the Revolution, Bernardin St. Pierre, the teller of the tale of "Paul and Virginia," with also that hero of a hundred romantic adventures, Beaumarchais, half Themistocles, half Alcibiades, the author of "The Barber of Seville." The line had to be drawn somewhere; and, whether wisely or not, at least thoughtfully, we drew it to run as it does.

A third, and a yet graver, occasion of regret was that we must stop short on the threshold, without crossing it, of the nineteenth-century literature of France. With so many shining names seen just ahead of us, beacon-like, to invite our advance, we felt it as a real self-denial to stay our steps at that point. We hope still to deal with Chateaubriand, Madame de Staël, Lamartine, Alfred de Musset, Sainte-Beuve, Victor Hugo, and perhaps others, in a future volume.

Our eye is caught with the antithetical terms, "classicism" and "romanticism," occurring here and there; and the observation is forced upon us, that these terms, in their mutual relation, are nowhere by us defined. The truth is, they scarcely, as thus used, admit of hard and fast definition. It is in a somewhat loose conventional sense of each term, that, in late literary language, they are set

off, one over against the other. They name two
different, but by no means necessarily antagonistic,
forces or tendencies in literature. Classicism stands
for what you might call the established order, against
which romanticism is a revolt. Paradoxical though
it be to say so, both the established order, and the
revolt against it, are good things. The established
order, which was never really any thing more or
less than the dominance in literature of rules and
standards derived through criticism from the acknowledged best models, especially the ancient,
tended at last to cramp and stifle the life which it
should, of course, only serve to shape and conform.
The mould, always too narrow perhaps, but at any
rate grown too rigid, needed itself to be fashioned
anew. Fresh life, a full measure, would do this.
Such is the true mission of romanticism, — not to
break the mould that classicism sought to impose
on literary production, but to expand that mould,
make it more pliant, more free. A mould, for
things living and growing, should be plastic in the
passive, as well as in the active, sense of that word,
— should accept form, as well as give form. Romanticism will accordingly have won its legitimate
victory, not when it shall have destroyed classicism
and replaced it, but when it shall have made classicism over, after the law of a larger life. To risk a
concrete illustration — among our American poets,
Bryant, in the perfectly self-consistent unity of his
whole intellectual development, may be said to rep-

resent classicism ; while in Lowell, as Lowell appears in the later, more protracted, phase of his genius, romanticism is represented. The "Thanatopsis" of Bryant and the "Cathedral" of Lowell may stand for individual examples respectively of the classic and the romantic styles in poetry. Compare these two productions, and in the difference between the chaste, well-pruned severity of the one, and the indulged, perhaps stimulated, luxuriance of the other, you will feel the difference between classicism and romanticism. But Victor Hugo is the great recent romanticist ; and when, hereafter, we come to speak somewhat at large of him, it will be seasonable to enter more fully into the question of these two tendencies in literature.

We cannot consent to have said here our very last word, without emphasizing once again our sense of the really extraordinary pervasiveness in French literature of that element in it which one does not like to name, even to condemn it, — we mean its impurity. The influence of French literary models, very strong among us just now, must not be permitted insensibly to pervert our own cleaner and sweeter national habit and taste in this matter. But we, all of us together, need to be both vigilant and firm ; for the beginnings of corruption here are very insidious. Let us never grow ashamed of our saving Saxon shamefacedness. They may nickname it prudery, if they will ; but let us, American and English, for our part, always take pride in such prudery.

INDEX.

[The merest approximation only can be attempted, in hinting here the pronunciation of French names. In general, the French distribute the accent pretty evenly among all the syllables of their words. We mark an accent on the final syllable, chiefly in order to correct a natural English tendency to slight that syllable in pronunciation. In a few cases, we let a well-established English pronunciation stand. N notes a peculiar nasal sound, ü, a peculiar vowel sound, having no equivalent in English.]

RECOMMENDED SUPPLEMENTARY READING.

Four new volumes in the Garnet Series.

READINGS FROM MILTON. With introduction by Bishop HENRY W. WARREN, D.D., LL.D. $0.75

READINGS FROM GOLDSMITH. With introduction by EDWARD EVERETT HALE, D.D., LL.D. 75

ASCHAM AND ARNOLD. With introduction by JAMES H. CARLISLE, D.D., President Wofford College 75

SELECTED ESSAYS OF ADDISON. With introduction by C. T. WINCHESTER, Professor of English Literature at Wesleyan University, .75

The Entire Set in a Neat Box, $3.00, by mail, postpaid.

"One can hardly say too much in praise of this little library." — *Boston Evening Transcript.*

"The Chautauqua Press has only to continue to publish such volumes as these to fulfil its promise to provide for its students a library of choice literature." — *New-York Observer.*

"The volumes are excellent, and deserve a very wide circulation. Beginners in the reading of our best literature should not fail to possess themselves of this GARNET SERIES, which is altogether unexceptionable, and cannot fail to do great good." — *The Beacon, Boston.*

THE NEW GAME OF MYTHOLOGY.
Roman and Greek.

Interesting and instructive. Contains one hundred cards, grouped into books of from three to six cards each, not arbitrarily, but according to a natural classification. This is a special feature of this game, and is a most valuable aid to the memory, and to an intelligent grasp of the subject. As an additional feature, well-executed outline cuts are given of the chief deities, taken in almost every case from some famous statue or picture. Beautifully printed in colors and put up in a neat box. PRICE 50 cts., by mail, postpaid.

HOME STATIONERY FOR C. L. S. C.

Each class printed in different color, on paper of the finest quality, and put up in attractive style, in one and two quire boxes.

See what High Praise it has Received.

Hon. HENDERSON ELLIOTT, Vice-President Class of 1882, writes: "The designs for the various classes are exceedingly neat and appropriate. That of the class of 1882 strikes me exactly, — 'Pioneers' we love to be called. Your paper is fine and easily impressed, and the prices very reasonable."

Rev. H. C. FARRAR, President Class of 1883, writes: "The C. L. S. C. paper is beautiful and worthy a large sale. I know it must make every true Chautauquan more thoroughly in love with the Chautauqua idea, for writing his C. L. S. C. letters on this paper."

J. B. UNDERWOOD, President Class of 1884, adds his testimony in these words: "It will be with great pleasure that each graduate 'Invincible' must welcome such superb taste as displayed in that prepared for their use, and the writer congratulates you and the C. L. S. C. upon finally having some stationery adapted to the home use of refined and cultivated firesides."

Miss CARRIE HART, Treasurer Class of 1885, writes: "I am enjoying using it very much, and advertising it to my friends as fast as my correspondence will permit. It is the only C. L. S. C. stationery that has met my ideas of elegance and beauty for home use."

One-quire box, 60 cents; two-quire box, $1.00, by mail, postpaid.

CHAUTAUQUA PRESS, 117 Franklin St., Boston.